THINKING THROUGH SOURCES

Documents and Images from the Global Past

for

Ways of the World

FIFTH EDITION

FOR THE AP® WORLD HISTORY: MODERN COURSE

SINCE 1200 C.E.

Robert W. Strayer

The College at Brockport: State University of New York

Eric W. Nelson

Missouri State University

bedford, freeman & worth
publishers

Boston | New York

Vice President, Social Sciences and High School: Shani Fisher
Executive Program Director, High School: Ann Heath
Program Manager, History & Government: Lee Benjamins
Associate Editor: Kelly Noll
Assistant Editor: Sophie Dora Tulchin
Executive Development Editor for Media: Lisa Samols
Senior Media Editor: Justin Perry
Associate Media Editor: Michael Emig
Director, High School Marketing: Janie Pierce-Bratcher
Marketing Manager: Claire Brantley
Marketing Assistant: Brianna DiGeronimo
Senior Director, Content Management Enhancement: Tracey Kuehn
Senior Managing Editor: Michael Granger
Executive Content Project Manager: Christina Horn
Senior Workflow Project Manager: Lisa McDowell
Production Supervisor: Jose Olivera
Director of Design, Content Management: Diana Blume
Cover Design: William Boardman
Director, Rights and Permissions: Hilary Newman
Text Permissions Researcher: Elaine Kosta, Lumina Datamatics, Inc.
Executive Permissions Editor: Cecilia Varas
Director of Digital Production: Keri deManigold
Lead Media Project Manager: Jodi Isman
Copyeditor: Susan Zorn
Composition: Lumina Datamatics, Inc.
Printing and Binding: Lakeside Book Company

Library of Congress Control Number: 2022948802

ISBN 978-1-319-51347-4

Printed in the United States of America.

2   3   4   5   6   28   27   26   25   24   23

Acknowledgments
Text acknowledgments and copyrights appear at the back of the book on page 207, which constitutes an extension of the copyright page. Art acknowledgments and copyrights appear on the same page as the art selections they cover.

AP® is a trademark registered by the College Board, which is not affiliated with, and does not endorse, this product.

For information, write: BFW Publishers, 120 Broadway, New York, NY 10271
hsmarketing@bfwpub.com

Preface

Designed specifically to be used with *Ways of the World* for the AP® World History: Modern Course, Fifth Edition, this collection of sources—both primary and secondary—complements and extends each chapter of the parent textbook. As the title of the collection suggests, these source projects enable students to "think through sources" and, in turn, begin to understand the craft of historians as well as their conclusions. Readers explore in greater depth a central theme from each chapter, using both documentary and visual sources as well as brief extracts from works by recent historians and other scholars. Each Historians' Voices feature and every primary source includes a brief headnote that provides context for the source and several questions to consider. The primary source projects include a series of integrative and probing essay questions appropriate for in-class discussion and writing assignments.

In addition to this print volume, we are delighted to offer *Thinking through Sources* in Bedford, Freeman & Worth Publishers' online learning platform. To learn more about the benefits of Bedford, Freeman & Worth Publishers' digital platform and the different *Ways of the World* packages, visit **bfwpub.com/wowmodern5e**.

New in This Edition

To align with the new student edition, there are now fourteen Working with Evidence and Historians' Voices features offering alternative primary and secondary sources for each chapter. Some source sets are new to *Thinking through Sources*, including Chapter 7: Debating Rights and Chapter 13: Global Feminism.

Acknowledgments

We extend our thanks to Senior Program Manager William Lombardo and Executive Content Project Manager Christina Horn of Bedford/St. Martin's, as well as Program Manager for History and Government Lee Benjamins and Associate Editor Kelly Noll of Bedford, Freeman & Worth Publishers.

Robert Strayer, La Selva Beach, California
Eric Nelson, Springfield, Missouri

Contents

3   Living and Dying during the Black Death

6 Renewal and Reform in the Early Modern World

9 Colonial India: Experience and Response

10 Japan and the West in the Nineteenth Century

11   Ideologies of the Axis Powers

12   Articulating Independence

13 Global Feminism   182

14 Experiencing International Migration   193

Representations of the Buddha

WORKING WITH EVIDENCE

Buddhism derived from a single individual, Siddhartha Gautama, who was born in north-ern India around the middle of the first millennium B.C.E. Over many centuries, the religion evolved as it spread within and beyond India, attracting growing numbers of fol-lowers and intersecting with various cultures throughout Asia, including those of China, Japan, Tibet, Korea, Thailand, Burma, and Vietnam. But the figure of the Buddha remained central to all versions and variations of the faith. Perceptions of the Buddha took on the flavor of the various cultures in which Buddhism took root. In China, for example, descriptions of the Buddha emphasized his "filial piety," citing the conversion of his father.

Understandings of the Buddha found expression in the titles and qualities attributed to him, such as "the teacher of gods and men," the Blessed One, the "great cosmic per-son," and many others. A proliferating body of written texts—sermons, biographies, sto-ries, and myths—also featured various understandings of the Buddha. Over time, these descriptions increasingly emphasized the superhuman and transcendent elements of the Buddha, portrayed his actions as miraculous and magical, and invoked numerous past and future Buddhas. He was also represented artistically in sculptures and paintings. But for almost five centuries after his death, artists depicted the Buddha as an empty throne, a horse with no rider, a tree, a wheel, a set of footprints, or in some other symbolic way, while largely shunning any image of him in human form. All of these symbols played a role in Buddhist worship, prayer, and meditation, allowing his followers to experience the Buddha as a living presence in their own lives.

SOURCE 1.1 A Greco-Indian Buddha

By the first century C.E., the impulse to show the Buddha in human form had surfaced, with some of the earliest examples coming from the region of South Asia in what is now northern Pakistan and eastern Afghanistan. That area had been a part of the empire of Alexander the Great and his Hellenistic successors during the three centuries before the birth of Jesus and had developed commercial ties to the Roman Empire. These early images of the Buddha reflect this Greco-Roman influence, portraying him with a face similar to that of the Greek god Apollo, dressed in a Roman-style toga, and with the curly hair characteristic of the Mediterranean region.

Such Greco-Roman influence is apparent in Source 1.1. Dating from the second or third century C.E., it comes from India and depicts a famous scene from the life of the Buddha—his temptation by the demon Mara and Mara's seductive daughters while he was meditating under the Bodhi tree.

1. How are Mara and his daughters, shown on the right, portrayed in this relief?

2. What attitude characterizes the Buddha, shown on the left and surrounded by attendants?

3. One scholar has recently argued that "statues of the Buddha started to appear only after the cult of Apollo became established [in the region]. Buddhists felt threatened by the success of the new religious practices and began to create their own visual images."[1] How might this possibility shape your understanding of Greco-Roman cultural influences on Buddhism? Can you imagine other possible explanations for the creation of the first physical representations of the Buddha?

4. Does the idea that competition from a Greek religious cult caused Buddhists to create early images of the Buddha affect your analysis of this image?

The Temptation of the Buddha | 2nd or 3rd century C.E.

■ ■ ■

SOURCE 1.2 A Classical Indian Buddha

By the time of India's Gupta dynasty (320–550 c.e.), Greco-Roman influence in Buddhist art was fading, replaced by more completely Indian images of the Buddha. Such representations became the "classic" model illustrated in Source 1.2, which dates from the sixth century c.e. The Buddha's right hand with palm facing the viewer indicates reassurance, or "have no fear." The partially webbed fingers are among the *lakshanas*, or signs of a Buddha image, that denote the Buddha's unique status. So too is the hair knot on the top of his head, symbolizing enlightenment.

1. The elongated earlobes reflect the heavy, luxurious earrings that the Buddha wore earlier in his life before becoming the enlightened one. Why might the artist have included this detail in his depiction of the Buddha?

2. The creator of this statue intended to convey the Buddha's calm and detached posture toward the world. What features of the statue might illustrate this posture? What similarities and differences can you observe between this depiction of the Buddha and that in Source 1.1?

An Indian Buddha | **6th century** c.e.

Image copyright © The Metropolitan Museum of Art. Image source: Art Resource, NY

■ ■ ■

SOURCE 1.3 The Reputation of the Buddha in Ancient Buddhist Stories

Various perceptions of the Buddha found expression not only in artistic form, but also in the growing body of Buddhist texts, known as the Pali Canon, originally passed on orally and reduced to writing during the first century B.C.E. Source 1.3 recounts a conversation derived from one of these texts between the Buddha and a wandering holy man, Sakuludayin, about the qualities of various religious leaders in the area.

1. How might you summarize the perception of the Buddha reflected in this source?

2. To what extent are these qualities expressed in the artistic representations of the Buddha?

The Greater Discourse to Sakuludayin | ca. 1st century B.C.E.

[Sakuludayin reported:] And some said this: This recluse Gotama [the Buddha] is the head of an order, the head of a group, the teacher of a group, the well-known and famous founder of a sect regarded by many as a saint. He is honoured, respected, revered, and venerated by his disciples, and his disciples live in dependence on him. . . .

Once the recluse Gotama was teaching his Dhamma [truth, wisdom, teachings] to an assembly of several hundred followers and there a certain disciple of his cleared his throat. Thereupon one of his companions in the holy life nudged him with his knee. "Be quiet, venerable sir, make no noise; the Blessed One, the Teacher, is teaching us the Dhamma."

When the recluse Gotama is teaching the Dhamma to an assembly of several hundred followers, on that occasion there is no sound of his disciples' coughing or clearing their throats. For then that large assembly is poised in expectancy . . . just as though a man were at a crossroads pressing out pure honey and a large group of people were poised in expectancy. . . .

"But, [asked the Buddha] how many qualities do you see in me because of which my disciples honour, respect, revere, and venerate me?" [Sakuludayin replied] "Venerable sir, I see five qualities in the Blessed One: . . . First, venerable sir, the Blessed One eats little. . . . Again, the Blessed One is content with any kind of robe. . . . Again, the Blessed One is content with any kind of resting place. . . . Again, venerable sir, the Blessed One is secluded and commends seclusion."

Source: Bhikkhu Nanamola and Bhikkhu Bodhi, trans., *The Middle Length Discourses of the Buddha* (Boston: Wisdom Publications, 1995), 631–32.

■ ■ ■

SOURCE 1.4 A Korean Bodhisattva of Compassion

Across the world of Asian Mahayana Buddhism, a popular artistic representation of Buddhist values found expression in numerous images of bodhisattvas, those spiritually developed beings who delayed their own entry into nirvana to assist others on the path.

The historical Buddha had on occasion described himself as a bodhisattva. In sculpture or painting, bodhisattvas became objects of worship and sources of comfort and assistance to many Buddhists. The most widely popular of the many bodhisattva figures was that of Avalokitesvara, known in China as Guanyin and in Japan as Kannon. This Bodhisattva of Compassion, often portrayed as a woman or with distinctly feminine characteristics, was known as "the one who hears the cries of the world."

Among the most striking of the many representations of this bodhisattva are those that portray him or her with numerous heads, with which to hear the many cries of a suffering humanity, or with multiple arms to aid them. Source 1.4 provides an illustration of such a figure, a gilded wooden statue from Korea dating to the tenth or eleventh century c.e.

1. What elements of Buddhist imagery can you identify in this statue?

2. To whom might such an image appeal? And why?

3. How does this image differ from the classical Indian Buddha shown in Source 1.2?

Avalokitesvara with a Thousand Arms | **10th or 11th** century c.e.

■ ■ ■

SOURCE 1.5   The Buddha and the Outcaste

According to Buddhist sacred texts, the Buddha himself both taught and practiced compassion. Among the most widely known of his teachings are those about loving-kindness or compassion: "Like a caring mother holding and guarding the life of her only child, so with a boundless heart of loving-kindness, hold yourself and all beings as your beloved children." The story in Source 1.5, contained in the Buddhist scriptures, conveys this sensibility in action from the perspective of an untouchable cleaner named Sunita. As an untouchable, Sunita was born into a social class outside of and below the traditional Indian caste system, making him an "outcaste"—literally someone outside the caste system. The English word "outcast" derives from this Indian term.

1. How does this story convey the Buddhist ideal of compassion?

2. In what ways was Sunita transformed by his encounter with the Buddha?

3. How does the Buddha define a genuine Brahmin? How might Hindu Brahmins, with whom the Buddha was in frequent dispute, respond to this story?

Sunita the Outcaste | **1st century B.C.E. to 2nd century C.E.**

In a lowly family I was born, poor, with next to no food. My work was degrading: I gathered the spoiled, the withered flowers from shrines and threw them away. People found me disgusting, despised me, disparaged me. Lowering my heart, I showed reverence to many.

Then I saw the One Self-awakened, arrayed with a squadron of monks, entering the city. . . . Throwing down my carrying pole, I approached him to do reverence. He—the supreme man—stood still out of sympathy just for me. After paying homage to the feet of the teacher [the Buddha], I stood to one side and requested the Going Forth [permission to enter the rank of monks] from him, supreme among all living beings. The compassionate Teacher, sympathetic to all the world, said: "Come, monk." That was my formal Acceptance.

Alone, I stayed in the wilds, untiring, I followed the Teacher's words, just as he, the Conqueror, had taught me. . . . Indra & Brahma [powerful Hindu/Buddhist deities] came to pay homage to me, hands palm-to-palm at their hearts: "Homage to you, O thoroughbred of men. . . . You, dear sir, are worthy of offerings."

Seeing me, arrayed with a squadron of devas [god-like spiritual beings], the Teacher smiled & said: "Through austerity, celibacy, restraint, and self-control: That's how one is a brahman. He is a brahman supreme."

Source: "Sunita the Outcaste" (Thag 12.2), translated from the Pali by Thanissaro Bhikkhu, *Access to Insight (BCBS Edition)*, November 30, 2013, http://www.accesstoinsight.org/tipitaka/kn/thag/thag. 12.02.than.html.

■ ■ ■

SOURCE 1.6 A Chinese Buddha

Mahayana Buddhism not only featured numerous bodhisattvas, but it also populated the spiritual universe with various Buddhas in addition to the historical Buddha. One of these is the Maitreya Buddha, or the Buddha of the Future, predicted to appear when the teachings of the historical Buddha have been lost or forgotten. In China, this Buddha of the future was sometimes portrayed as the "laughing Buddha," a fat, smiling, contented figure, said to be modeled on a tenth-century monk named Budai who wandered the country merrily spreading happiness and good cheer while evoking contentment and abundance. Source 1.6 illustrates this Chinese Maitreya Buddha, together with some of his disciples, in a carving dating to the tenth through fourteenth centuries, in China's Feilai Feng caves.

1. How does this Buddha image differ, both physically and in its religious implications, from the other Buddhas already discussed in this feature? Why might this image be appealing to some Buddhists, and why might others object to it?

2. In what ways does this figure represent an adaptation of Buddhist imagery to Chinese culture? Consider what you know about Confucian and Daoist postures to the world.

The Chinese Maitreya Buddha | 10th to 14th century C.E.

Earl & Nazima Kowall/Getty Images

DOING HISTORY

1. **Tracing change:** What transformations in Buddhist belief and practice are disclosed in these sources?

2. **Identifying cultural adaptation:** What evidence do these sources provide about the blending of Buddhism into a variety of cultural settings?

3. **Understanding the growth of Buddhism:** What do these sources suggest about the appeal of Buddhism to growing numbers of people across Asia?

4. **Considering cultural boundaries:** To what extent are these sources meaningful to people outside the Buddhist tradition? In what ways might they speak to universal human needs or desires? What is specifically Buddhist or Asian about them?

HISTORIANS' VOICES

On the Buddha

All of the preceding sources were the work of "insiders," reflecting the perceptions of the Buddha among those who operated within the Buddhist world at varying times and places in the distant past. Modern historians, particularly those from the Western world, are "outsiders," even if they are personally sympathetic with Buddhism. The following selections come to us from such historians, one American and the other British. Both John Strong (Voice 1.1) and Karen Armstrong (Voice 1.2) have written early-twenty-first-century biographies of the Buddha.

1. What features of the Buddha's life does John Strong (Voice 1.1) emphasize? Why does he largely omit the supernatural and miraculous elements that so often accompany "insider" understandings of the Buddha?

2. Why does Karen Armstrong in Voice 1.2 suggest that some Buddhists might be skeptical of any effort to create a modern biography of the Buddha? What aspects of the Buddha's life does she highlight?

3. **Integrating primary and secondary sources:** How do these modern scholarly reflections on the Buddha differ from the much earlier insider accounts and images? Which do you find more useful in understanding the life of Siddhartha Gautama?

VOICE 1.1

John Strong on the Context of the Buddha's Life | 2001

Historically speaking, we know very little for certain about the life of Siddhartha Gautama, the man who came to be known as the Buddha. Although no one today seriously questions his actual existence, debates still rage over the dates of his life . . . the contents of his teaching, and the nature of the religious community he is said to have founded. . . .

We know that the India of his day was caught up in a period of ferment and religious questioning spawned by the rise of new urban centers and the breakdown of old political systems. As two contemporary religious scholars put it: "The historical Buddha responded to this kind of situation. . . . He was a renouncer and an ascetic . . . although it seems mild by Indian standards. He shared with other renunciants an ultimately somber view of life and its pleasures, and he practiced and recommended a mode of religious life in which individual participation in a specifically religious community was of primary importance. He experimented with the practices of . . . begging, wandering, celibacy, . . . self-restraint (yoga) and the like, and he organized a community in which discipline played a central role. Judging from the movement he inspired, he was not only an innovator but also a charismatic personality. Through the course of his ministry, he gathered around him a group of wandering mendicants and nuns as well as men and women who continued to live the life of householders."

Source: John S. Strong, *The Buddha: A Short Biography* (Oxford: Oneworld Publications, 2001), 1–2. Quotation from Frank E. Reynolds and Charles Hallisey, "Buddha," in *Encyclopedia of Religion* (New York: Macmillan, 1987), 2:321.

VOICE 1.2

Karen Armstrong on the Buddha and Biography | 2001

Some Buddhists might say that to write a biography of Sidhatta Gotama is a very un-Buddhist thing to do. In their view no authority should be revered, however august; Buddhists must rely on their own efforts and motivate themselves, not on a charismatic leader. One ninth century master . . . even went so far as to command his disciples: "If you meet the Buddha, kill the Buddha!" to emphasize the importance of maintaining this independence from authority figures. . . . Throughout his life, he [the Buddha] fought against the cult of personality and endlessly deflected the attention of his disciples from himself. It was not his life and personality, but his teaching that was important. He believed he had woken up to a truth that was inscribed in the deepest structure of existence. It was a *dhamma*, . . . a fundamental law of life for gods, humans, and animals alike. By discovering this truth, he had become enlightened and had experienced a profound inner transformation; he had won peace and immunity in the midst of life's sufferings. Gotama has thus become a Buddha, an Enlightened or Awakened One. Any one of his disciples could achieve the same enlightenment if he or she followed this method. But if people start to revere Gotama the man, they would distract themselves from their task and the cult could become a prop, causing an unworthy dependence that could only impede spiritual progress.

Source: Karen Armstrong, *Buddha* (New York: Penguin Books, 2001), xi–xii.

NOTE

1. William Theodore de Bary and Irene Bloom, compilers, *Sources of Chinese Tradition*, 2nd ed., vol. 1 (New York: Columbia University Press, 1999), 326–29.

CHAPTER 2

The Making of
Japanese Civilization

Japan was among the new third-wave civilizations that took shape between 500 and 1500 C.E. Each of them was distinctive in particular ways, but all of them followed the general patterns of earlier civilizations in the creation of cities, states, stratified societies, patriarchies, written languages, and more. Furthermore, many of them borrowed extensively from nearby and older civilizations. In the case of Japan, that borrowing was primarily from China, its towering neighbor to the west. The sources that follow provide glimpses of a distinctive Japanese civilization in the making, even as that civilization selectively incorporated elements of Chinese thinking and practice.

SOURCE 2.1 Japanese Political Thinking

As an early Japanese state gradually took shape in the sixth and seventh centuries, it was confronted by serious internal divisions of clan, faction, and religion. Externally, Japanese forces had been expelled from their footholds in Korea, while Japan also faced the immense power and attractiveness of a reunified China under the Sui and Tang dynasties. In these circumstances, Japanese authorities sought to strengthen their own emerging state by adopting a range of Chinese political values and practices. This Chinese influence in Japanese political thinking was particularly apparent in the so-called Seventeen Article Constitution issued by Prince Shotoku, a prominent political figure, in 604 C.E., which comprised a set of general guidelines for court officials.

Despite this apparent embrace of all things Chinese, Shotoku's attitude toward China itself is less clear. He inscribed various letters that he sent to the Chinese Sui dynasty ruler as follows: "The Son of Heaven of the Land of the Rising Sun to the Son of Heaven of the Land of the Setting Sun." Another read: "The Eastern Emperor Greets the Western Emperor."[1] Considering their country to be the Middle Kingdom, greatly superior to all its neighbors, Chinese court officials were incensed at these apparent assertions of equality. It is not clear whether Shotoku was deliberately claiming equivalence with China or if he was simply unaware of how such language might be viewed in China.

1. What elements of Confucian, Legalist, or Buddhist thinking are reflected in this document?

2. What can you infer about the internal problems that Japanese rulers faced?

3. How might Shotoku define an ideal Japanese state?

SHOTOKU | *The Seventeen Article Constitution* | 604 C.E.

1. Harmony is to be valued, and an avoidance of wanton opposition to be honored. All men are influenced by class feelings, and there are few who are intelligent. Hence there are some who disobey their lords and fathers, or who maintain feuds with the neighboring villages. But when those above are harmonious and those below are friendly, and there is concord in the discussion of business, right views of things spontaneously gain acceptance. . . .

2. Sincerely reverence the three treasures . . . the Buddha, the Law [teachings], and the Priesthood [community of monks]. . . .

3. When you receive the Imperial commands, fail not scrupulously to obey them. The lord is Heaven, the vassal is Earth. Heaven overspreads, and Earth upbears. . . . [W]hen the superior acts, the inferior yields compliance.

4. The Ministers and functionaries should make decorous behavior their leading principle. . . . If the superiors do not behave with decorum, the inferiors are disorderly. . . .

5. Ceasing from gluttony and abandoning covetous desires, deal impartially with the [legal] suits which are submitted to you. . . .

6. Chastise that which is evil and encourage that which is good. This was the excellent rule of antiquity. . . .

7. Let every man have his own charge, and let not the spheres of duty be confused. When wise men are entrusted with office, the sound of praise arises. If unprincipled men hold office, disasters and tumults are multiplied. In this world, few are born with knowledge: wisdom is the product of earnest meditation. In all things, whether great or small, find the right man, and they will surely be well managed. . . .

10. Let us cease from wrath, and refrain from angry looks. Nor let us be resentful when others differ from us. For all men have hearts, and each heart has its own leanings. . . . [All] of us are simply ordinary men. . . .

11. Give clear appreciation to merit and demerit, and deal out to each its sure reward or punishment. In these days, reward does not attend upon merit, nor punishment upon crime. You high functionaries, who have charge of public affairs, let it be your task to make clear rewards and punishments. . . .

12. Let not the provincial authorities or the [local nobles] levy exactions on the people. In a country, there are not two lords. . . . The sovereign is the master of the people of the whole country. . . .

15. To turn away from that which is private, and to set our faces toward that which is public — this is the path of a Minister. . . .

16. Let the people be employed [in forced labor] at seasonable times. This is an ancient and excellent rule. Let them be employed, therefore, in the winter months, when they are at leisure. But from spring to autumn, when they are engaged in agriculture or with the mulberry trees, the people should not be so employed. For if they do not attend to agriculture, what will they have to eat? If they do not attend the mulberry trees, what will they do for clothing?

17. Decisions on important matters should not be made by one person alone. They should be discussed with many.

Source: W. G. Aston, trans., *Nihongi: Chronicles of Japan from the Earliest Times to A.D. 697* (London, UK: Paul, Trench, Truebner, 1896), 2:129–33.

■ ■ ■

SOURCE 2.2 The Uniqueness of Japan

Despite Japan's extensive cultural borrowing from abroad — or perhaps because of it — Japanese writers often stressed the unique and superior features of their own country. Nowhere is this theme echoed more clearly than in *The Chronicle of the Direct Descent of Gods and Sovereigns*, written by Kitabatake Chikafusa (1293–1354). A longtime court official and member of one branch of Japan's imperial family, Kitabatake wrote at a time of declining imperial authority in Japan, when two court centers competed in an extended "war of the courts." As an advocate for the southern court, Kitabatake sought to prove that the emperor he served was legitimate because he had descended in an unbroken line from the Age of the Gods. In making this argument, Kitabatake also served as a spokesman for the revival of Japan's earlier religious tradition of numerous gods and spirits, known later as Shintoism.

1. In Kitabatake's view, what was distinctive about Japan in comparison to China and India?

2. How might the use of Japan's indigenous religious tradition, especially the Sun Goddess, serve to legitimize the imperial rule of Kitabatake's family?

3. How did Kitabatake understand the place of Confucianism and Buddhism in Japan and their relationship to Shinto beliefs?

KITABATAKE CHIKAFUSA | *The Chronicle of the Direct Descent of Gods and Sovereigns* | 1339

Japan is the divine country. The heavenly ancestor it was who first laid its foundations, and the Sun Goddess left her descendants to reign over it forever and ever. This is true only of our country, and nothing similar may be found in foreign lands. That is why it is called the divine country.

In the age of the gods, Japan was known as the "ever-fruitful land of reed-covered plains and luxuriant rice fields." This name has existed since the creation of heaven and earth.... [I]t may thus be considered the prime name of Japan. It is also called the country of the great eight islands. This name was given because eight islands were produced when the Male Deity and the Female Deity begot Japan.... Japan is the land of the Sun Goddess [Amaterasu]. Or it may have thus been called because it is near the place where the sun rises.... Thus, since Japan is a separate continent, distinct from both India and China and lying in a great ocean, it is the country where the divine illustrious imperial line has been transmitted.

The creation of heaven and earth must everywhere have been the same, for it occurred within the same universe, but the Indian, Chinese, and Japanese traditions are each different....

In China, nothing positive is stated concerning the creation of the world, even though China is a country which accords special importance to the keeping of records....

The beginnings of Japan in some ways resemble the Indian descriptions, telling as it does of the world's creation from the seed of the heavenly gods. However, whereas in our country the succession to the throne has followed a single undeviating line since the first divine ancestor, nothing of the kind has existed in India. After their first ruler, King People's Lord, had been chosen and raised to power by the populace, his dynasty succeeded, but in later times most of his descendants perished, and men of inferior genealogy who had powerful forces became the rulers, some of them even controlling the whole of India. China is also a country of notorious disorders. Even in ancient times, when life was simple and conduct was proper, the throne was offered to wise men, and no single lineage was established. Later, in times of disorder, men fought for control of the country. Thus some of the rulers rose from the ranks of the plebeians [commoners], and there were even some of barbarian origin who usurped power. Or some families after generations of service as ministers surpassed their princes and eventually supplanted them. There have already been thirty-six changes of dynasty since Fuxi, and unspeakable disorders have occurred.

Only in our country has the succession remained inviolate from the beginning of heaven and earth to the present. It has been maintained within a single lineage, and even when, as inevitably has happened, the succession has been transmitted collaterally, it has returned to the true line. This is due to the ever-renewed Divine Oath and makes Japan unlike all other countries....

Then the Great Sun Goddess ... sent her grandchild to the world below.... [The Sun Goddess] uttered these words of command: "Thou, my illustrious grandchild, proceed thither and govern the land. Go, and may prosperity attend thy dynasty, and may it, like Heaven and Earth, endure forever." ...

Because our Great Goddess is the spirit of the sun, she illuminates with a bright virtue which is incomprehensible in all its aspects but dependable alike in the realm of the visible and invisible. All sovereigns and ministers have inherited the bright seeds of the divine light, or they are descendants of the deities who received personal instruction from the Great Goddess. Who would not stand in reverence before this fact? The highest object of all teachings, Buddhist and Confucian included, consists in realizing this fact and obeying in perfect consonance its principles. It has been the power of the dissemination of the Buddhist and Confucian texts which has spread these principles. . . . Since the reign of the Emperor Ojin, the Confucian writings have been disseminated, and since Prince Shotoku's time Buddhism has flourished in Japan. Both these men were sages incarnate, and it must have been their intention to spread a knowledge of the way of our country, in accordance with the wishes of the Great Sun Goddess.

Source: *Sources of Japanese Tradition*, Volume 1, compiled by William De Bary et al. Copyright © 2001 Columbia University Press, 358–363.

■ ■ ■

SOURCE 2.3 Social Life at Court

For many centuries, high culture in Japan—art, music, poetry, and literature—found a home in the imperial court, where men and women of the royal family and nobility, together with various attendants, mixed and mingled. That aristocratic culture reached its high point between the ninth and twelfth centuries, but, according to one prominent scholar, it "has shaped the aesthetic and emotional life of the entire Japanese people for a millennium."[2] Women played a prominent role in that culture, both creating it and describing it. Among them was Sei Shonagon (966–1017), a lady-in-waiting to Empress Sadako. In her *Pillow Book*, a series of brief and often witty observations, Sei Shonagon described court life as well as her own likes and dislikes.

1. What impression does Sei Shonagon convey about the relationship of men and women at court?

2. How would you describe Sei Shonagon's own posture toward men, toward women, and toward ordinary people? What insight can you gain about class differences from her writing?

3. In what ways does court life, as Sei Shonagon describes it, reflect Buddhist and Confucian influences, and in what ways does it depart from, and even challenge, those traditions?

SEI SHONAGON | *Pillow Book* | ca. 1000

That parents should bring up some beloved son of theirs to be a priest is really distressing. No doubt it is an auspicious thing to do; but unfortunately most people are convinced that a priest is as unimportant as a piece of wood, and they treat him accordingly. A priest lives poorly on meager food, and cannot even sleep without being criticized. While he is young, it is only natural that he should be curious about all sorts of things, and, if there are women about, he will probably peep in their direction (though, to be sure, with a look of aversion on his face). What is wrong about that? Yet people immediately find fault with him for even so small a lapse. . . .

A preacher ought to be good-looking. For, if we are properly to understand his worthy sentiments, we must keep our eyes on him while he speaks; should we look away, we may forget to listen. Accordingly an ugly preacher may well be the source of sin. . . .

When I make myself imagine what it is like to be one of those women who live at home, faithfully serving their husbands—women who have not a single exciting prospect in life yet who believe that they are perfectly happy—I am filled with scorn. . . .

I cannot bear men who believe that women serving in the Palace are bound to be frivolous and wicked. Yet I suppose their prejudice is understandable. After all, women at Court do not spend their time hiding modestly behind fans and screens, but walk about, looking openly at people they chance to meet. Yes, they see everyone face to face, not only ladies-in-waiting like themselves, but even Their Imperial Majesties (whose august names I hardly dare mention), High Court Nobles, senior courtiers, and other gentlemen of high rank. In the presence of such exalted personages the women in the Palace are all equally brazen, whether they be the maids of ladies-in-waiting, or the relations of Court ladies who have come to visit them, or housekeepers, or latrine-cleaners, or women who are of no more value than a roof-tile or a pebble. Small wonder that the young men regard them as immodest! Yet are the gentlemen themselves any less so? They are not exactly bashful when it comes to looking at the great people in the Palace. No, everyone at Court is much the same in this respect. . . .

Hateful Things

. . . A man who has nothing in particular to recommend him discusses all sorts of subjects at random as though he knew everything. . . .

An admirer has come on a clandestine visit, but a dog catches sight of him and starts barking. One feels like killing the beast.

One has been foolish enough to invite a man to spend the night in an unsuitable place—and then he starts snoring.

A gentleman has visited one secretly. Though he is wearing a tall, lacquered hat, he nevertheless wants no one to see him. He is so flurried, in fact, that upon leaving he bangs into something with his hat. Most hateful! . . .

A man with whom one is having an affair keeps singing the praises of some woman he used to know. Even if it is a thing of the past, this can be very annoying. How much more so if he is still seeing the woman! . . .

A good lover will behave as elegantly at dawn as at any other time. He drags himself out of bed with a look of dismay on his face. The lady urges him on: "Come, my friend, it's getting light. You don't want anyone to find you here." He gives a deep sigh, as if to say that the night has not been nearly long enough and that it is agony to leave. Once up, he does not instantly pull on his trousers. Instead he comes close to the lady and whispers whatever was left unsaid during the night. Even when he is dressed, he still lingers, vaguely pretending to be fastening his sash. . . .

Indeed, one's attachment to a man depends largely on the elegance of his leave-taking. When he jumps out of bed, scurries about the room, tightly fastens his trouser-sash, rolls up the sleeves of his Court cloak, over-robe, or hunting costume, stuffs his belongings into the breast of his robe and then briskly secures the outer sash—one really begins to hate him. . . .

It is very annoying, when one has visited Hase Temple and has retired into one's enclosure, to be disturbed by a herd of common people who come and sit outside in a row, crowded so close together that the tails of their robes fall over each other in utter disarray. I remember that once I was overcome by a great desire to go on a pilgrimage. Having made my way up the log steps, deafened by the fearful roar of the river, I hurried into my enclosure, longing to gaze upon the sacred countenance of Buddha. To my dismay I found that a throng of commoners had settled themselves directly in front of me, where they were incessantly standing up, prostrating themselves, and squatting down again. They looked like so many basket-worms as they crowded together in their hideous clothes, leaving hardly an inch of space between themselves and me. I really felt like pushing them all over sideways.

Source: From *The Pillow Book of Sei Shonagon* by Sei Shonagon, translated by Ivan I. Morris, Copyright © 1991 Columbia University Press. Reprinted with permission of Columbia University Press and reproduced with permission of Oxford University Press through PLSclear.

■ ■ ■

SOURCE 2.4 Japanese Zen Buddhism

Among Japan's imports from China, none has been received more eagerly and thoroughly than Buddhism. And among the various forms of Buddhism, none has become more Japanese than Zen, which was firmly established in Japan by the twelfth and thirteenth centuries. Like all Buddhist teachings, it offers a path to the end of suffering, or to enlightenment. But for Zen practitioners, nothing external, such as deities or sacred texts, is of much help. Rather, the key practice is an inward-looking meditation, conducted under the guidance of often stern and rigorous teachers who are linked to a long lineage of transmission. In a classic formulation of Zen, there is "no dependence on words and letters; direct pointing to the mind of man; seeing into one's nature and attaining Buddhahood." In this way, individuals come to realize that they are already enlightened, that they already possess a Buddha nature. Sometimes this occurs gradually, but at other times this realization emerges in a flash of insight while doing something ordinary such as catching a shrimp or cutting a piece of bamboo. Thus Zen emphasizes simplicity, spontaneity, and the profundity of the ordinary, and it leads to compassion and tranquility, amid all the changing and difficult circumstances of life.

In Japan, Zen became associated in particular with the samurai, who appreciated its emphasis on rigorous practice and intuitive action. It also informed much of Japanese secular culture, especially painting, poetry, theater, and the elaborate simplicity of the tea ceremony.

In this image by an unknown Japanese artist from the second half of the fifteenth century, something of the style and substance of Zen finds expression. With a few quick and simple brushstrokes, the artist sets the scene of a story about a famous Chinese scholar-official named Su Dongpo, living in exile, caught in a sudden rainstorm, and forced to borrow a peasant's straw hat and wooden sandals. While local people laughed uproariously at the sight of a highly educated scholar in peasant attire, Su himself remained calm and unperturbed. The poetic text in the image reflects the Zen conception of "the essential oneness of all things, good and bad, whether in office or in lonely exile."[3]

1. What significance do you see in a Japanese Zen artist's referencing the story of a Chinese scholar?

2. What distinctive features of a Zen Buddhist outlook are expressed in this image of a solitary figure?

3. Why might members of the samurai class be attracted to such images and teachings?

Su Dongpo in Straw Hat and Wooden Shoes │ **15th century**

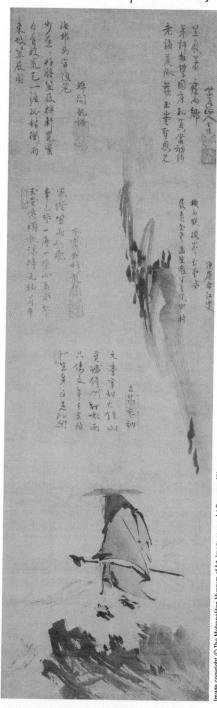

■ ■ ■

SOURCE 2.5 The Way of the Warrior

As the Japanese imperial court gradually lost power to military authorities in the countryside, a further distinctive feature of Japanese civilization emerged in the celebration of martial virtues and the warrior class—the samurai—that embodied those values. From the twelfth century through the mid-nineteenth century, public life and government in Japan were dominated by the samurai, while their culture and values, known as bushido, expressed the highest ideals of political leadership and of personal conduct. At least in the West, the samurai are perhaps best known for preferring death over dishonor, a posture expressed in seppuku (ritual suicide). But there was much more to bushido, for the samurai served not only as warriors but also as bureaucrats—magistrates, land managers, and provincial governors—acting on behalf of their lords (daimyo) or in service to military rulers, the shoguns. Furthermore, although bushido remained a distinctively Japanese cultural expression, it absorbed both Confucian and Buddhist values as well as those of the indigenous Shinto tradition.

The two selections that follow reflect major themes of an emerging bushido culture, the way of the warrior. The first excerpt comes from the writings of Shiba Yoshimasa (1349–1410), a feudal lord, general, and administrator as well as a noted poet, who wrote a manual of advice for the young warriors of his own lineage. Probably the man who most closely approximated in his own life the emerging ideal of a cultivated warrior was Imagawa Ryoshun (1325–1420), famous as a poet, a military commander, and a devout Buddhist. The second excerpt contains passages from a famous and highly critical letter Imagawa wrote to his adopted son (who was also his younger brother). The letter was published and republished hundreds of times and used for centuries as a primer or school text for the instruction of young samurai.

1. Based on these accounts, how would you define the ideal samurai?

2. What elements of Confucian, Buddhist, or Shinto thinking can you find in these selections? How do these writers reconcile the peaceful emphasis of Confucian and Buddhist teachings with the military dimension of bushido?

3. What does the Imagawa letter suggest about the problems facing the military rulers of Japan in the early fifteenth century?

SOURCE 2.5A

SHIBA YOSHIMASA │ *Advice to Young Samurai* │ ca. 1400

Wielders of bow and arrow should behave in a manner considerate not only of their own honor, of course, but also of the honor of their descendants. They should not bring on eternal disgrace by solicitude for their limited lives.

. . . [T]o regard your one and only life as like dust or ashes and die when you shouldn't is to acquire a worthless reputation. A genuine motive would be, for example, to give up your life for the sake of the sole sovereign, or serving under the commander of the military in a time of need; these would convey an exalted name to children and descendants. Something like a strategy of the moment, whether good or bad, cannot raise the family reputation much.

Warriors should never be thoughtless or absentminded but handle all things with forethought. . . .

It is said that good warriors and good Buddhists are similarly circumspect. Whatever the matter, it is vexing for the mind not to be calm. Putting others' minds at ease too is something found only in the considerate. . . .

When you begin to think of yourself, you'll get irritated at your parents' concern and defy their instructions. Even if your parents may be stupid, if you obey their instructions, at least you won't be violating the principle of nature. What is more, eighty to ninety percent of the time what parents say makes sense for their children. It builds up in oneself to become obvious. The words of our parents we defied in irritation long ago are all essential. You should emulate even a bad parent rather than a good stranger; that's how a family culture is transmitted and comes to be known as a person's legacy. . . .

Even if one doesn't perform any religious exercises and never makes a visit to a shrine, neither deities nor buddhas will disregard a person whose mind is honest and compassionate.

Source: Thomas Cleary, trans. and ed., *Training the Samurai Mind* (Boston, MA: Shambhala, 2008), 18–20.

SOURCE 2.5B

IMAGAWA RYOSHUN | *The Imagawa Letter* | **1412**

As you do not understand the Arts of Peace [literary skills including poetry, history, philosophy, and ritual] your skill in the Arts of War [horsemanship, archery, swordsmanship] will not, in the end, achieve victory.

You like to roam about, hawking and cormorant fishing, relishing the purposelessness of taking life.

You live in luxury by fleecing the people and plundering the shrines.

To build your own dwelling you razed the pagoda and other buildings of the memorial temple of our ancestors.

You do not distinguish between good and bad behavior of your retainers, but reward or punish them without justice.

You permit yourself to forget the kindness that our lord and father showed us; thus you destroy the principles of loyalty and filial piety.

You do not understand the difference in status between yourself and others; sometimes you make too much of other people, sometimes too little.

You disregard other people's viewpoints; you bully them and rely on force.

You excel at drinking bouts, amusements, and gambling, but you forget the business of our clan.

You provide yourself lavishly with clothes and weapons, but your retainers are poorly equipped.

You ought to show utmost respect to Buddhist monks and priests and carry out ceremonies properly.

You impede the flow of travelers by erecting barriers everywhere in your territory.

Whether you are in charge of anything—such as a province or a district—or not, it will be difficult to put your abilities to any use if you have not won the sympathy and respect of ordinary people.

Just as the Buddhist scriptures tell us that the Buddha incessantly strives to save mankind, in the same way you should exert your mind to the utmost in all your activities, be they civil or military, and never fall into negligence.

It should be regarded as dangerous if the ruler of the people in a province is deficient even in a single [one] of the cardinal virtues of human-heartedness, righteousness, propriety, wisdom, and good faith.

You were born to be a warrior, but you mismanage your territory, do not maintain the army, and are not ashamed although people laugh at you. It is, indeed, a mortifying situation for you and our whole clan.

Source: Carl Steenstrup, trans., "The Imagawa Letter," *Monumenta Nipponica* 28, no. 3 (1973), 295–316. Copyright © 1973 by Sophia University.

■ ■ ■

SOURCE 2.6 Samurai and the "Arts of Peace"

Beyond their skills in military and political matters, samurai were expected to master the arts of peace as well as those of war. According to a leading samurai of the sixteenth century, such a person is "renowned for his elegant pursuits, he is a complete man combining arts [*bun*] and arms [*bu*]. A man of nobility . . . he was a ruler endowed with awesome dignity and inspiring decorum. . . . He discussed Chinese poetic styles and recited by heart the secret teachings of Japanese poetry."[4] Such cultural attainments added to the authority of the samurai and allowed them to mix with nobility in settings where the arts were of great importance. Thus many samurai took up poetry, painting, classical *noh* theater, Zen Buddhist meditation, and the tea ceremony.

This woodblock print shows a loyal and probably mythical fourteenth-century samurai warrior, Kojima Takanori, who had just failed to rescue his captured emperor. In the immediate aftermath of his unsuccessful attempt, Kojima stripped some bark from a nearby cherry tree and wrote a Chinese poem comparing the emperor to an ancient Chinese ruler, declaring himself a loyal subject, and promising eventual victory. Kojima expected that his emperor would see the message as he was being led into exile and know that help was on the way.

1. How does this image fit with your perception of samurai warriors?

2. In Source 2.5B, Imagawa writes, "As you do not understand the Arts of Peace, your skill in the Arts of War will not, in the end, achieve victory." How does this image help you understand Imagawa's statement?

3. Why do you think Kojima is writing in Chinese and comparing his ruler to the Chinese monarch?

Kojima Takanori Writing a Poem on a Cherry Tree | 14th century

Kojima Takanori Writing a Poem on a Cherry Tree, from the series, "Pictures of Flowers of Japan," 1895 (woodblock print)/Ogata Gekko (1859-1920)/FITZWILLIAM MUSEUM/Fitzwilliam Museum, University of Cambridge, UK/Bridgeman Images

DOING HISTORY

1. **Looking for continuities:** What older patterns of Japanese thought and practice persisted despite much cultural borrowing from China? To what extent did borrowed elements of Chinese culture come to be regarded as Japanese?

2. **Noticing inconsistencies and change:** No national culture develops as a single set of ideas and practices. What inconsistencies, tensions, or differences in emphasis can you identify in these documents and images? What changes over time can you find in these selections?

3. **Considering Confucian reactions:** How might Confucian scholars respond to each of these documents and images?

China's Influence in the Making of Japanese Civilization

Japan was one of several third-wave civilizations that emerged in East Asia within the cultural orbit of China. Like Korea and Vietnam, it was heavily influenced by Chinese culture, political thought, and religious traditions, but at the same time developed into a distinct civilization. The two voices that follow assess the influence of China on this emerging Japanese civilization. In Voice 2.1, Milton Walter Meyer, who has written extensively on East Asia, examines first the profound impact of China and then the limitations of its influence. In Voice 2.2, Matthew Stavros, an Australian historian of early Japan, explores the relationship between Chinese ideas and the planning and construction of the Japanese capital Kyoto.

1. According to Meyer, what Chinese practices and concepts were most easily adopted in Japan?

2. In what ways does Stavros's description of Kyoto reflect aspects of Chinese influence raised by Meyer?

3. **Integrating primary and secondary sources:** In what ways do these two voices reinforce or add to the picture of Chinese influence on Japanese society provided by the sources in this feature?

VOICE 2.1

Milton Walter Meyer on China's Influence on Japan's First Imperial State | 2009

The Nara epoch [710–794 c.e.] saw the peak and the beginning of the decline in borrowing from the Chinese. . . . [T]he central government zealously promoted Buddhist religion and art, which existed in concrete, recognizable, and vivid forms. The transplantation of the more complex, detailed, and less vivid Chinese political and economic concepts proved more difficult. Those Chinese ideas that could be pragmatically adopted or those that were similar or understandable to Japanese concepts persisted, such as the notions of hierarchy, titles, and court rituals. Those ideas that proved impractical or unassimilable died out, such as the concept of a strong state based on extended and well-structured economic, political, and administrative forms.

While the Japanese borrowed wholesale, they also insisted on retaining their own traditions. Bureaucracy was maintained through hereditary aristocracy and not through the Chinese Confucian system of education, examination, and meritocracy. The Japanese continued to emphasize the divinity of the emperor. They never accepted the Chinese idea of the mandate of heaven, which implied the right to revolt. As propounded in China by Confucian scholars, the mandate could be used against evil emperors, who, because of their immorality and injustice, became unfit for office, which required, in theory, virtuous men to perform virtuous functions amenable to the gods. The Japanese retained their emperors and only changed their ruling families behind the throne. Despite heavy doses of sinification [Chinese influence], Nara traveled its own cultural path.

Source: Milton Walter Meyer, *Japan: A Concise History* (Lanham, MD: Rowman and Littlefield, 2009), 56.

VOICE 2.2

Matthew Stavros on China's Influence on the Capital City of Kyoto | 2014

When Emperor Kanmu (737–806) founded Heian-kyō [Kyoto] in 794, the new capital was meant to be the permanent bureaucratic and ritual seat of a strong, centralized, Chinese style state. The scale and opulence of the plan was grand and ambitious, in fact probably too much so. Some of the key traits meant to define Heian-kyō's appearance were never entirely realized, while many of those that were rapidly disintegrated. Not only did the Japanese polity [state] function very differently from its Chinese prototype, real power, even from the outset, rested more with private political actors than the state. . . .

It was to be a capital in the purest sense of the word: the seat of the statutory government, home and ritual center of the emperor and the civil aristocracy, and the location of numerous official buildings and monuments that facilitated imperial pageantry, bureaucratic administration, and diplomacy. Buddhist temples and shrines were excluded, and the presence of warriors in the city was, in principle, taboo. Due to their polluting effects, killing and burial were also formally proscribed. Commercial activity was limited, while farming was generally not allowed. . . .

In closing, it should be emphasized that the narrative thus far has described how Heian-kyō was *meant* to be; how it was planned; how it was idealized. The reality, however, is that the city never lived up to the grand vision of its founders. . . . Heian-kyō did indeed become Japan's eternal capital, but the city envisioned by Kanmu never fully materialized.

Source: Matthew Gerald Stavros, *Kyoto: An Urban History of Japan's Premodern Capital* (Honolulu, HI: University of Hawai'i Press, 2014), 1–2, 27.

NOTES

1. Wm. Theodore de Bary et al., eds., *Sources of Japanese Tradition*, 2nd ed. (New York, NY: Columbia University Press, 2001), 1:42.

2. Donald Keene, *Seeds in the Heart* (New York, NY: Henry Holt, 1993), 477–78.

3. "Su Dongpo in Straw Hat and Wooden Shoes," *Heilbrunn Timeline of Art History*, Metropolitan Museum of Art, accessed March 7, 2018, http://www.metmuseum.org/toah/works-of-art/1975.268.39.

4. Yoshiaki Shimizu, ed., *Japan: The Shaping of Daimyo Culture, 1185–1868* (Washington, DC: National Gallery, 1988), 78.

Living and Dying during the Black Death

CHAPTER 3

Among the most far-reaching outcomes of the Mongol moment in world history was the spread all across Asia, the Middle East, Europe, and North Africa of the deadly disease known as the plague or the Black Death. While the Mongols certainly did not intend to cause the plague, their empire facilitated the movement not only of goods and people, but also of the microorganisms responsible for this pestilence. Its sudden arrival in the late 1340s, the enormity of its death toll, the social trauma it generated, the absence of any remembered frame of reference for an event so devastating—all of this left people everywhere bewildered, imagining the end of the world. The sources that follow illustrate how people in various cultural settings experienced this initial phase of the catastrophe, sought to understand what was happening, and tried to cope with it. The feature begins with three general accounts of the arrival of the plague—in the Islamic Middle East, Western Europe, and the Byzantine Empire—followed by five sources that focus on more specific aspects of this hemispheric pandemic.

SOURCE 3.1 The Black Death in the Islamic World

Ibn al-Wardi was an Arab Muslim writer living in Aleppo, Syria, when the plague struck. He wrote extensively about what he witnessed and then died from the pestilence in 1349. As the only major contemporary account of the Black Death to survive from the Middle East, his description was widely quoted by later Muslim writers and remains a major source for modern historians. His account is thoroughly informed by an Islamic religious sensibility, especially when Ibn al-Wardi refers to the "noble tradition" that prohibits fleeing an outbreak of disease. Three passages from the hadiths, sayings attributed to Muhammad, were especially important for Muslims:

When you learn that epidemic disease exists in a country, do not go there, but if it breaks out in the country where you are, do not leave.
He who dies of epidemic disease is a martyr.
It is a punishment that God inflicts on whom he wills, but He has granted a modicum of clemency with respect to Believers.[1]

These teachings made it a matter of faith for many Muslims to trust in God to protect them from the plague.

1. How does Ibn al-Wardi seek to explain the plague?

2. What does this document reveal about the range of initial responses to the pandemic?

3. In what ways does Islam inform Ibn al-Wardi's account of these events?

IBN AL-WARDI | *Report of the Pestilence* | 1348

The plague frightened and killed. It began in the land of darkness [Northern Asia]. Oh, what a visitor! . . . China was not preserved from it. The plague afflicted the Indians in India. . . . It attacked the Persians . . . and gnawed away at the Crimea. . . . The plague destroyed mankind in Cairo . . . the scourge came to Jerusalem. . . . It overtook those people who fled to the al-Aqsa Mosque. . . .

How amazingly does it pursue the people of each house. One of them spits blood and everyone in the household is certain of death . . . after two or three nights.

Oh God, it is acting by your command. Lift this from us.

The pestilence caused the people of Aleppo the same disturbance. . . . Oh, if you could see the nobles of Aleppo studying their inscrutable books of medicine. They multiply its remedies by eating dried and sour food. . . . They perfumed their homes with ambergris and camphor. . . . They wore ruby rings and put onions, vinegar, and sardines together with the daily meal. . . .

If you see many biers and their carriers and hear in every quarter of Aleppo the announcements of death and cries, you run from them and refuse to stay with them. The profits of the undertakers have greatly increased. . . . Those who sweat from carrying coffins enjoy this plague-time.

We ask God's forgiveness for our souls' bad inclinations; the plague is surely part of His punishment.

The plague is for the Muslims a martyrdom and a reward, and for the disbelievers a punishment and a rebuke. . . . It has been established by our Prophet . . . that the plague-stricken are martyrs. . . . And this secret should be pleasing to the true believer. If someone says that it causes infection and destruction, say: God creates and recreates. . . . If we acknowledge the plague's devastation of the people, it is the will of the Chosen Doer. I take refuge in God from the yoke of the plague.

One man begs another to take care of his children, and one says goodbye to his neighbors. A third perfects his work, and another prepares his shroud. A fifth is reconciled with his enemies, and another treats his friends with kindness. . . . One man puts aside his property [in a religious endowment called a *waqf*]; one frees his servants. One man changes his character, while another amends his ways. There is no protection today from it other than His mercy, praise be to God.

Nothing prevented us from running away from the plague, except our devotion to the noble tradition [prohibiting flight from a plague-stricken land]. Come then, seek the aid of God Almighty for raising the plague, for He is the best helper. . . . We do not depend on our good health against the plague, but on You [God].

[*Somewhat later, a fifteenth-century account of the plague in Cairo by the Egyptian scholar al-Maqrizi reported that people received very high wages for reciting the Quran at funerals, caring for the ill, and washing the dead. Many trades disappeared as artisans found more lucrative employment in plague-related occupations. Fields went unharvested for lack of peasants to do the work. Weddings and family feasts vanished, and even the call to prayer was sometimes canceled. Al-Maqrizi reported that in Cairo, "some people appropriated for themselves without scruple the immovable and movable goods and cash of their former owners after their demise. But very few lived long enough to profit thereby."[2]*]

Source: Michael Dols, "Ibn al-Wardi's Risalah al-Naba' 'an al-Waba', a Translation of a Major Source for the History of the Black Death in the Middle East," in *Near Eastern Numismatics, Iconography, Epigraphy and History: Studies in Honor of George C. Miles*, ed. Dickran K. Kouymjian (Beirut, Lebanon: American University of Beirut, 1974), 448–55.

■ ■ ■

SOURCE 3.2 **The Black Death in Western Europe**

Like Ibn al-Wardi in Aleppo, the Italian writer Giovanni Boccaccio of Florence, Italy, was an eyewitness to the plague in his city. He recorded his impressions of the plague, which claimed the lives of his father and stepmother, in a preface to *The Decameron*, completed around 1353. This fictional collection of tales was set in a villa outside Florence, where a group of seven women and three men took turns telling stories to one another while escaping the plague that was ravaging their city.

1. How does Boccaccio describe the social breakdown that accompanied the plague in Florence?

2. What different responses to the plague does he identify?

3. In what ways does Boccaccio's account overlap with that of Ibn al-Wardi? How does it differ?

GIOVANNI BOCCACCIO | *The Decameron* | **mid-14th century**

In the year of our Lord 1348, there happened at Florence, the finest city in all Italy, a most terrible plague; . . . [In] spite of all the means that art and human foresight could suggest, such as keeping the city clear from filth, the exclusion of all suspected [sick] persons, and the publication of copious instructions for the preservation of health; and notwithstanding manifold humble supplications offered to God in processions and otherwise; it [the plague] began to show itself in the spring. . . .

To the cure of this malady, neither medical knowledge nor the power of drugs was of any effect; whether because the disease was in its own nature mortal, or that the physicians (the number of whom, taking quacks and women pretenders into the account, was grown very great,) could form no just idea of the cause, nor consequently devise a true method of cure; whichever was the reason, few escaped; but nearly all died the third day from the first appearance of the symptoms. . . .

. . . These facts [the incurable and horrible nature of the disease] . . . occasioned various fears and devices amongst those who survived, all tending to the same uncharitable and cruel end, which was, to avoid the sick, and every thing that had been near them, expecting by that means to save themselves. And some holding it best to live temperately, and to avoid excesses of all kinds, made parties, and shut themselves up from the rest of the world; eating and drinking moderately of the best, and diverting themselves with music, and such other entertainments as they might have within doors; never listening to anything from without, to make them uneasy. Others maintained free living to be a better preservative, and would baulk no passion or appetite they wished to gratify, drinking and reveling incessantly from tavern to tavern, or in private houses (which were frequently found deserted by the owners, and therefore common to everyone), yet strenuously avoiding, with all this brutal indulgence, to come near the infected. And such, at that time, was the public distress, that the laws, human and divine, were no more regarded; for the officers, to put them in force, being either dead, sick, or in want of persons to assist them, every one did just as he pleased. . . .

Others with less humanity, but perchance, as they supposed, with more security from danger, decided that the only remedy for the pestilence was to avoid it: persuaded therefore, of this, and taking care for themselves only, men and women in great numbers left the city, their houses, relations, and effects, and fled into the country: as if the wrath of God had been restrained to visit those only within the walls of the city . . . their terror was such, that a brother even fled from his brother, a wife from her husband, and, what is more uncommon, a parent from his own child. . . .

From this desertion of friends, and scarcity of servants, an unheard-of custom prevailed; no lady, however young or handsome, would scruple to be attended by a man-servant, whether young or old it mattered not, and to expose herself naked to him, the necessity of the distemper [disease] requiring it, . . . which might make those who recovered, less modest for the time to come.

[Traditional burial customs were] now laid aside, and, so far from having a crowd of women to lament over them, great numbers passed out of the world without a witness. Few were they who had the tears of their friends at their departure. . . . Nor was a corpse attended by . . . citizens of credit, but [rather] fellows hired for the purpose; who would . . . carry it [the body] with all possible haste to the nearest church; and the corpse was interred without any great ceremony, where they could find room.

[S]ome breathed their last in the streets, and others shut up in their own houses, where the stench that came from them made the first discovery of their deaths to the neighborhood. And, indeed, every place was filled with the dead. . . . The consecrated ground [cemeteries] no longer containing the numbers which were continually brought thither. . . they were forced to dig trenches, and to put them in by hundreds, piling them up in rows, as goods are stowed in a ship. . . .

[In the surrounding countryside] distressed labourers, with their families, without either the aid of physicians, or help of servants, languishing on the highways, in the fields, and in their own houses, and dying rather like cattle than human creatures. . . . [S]upposing every day to be their last, their thoughts were not so much employed how to improve, as how to use their substance for their present support. [Domesticated animals] were left to roam at will about the fields, and among the standing corn, which no one cared to gather, or even to reap. . . .

Such was the cruelty of Heaven, and perhaps of men, that between March and July following, according to authentic reckonings, upwards of a hundred thousand souls perished in the city. . .

Source: *The Decameron, or, Ten Days' Entertainment of Boccaccio.* A revised translation, by Walter Keating Kelly. (London, UK: Henry G. Bohn, 1855), xii, frontis. (port.). (Bohn's Extra Volume) Extra Volume: 5 (pp. 1–6).

■ ■ ■

SOURCE 3.3 The Black Death in Byzantium

In 1347, the plague struck Constantinople, capital of the Byzantine Empire. It quickly touched the royal family, as the young son of Emperor John VI and Empress Irene perished from the disease. Eight years later, the emperor abdicated his throne, retiring to a monastery, where he wrote a history of the Byzantine Empire. That work contained a description of the plague as it arrived in Constantinople.

1. In what larger context did Emperor John VI place the plague and his own personal tragedy?

2. How did the emperor describe the outcomes of the plague?

3. Does this account have more in common with that of Ibn al-Wardi or that of Boccaccio?

EMPEROR JOHN VI OF BYZANTIUM | *Historiarum* | mid- to late 14th century

---

Upon arrival in Byzantium, she [the empress Irene] found Andronikos, the youngest born, dead from the invading plague. . . . [It has] spread throughout almost the entire world.

So incurable was the evil that neither any regularity of life, nor any bodily strength could resist it. Strong and weak bodies were all similarly carried away and those best cared for died in the same manner as the poor. . . . Neither did the disease take the same course in all persons.

Great abscesses were formed on the legs or the arms, from which, when cut, a large quantity of foul-smelling pus flowed. . . . Even many who were seized by all the symptoms unexpectedly recovered. There was no help from anywhere; if someone brought to another a remedy useful to himself, this became poison to the other patient. Some, by treating others, became infected with the disease.

It caused great destruction and many homes were deserted by their inhabitants. Domestic animals died together with their masters. Most terrible was the discouragement. Whenever people felt sick there was no hope left for recovery, but by turning to despair, adding to their prostration and severely aggravating their sickness, they died at once.

No words could express the nature of the disease. All that can be pointed out is that it had nothing in common with the everyday evils to which the nature of man is subject, but was something else sent by God to restore chastity. Many of the sick turned to better things in their minds, by being chastened, not only those who died, but also those who overcame the disease. They abstained from all vice during that time and they lived virtuously; many divided their property among the poor, even before they were attacked by the disease. If he ever felt himself seized, no one was so ruthless as not to show repentance of his faults and to appear before the judgment seat of God with the best chance of salvation, not believing that the soul was incurable or unhealed.

Many died in Byzantium then, and the king's son, Andronikos, was attacked and died the third day.

Source: Christos S. Bartsocas, "Two Fourteenth-Century Descriptions of the 'Black Death,'" *Journal of the History of Medicine and Allied Sciences* (Oxford University Press) 21, no. 4 (October 1966): 395-97.

■ ■ ■

SOURCE 3.4 Religious Responses in the Islamic World

Religion permeated the worlds of both Islam and Christianity during the fourteenth century. It is hardly surprising, then, that many people would turn to religious practices in their efforts to understand and cope with a catastrophe of such immense proportions as the Black Death. And yet for a few, the plague challenged established religious understandings. Some Islamic scholars had long opposed the idea of contagion as an explanation for the spread of disease, as that theory seemed to grant human actions, rather than God's decree, the primary role in this process. The plague, however, persuaded one Muslim scholar and physician, al-Khatib, to reject this teaching. "The existence of contagion," he wrote, "has been proved by experience, deduction, the senses, observation, and by unanimous reports."[3]

Most people, however, turned to traditional religious practices to find some sense of meaning, comfort, and protection in the face of the unimaginable tragedy. Source 3.4, written by Ibn Kathir, an Islamic teacher from Damascus, describes one such event.

1. What specific practices did the Muslims of Damascus undertake? Why might they have chanted the Quran's account of the flood of Noah in particular?

2. What assumptions underlay these practices?

3. What might you infer from Ibn Kathir's description of the composition of the gathered crowd?

IBN KATHIR | *The Beginning and the End: On History* | ca. 1350–1351

At Damascus, a reading of the *Traditions* of Bukhari [a collection of the sayings of Muhammad] took place on June 5 of this year [1348] after the public prayer—with the great magistrates there assisting in the presence of a very dense crowd. The ceremony continued with a recitation of a section of the Koran, and the people poured out their supplication that the city be spared the plague.... It was predicted and feared that it would become a menace to Damascus.... On the morning of June 7, the crowd reassembled ... and resumed the recitation of the flood of Noah.... During this month, the mortality increased among the population of Damascus, until it reached a daily average of more than 100 persons.

On Monday July 21, a proclamation made in the city invited the population to fast for three days; they were further asked to go on the fourth day, a Friday, to the Mosque of the Foot in order to humbly beseech God to take away this plague.... On the morning of July 25, the inhabitants threw themselves [into these ceremonies] at every opportunity.... One saw in this multitude Jews, Christians, Samaritans, old men, old women, young children, poor men, emirs, notables, magistrates, who processed after the morning prayer, not ceasing to chant their prayers until daybreak. That was a memorable ceremony....

[By October] in the environs of the capital, the dead were innumerable, a thousand in a few days.

Source: Gaston Wiet, "La Grande Peste Noire en Syrie et en Egypt," *Études d'Orientalisme dédiées à la memoire de Lévi Provençal*, 2 vols. (Paris, France: G.-P. Maisonneuve et Larose, 1962), 1:381–83.

■ ■ ■

SOURCE 3.5 Picturing Religious Responses in the Christian World

The horrific experience of the Black Death caused some people in the Christian world to question fundamental teachings about the mercy and power of God or the usefulness of religious rituals. For some, the plague prompted an orgy of hedonism, perhaps to affirm life in the face of endless death or simply to live life to the fullest in what time remained to them. Most European Christians, however, relied on familiar practices: seeking the aid of parish priests, invoking the intercession of the Virgin Mary, participating in religious processions and pilgrimages, attending mass regularly, and increasing attention to private devotion. From church leaders, the faithful heard the message that the plague was God's punishment for sins. Accompanying such ideas were religiously based attacks on prostitutes, homosexuals, and Jews—people whose allegedly immoral behavior or alien beliefs had invited God's retribution.

The most well-known movement reflecting an understanding of the plague as God's judgment on a sinful world was that of the flagellants, whose name derived from the Latin word *flagella*, meaning "whips." The practice of flagellation—whipping oneself or allowing oneself to be whipped—had a long tradition within the Christian world and elsewhere. It reemerged as a fairly widespread practice, especially in Germany, between 1348 and 1350 in response to the initial outbreak of the plague. Its adherents believed that perhaps the terrible wrath of God could be averted by performing this extraordinary act of atonement or penance. Groups of flagellants moved from city to city, where they called for repentance, confessed their sins, sang hymns, and participated in ritual dances, which climaxed in the participants whipping themselves with knotted cords sometimes embedded with iron points. Source 3.5A is a contemporary representation of the flagellants in the town of Doornik in the Netherlands in 1349.

1. Does this procession seem spontaneous or organized? Does it seem to be led by major church authorities or by ordinary people?

2. Why might the flagellants identify with the image of the crucified Jesus carried in the procession?

SOURCE 3.5A

The Flagellants | 1349

The Flagellants at Doornik in 1349, copy of a miniature from the Chronicle of Aegidius Li Muisis/Private Collection/Bridgeman Images

The initial and subsequent outbreaks of the plague in Western Europe generated an understandable preoccupation with death and its apparently indiscriminate occurrence. This concern, or obsession, found expression in the Dance of Death, a ritual intended to prevent the plague or to cure the afflicted, which began in France in 1348. During the performance, people would periodically fall to the ground, allowing others to trample on them. By 1400, such performances took place in a number of parish churches and subsequently in more secular settings.

The Dance of Death also received artistic expression in a variety of poems and sketches, along with paintings like Source 3.5B. This painting was created by the German artist Berndt Notke in 1463 and subsequently restored and reproduced many times. In the inscriptions at the bottom of the painting, each living character addresses a skeletal figure, who in turn makes a reply. In the exchange between the Empress (shown in a red dress and an elaborate headgear) and the skeletal figure of Death, the terrified empress begs for more time on the basis of her high status. But Death reminds her that she must bear the fate of all humans.

1. What can you infer about the status of the living figures in this painting?

2. Notice that the living figures face outward toward the viewer, rather than toward the entreating death figures on either side of them. What might this mean?

3. What lesson was the exchange between the empress and Death intended to convey?

SOURCE 3.5B

A Culture of Death | 1463

Macabre (oil on canvas) (see 197685, 197687)/Bernt Notke (c.1440–1509)/ART MUSEUM OF ESTONIA/St Nicholas' Church, Art Museum of Estonia, Tallinn, Estonia/Bridgeman Images

■ ■ ■

The Black Death and European Jews

Extreme and traumatic events such as the plague cry out for explanation so that people can find some sense of stability in a bewildering and chaotic environment. One such explanation lay in the scapegoating of minorities or outsiders, about whom conspiracies were constructed to account for the inexplicable. In France, "beggars and mendicants of various countries" were accused of poisoning wells, tortured to produce confessions, and then burned to death. More frequently the targets of such attacks were Jews, who had long been damned as "Christ killers," prohibited from practicing certain occupations, and stereotyped as greedy moneylenders. Many church authorities had encouraged tolerance of Jews, hoping that they might finally convert to Christianity. But as the plague took hold, accusations against Jews for poisoning wells mounted, as did attacks upon them, confessions extracted under torture, and executions by burning. Conflicting economic interests played an important role in these events. Rulers and city fathers often wanted to keep Jews in their cities as a source of tax revenue, while those indebted to Jewish lenders might well benefit from their death. This account by the German chronicler Jacob Von Königshofen (1346–1420) illustrates that horrendous process of burning innocent Jews to death.

1. What differences of opinion on dealing with Jews appear in this source?

2. What mix of motives lay behind these attacks on Jews?

3. How do these attacks on Jews compare with those that occurred during the Crusades?

JACOB VON KÖNIGSHOFEN | *About the Great Plague and the Burning of the Jews*
| *ca. early 15th century*

In the matter of this plague the Jews throughout the world were reviled and accused in all lands of having caused it through the poison which they are said to have put into the water and the wells. . . . For this reason the Jews were burnt all the way from the Mediterranean into Germany . . . , but not in Avignon, for the pope protected them there.

[I]n Basel the citizens marched to the city hall and compelled the council to take an oath that they would burn the Jews, and that they would allow no Jew to enter the city for the next two hundred years. . . . And there was a great indignation and clamor against the deputies from Strasbourg. So finally the Bishop and the lords and the Imperial Cities agreed to do away with the Jews. On . . . St. Valentine's Day [1349] they burnt the Jews on a wooden platform in their cemetery. There were about two thousand people of them. Those who wanted to baptize themselves were spared. Many small children were taken out of the fire and baptized against the will of their fathers and mothers. And everything that was owed to the Jews was cancelled, and the Jews had to surrender all pledges and notes that they had taken for debts. The council, however, took the cash that the Jews possessed and divided it among the workingmen proportionately. The money was indeed the thing that killed the Jews. If they had been poor and if the feudal lords had not been in debt to them, they would not have been burnt. After this wealth was divided among the artisans, some gave their share to the Cathedral or to the Church on the advice of their confessors. . . .

In some cities the Jews themselves set fire to their houses and cremated themselves.

Source: Jacob Marcus, *The Jew in the Medieval World: A Sourcebook, 315–1791* (New York, NY: JPS, 1938), 43–48.

■ ■ ■

SOURCE 3.7 A Government's Response to the Plague

Just as individuals and families found themselves required to respond to the Black Death, so, too, did communities and cities. Various urban authorities issued regulations that they hoped might slow or prevent the spread of the disease. A particularly detailed set of ordinances was issued in the northern Italian city of Pistoia in May 1348. Interestingly, these ordinances were revised several times over the coming weeks as the authorities adapted their regulations in an effort to address the growing crisis.

1. What assumptions underlay these regulations?

2. What difficulties might these ordinances have created for the living residents of Pistoia?

3. What social distinctions are reflected in these regulations?

Ordinances against the Spread of Plague, Pistoia | 1348

[N]o citizen of Pistoia or dweller in the district or the county of Pistoia . . . shall in any way dare or presume to go to Pisa or Lucca or to the county or district of either. And that no one can or ought to come from either of them or their districts . . . to the said city of Pistoia or its district or county on penalty of £ 50.

[N]o person whether citizen, inhabitant of the district or county of the city of Pistoia or foreigner shall dare or presume in any way to bring . . . to the city of Pistoia, its district or county, any used cloth, either linen or woolen, for use as clothing for men or women or for bedclothes on penalty of £ 200. . . . the bodies of the dead, after they had died, cannot be nor ought to be removed from the place in which they are found unless first such a body has been placed in a wooden casket covered by a lid secured with nails, so that no stench can issue forth from it; nor can it be covered except by a canopy, blanket or drape under a penalty for £ 50 of pennies paid by the heirs of the dead person. . . . [T]o avoid the foul stench which the bodies of the dead give off they have provided and ordered that any ditch in which a dead body is to be buried must be dug under ground to a depth of 2½ braccia [the length of an arm] by the measure of the city of Pistoia.

[A]ny person who will have come for the burial or to bury any dead person can not and may not be in the presence of the body itself nor with the relatives of such a dead person except for the procession to the church where it will be buried. Nor shall such persons return to the house where the defunct person lived. . . . when anyone has died no person should dare or presume to present or to send any gift before or after burial to the former dwelling place of such a dead person . . . .

[T]o avoid useless or fruitless expenses no person should dare or presume to dress in new clothing during the period of mourning for any dead person or during the eight days after that, on penalty of £ 25 of pennies for whoever contravenes [this] and for each time. Wives of such dead persons however, shall be exempted; they can be dressed in whatever new clothing they wish without penalty. So that the sounds of bells might not depress the infirm nor fear arise in them [the Wise Men] have provided and ordered that the bellringers or custodians in charge of the belltower of the cathedral of Pistoia shall not permit any bell in the said campanile to be rung for the funeral of the dead. . . . At the chapel or parish church of the said dead person or at the friary if the person is to be buried at a church of the friars, they can ring the bell of the chapel, parish church or the church of the friars so long as it is rung only one time and moderately. . . .

[N]o person should dare or presume to raise or cause to be raised any wailing or clamor over any person or because of any person who has died outside the city, district or county of Pistoia; nor on the said occasion should any persons be brought together in any place except blood relatives and associates of such a dead person. . . . It must be understood, however, in any written ordinances speaking of the dead and of honoring the burial of the dead that the foresaid shall not have force in the burial of the body of any soldiers of the militia, doctors of laws, judges or physicians whose bodies, because of their dignity, may be honored licitly at burial in a manner pleasing to their heirs.

They have provided and ordered that butchers and retail vendors of meat, individually and in common, can not, nor ought to hold or maintain near a tavern or other place where they sell meats, or near a shop or beside or behind a shop any stable, pen or any other thing which will give off a putrid smell; nor can they slaughter meat animals nor hang them after slaughter in any stable or other place in which there is any stench on a penalty of £ 10. So that stench and putrefaction shall not be harmful to men, henceforth tanning of hides can not and must not be done within the walls of the city of Pistoia on penalty of £ 25. . . .

Source: Duane Osheim, trans., Pistoia, "Ordinances for Sanitation in a Time of Mortality," October 28, 1994. Accessed at http://www2.iath.virginia.edu/osheim/pistoia.html.

DOING HISTORY

1. **Making comparisons:** What similarities and differences can you identify in how people experienced and understood the plague, both between and within particular societies?

2. **Religion and the plague:** How might you assess the role of religion in shaping responses to the plague? In what ways might religion have been helpful? How might it have exacerbated the suffering associated with the plague?

3. **Reflecting on disasters:** What can we learn about how humans react to natural disasters from studying the Black Death? What do these sources reveal about the extent to which humans feel in control of their own lives and their own history? In what ways do larger impersonal forces shape our individual lives and our collective histories?

Winners and Losers in Europe after the Plague

Everywhere that it spread, the plague caused horrific death and suffering, leading to demographic collapse across much of Europe. For those who survived, though, the plague created a radically different social landscape that offered new opportunities for some. The Voices presented here examine the fortunes of three major groups in medieval European society: farmers, tradesmen, and commoner women. In Voice 3.1, the economic historian Harry A. Miskimin considers the relative productivity of tillers of the soil versus urban artisans after the initial demographic collapse of the 1340s. In Voice 3.2, the social historian Mavis Mate assesses whether the period after the outbreak of the plague offered a "golden age" for women in the workplace.

1. According to Miskimin, why did farmers benefit more than urban artisans from the demographic collapse caused by the plague?

2. How would you describe Mate's assessment of changes caused by the plague in the working lives of women?

3. **Integrating primary and secondary sources:** What do these two voices add to perspectives of the plague's effects on society in Western Europe that are not offered in Sources 3.2, 3.5, 3.6, and 3.7?

VOICE 3.1

Harry Miskimin on the Rural Economy after the Plague │ 1975

. . . Capital equipment in medieval industry consisted mainly of simple tools closely keyed to the man who used them; the skill of the individual artisan was of the utmost importance in the production process. These facts are crucial for understanding the impact of the vast late-fourteenth century population decline upon industry and the urban economy. In agriculture, the reduction of the rural population allowed the survivors to redistribute the land, to acquire larger holdings, and to abandon land that was not fully productive. For this reason, it is highly probable that the average productivity of agricultural workers rose substantially [as] each rural worker [had] a larger and more fertile endowment of land whether he owned it or simply worked on it for others. In towns, on the contrary, the inheritance effects on average productivity were far less noticeable. Where there was a one-to-one relationship between the worker and his tools, little additional benefit was gained from access to capital goods left by victims of the plague. A farmer with twice as many acres as he held before the plague might be much, though probably not twice as much, more productive, but a carpenter with two hammers, or a shoemaker with two benches, gained little. Indeed, since the skill factor was crucial in medieval industry, it is very likely that the average productivity of artisans fell in the immediate wake of each successive visitation of plague or famine. The rapid increase in the death rate during such periods may well have outstripped the ability of society, hampered as it was by long terms of apprenticeship and limitations upon the number of apprentices, to train adequate replacements at the old level of skill.

Source: Harry A. Miskimin, *The Economy of Early Renaissance Europe, 1300–1460* (Cambridge, UK: Cambridge University Press, 1975), 82–83.

VOICE 3.2

Mavis Mate on the Effects of the Black Death on Women | 1998

[Women] were likely to earn more money than in the pre-plague economy, but the kind of work available to them basically did not change. In the countryside they helped to bring in the harvest: they weeded, harrowed and winnowed and in pastoral districts they milked the cows and sheared sheep. In the towns they worked as servants in private houses, in inns, taverns, and shops, and in some industrial establishments like breweries and dye-houses. Women, in both urban and rural areas, also carded and spun on a piece-work basis, worked as independent traders, as brewsters, petty retailers, shepsters [seamstresses] or dressmakers, and laundresses. . . .

Historians like Hilton and Barron, who believe that the late Middle Ages was to some extent a "golden age" for women, stress the independence enjoyed by married women and widows who worked as labourers and traders. Barron, for example, believes that married women in London "were frequently working partners in marriages between economic equals." There are some Sussex [a region of England] couples who might fit that description. . . . Yet the economic contribution of these women did not lead to any public recognition. Legally their husbands remained heads of household. . . .

[T]hey rarely achieved economic parity with men. Only for a few tasks such as weeding were women paid the same rate as men. . . . Management positions. . . . were always taken by men. No Sussex woman, not even a widow, is known to have controlled a lucrative business such as a tannery and there is no evidence that Sussex women were ever hired for such high-paid, high skilled jobs as carpenter, tiler or mason.

Source: Mavis E. Mate, *Daughters, Wives, and Widows after the Black Death* (Suffolk, UK: Boydell Press, 1998), 193–95.

NOTES

1. Manfred Ullman, *Islamic Medicine* (Edinburgh, UK: Edinburgh University Press, 1978), 94–95.

2. Quoted in John Aberth, *The Black Death* (Boston, MA: Bedford/St. Martin's, 2005), 85.

3. Quoted in Aberth, *The Black Death,* 115.

CHAPTER

4

The Spanish and the Aztecs: From Encounter to Conquest

WORKING WITH EVIDENCE

Among the sagas of early modern empire building, few have been more dramatic, more tragic, or better documented than the Spanish conquest of the Aztec Empire during the early sixteenth century. In recounting this story, historians are fortunate in having considerable evidence from both the Spanish and the Aztec sides of the encounter.

SOURCE 4.1 The Meeting of Cortés and Moctezuma: A Spanish View

In February 1519, twenty-seven years after Columbus first claimed the New World for Spain, Hernán Cortés, accompanied by some 350 Spanish soldiers, set off from Cuba with a fleet of eleven ships. He stopped at several places along the Gulf of Mexico before proceeding to march inland toward Tenochtitlán (te-nawch-tee-TLAHN), the capital of the Aztec Empire. Along the way, Cortés learned something about the fabulous wealth of this empire and about the fragility of its political structure. He also received various emissaries from the Aztec ruler Moctezuma, bearing rich gifts and warm greetings. Through a combination of force and astute diplomacy, Cortés was able to negotiate alliances with a number of the Aztecs' restive subject peoples and with the Aztecs' many rivals or enemies, especially the Tlaxcalans. With his modest forces thus greatly reinforced, Cortés arrived on November 8, 1519, in Tenochtitlán, where his famous meeting with Moctezuma took place. Bernal Díaz, a Spanish soldier who took part in the expedition, recounted his recollection of this encounter some thirty years later.

1. How would you describe the Spanish posture toward the Aztecs? What amazed the Spaniards, and what appalled them?

2. Does the account by Díaz confirm or challenge the controversial notion that the Aztecs viewed the Spanish as divine beings of some kind?

3. What differences in religious understanding emerged in the conversations between the two leaders? Were there any areas of agreement?

42

BERNAL DÍAZ | *The True History of the Conquest of New Spain* | mid-16th century

We proceeded along the Causeway which . . . runs straight to the City of Mexico. It was so crowded with people that there was hardly room for them all. They had never before seen horses or men such as we are.

Gazing on such wonderful sights, we did not know what to say, . . . for on one side, on the land, there were great cities, and in the lake ever so many more, and the lake itself was crowded with canoes, and in the Causeway were many bridges at intervals, and in front of us stood the great City of Mexico, and we,—we did not even number four hundred soldiers!

When we arrived, . . . many more chieftains and Caciques approached clad in very rich mantles. The Great Moctezuma had sent these great Caciques in advance to receive us, and when they came before Cortés they bade us welcome in their language, and as a sign of peace, they touched their hands against the ground, and kissed the ground with the hand.

When we arrived near to Mexico, the Great Moctezuma got down from his litter, and those great Caciques supported him with their arms beneath a marvellously rich canopy of green coloured feathers with much gold and silver embroidery and with pearls suspended from a sort of bordering, which was wonderful to look at. Besides these four Chieftains, there were four other great Caciques, who supported the canopy over their heads, and many other Lords who walked before the Great Moctezuma, sweeping the ground where he would tread and spreading cloths on it, so that he should not tread on the earth. Not one of these chieftains dared even to think of looking him in the face, but kept their eyes lowered with great reverence, except those four relations, his nephews, who supported him with their arms.

When Cortés was told that the Great Moctezuma was approaching, he dismounted from his horse, and when he was near Moctezuma, they simultaneously paid great reverence to one another. Moctezuma bade him welcome, and our Cortés replied through Doña Marina wishing him very good health. And it seems to me that Cortés, through Doña Marina, offered him his right hand, and Moctezuma did not wish to take it, but he did give his hand to Cortés and Cortés brought out a necklace which he had ready at hand, made of glass stones, . . . and he placed it round the neck of the Great Moctezuma and when he had so placed it he was going to embrace him, and those great Princes who accompanied Moctezuma held back Cortés by the arm so that he should not embrace him, for they considered it an indignity.

Then Cortés through the mouth of Doña Marina told him that now his heart rejoiced at having seen such a great Prince, and that he took it as a great honour that he had come in person to meet him and had frequently shown him such favour. Then Moctezuma spoke other words of politeness to him, and told two of his nephews . . . to go with us and show us to our quarters. . . . They took us to lodge in some large houses, where there were apartments for all of us. . . . They took us to lodge in that house, because they called us Teules [the Spanish took this word to mean "gods"], and took us for such, so that we should be with the Idols or Teules which were kept there....

[*After a "sumptuous dinner" and more "polite speech," everyone retired for the night. The next day Cortés and Moctezuma met again and exchanged views on religion. After Cortés outlined the basics of the Christian faith, he invited Moctezuma to embrace it.*]

[Cortés told] how such a brother as our great Emperor, grieving for the perdition of so many souls, such as those which their idols were leading to Hell, where they burn in living flames, had sent us, so that after what he [Moctezuma] had now heard he would put a stop to it and they would no longer adore these Idols or sacrifice Indian men and women to them, for we were all brethren, nor should they commit sodomy or thefts....At present we merely came to give them due warning, and so he prayed him to do what he was asked and carry it into effect.

Moctezuma replied—"Señor Malinche, I have understood your words and arguments very well before now, from what you said to my servants....We have not made any answer to it because here throughout all time we have worshipped our own gods, and thought they were good, as no doubt yours are, so do not trouble to speak to us any more about them at present. Regarding the creation of the world, we have held the same belief for ages past, and for this reason we take it for certain that you are those whom our ancestors predicted would come from the direction of the sunrise. As for your great King, I feel that I am indebted to him, and I will give him of what I possess...."

And Moctezuma said, laughing, for he was very merry in his princely way of speaking: "Malinche, I know very well that these people of Tlaxcala with whom you are such good friends have told you that I am a sort of God or Teul, and that everything in my houses is made of gold and silver and precious stones, I know well enough that you are wise and did not believe it but took it as a joke. Behold now, Señor Malinche, my body is of flesh and bone like yours, my houses and palaces of stone and wood and lime; that I am a great king and inherit the riches of my ancestors is true, but not all the nonsense and lies that they have told you about me, although of course you treated it as a joke, as I did your thunder and lightning."

[*A few days later Cortés asked Moctezuma to "show us your gods and Teules." On a visit to the main temple, Díaz described the many grotesquely carved "idols" and recalled evidence of recent human sacrifices.*]

They had offered to this Idol five hearts from that day's sacrifices....Everything was covered with blood, both walls and altar, and the stench was such that we could hardly wait the moment to get out of it.

Our Captain said to Moctezuma through our interpreter, half laughing: "Señor Moctezuma, I do not understand how such a great Prince and wise man as you are has not come to the conclusion, in your mind, that these idols of yours are not gods, but evil things that are called devils, and so that you may know it and all your priests may see it clearly, do me the favour to approve of my placing a cross ... [and] divide off a space where we can set up an image of Our Lady."

Moctezuma replied half angrily (and the two priests who were with him showed great annoyance), and said: "Señor Malinche, if I had known that you would have said such defamatory things I would not have shown you my gods, we consider them to be very good, for they give us health and rains and good seed times and seasons and as many victories as we desire, and we are obliged to worship them and make sacrifices, and I pray you not to say another word to their dishonour."

When our Captain heard that and noted the angry looks he did not refer again to the subject, but said with a cheerful manner: "It is time for your Excellency and for us to return." And Moctezuma replied that it was well, but that he had to pray and offer certain sacrifices on account of the great tatacul, that is to say sin, which he had committed in allowing us to ascend his great Cue [temple], and being the cause of our being permitted to see his gods, and of our dishonouring them by speaking evil of them, so that before he left he must pray and worship.

Then Cortés said "I ask your pardon if it be so. . . ." After our Captain and all of us were tired of walking about and seeing such a diversity of Idols and their sacrifices, we returned to our quarters.

Source: Bernal Díaz, *The True History of the Conquest of New Spain* (London, UK: Hakluyt Society, 1908). Excerpt taken from Bedford series book Stuart B. Schwartz, *Victors and Vanquished* (Boston, MA: Bedford/St. Martin's, 2000), 133–55.

■ ■ ■

The Meeting of Cortés and Moctezuma: An Aztec Account

Another account of this initial encounter comes from *The Florentine Codex*, a compilation of text and images collected under the leadership of Fray Bernardino de Sahagún, a Franciscan missionary who believed that an understanding of Aztec culture was essential to the task of conversion. Because Sahagún relied on Aztec informants and artists, many scholars believe that *The Florentine Codex* and other codices represent Indigenous understandings of the conquest. Even so, these sources require a critical reading, because they date from several decades after the events they describe. At that point, many contributors to the codices had been influenced by the Christian and European culture of their missionary mentors, and they were writing or painting in a society thoroughly dominated by Spanish colonial rule. Furthermore, the codices reflect the ethnic and regional diversity of Mesoamerica rather than a single Aztec perspective. Despite such limitations, these codices represent a unique window into Mesoamerican understandings of the conquest.

1. How does this account differ from that of Díaz (Source 4.1)? In what ways does it overlap with or supplement Díaz's understanding?

2. What, in particular, did the author of this report notice about the Spanish?

3. This text and that of Díaz were composed some thirty years or so after the events they describe. How might this fact affect our understanding of these documents?

FRAY BERNARDINO DE SAHAGÚN | *The Florentine Codex* | mid-16th century

The Spaniards parted from the city of Itztapalapa, all dressed out for war, marching in their orders and ranks by squadrons. Some of them were mounted on horses to scout ahead and discover if there was an ambush.

[*Details from the Nahuatl text*] Four mounted horsemen went ahead in the lead. They kept vigilant, turning to look about as they went, peering at people, looking this and that way, examining everywhere between the houses, looking up at the roofs. Their war dogs also went ahead.

In the rearguard went Don Hernando Cortés with many other Spaniards, all of them armed and in their order. Behind them went the baggage train and the artillery in their carriages. Many Indian warriors also went along with them with their weapons, many *Tlaxcaltecas* and *Huexotzincas* [Indigenous allies of the Spaniards] and in this manner and order they went into Mexico [Tenochtitlan].*

All alone marching out ahead came the standard bearer who bore the standard. He came waving it about, making it twirl, and tossing it about. It came rigidly rising up like a warrior, twisting and turning about. . . .

Following behind him closely came those [Spaniards] with iron swords, which were bare and shiny. They bore their shields of wood and leather on their shoulders.

In the second file or rank came the horses carrying people, each one with their cotton armor, their leather shield and an iron lance, with their iron swords hanging down from their horses' necks. They came with bells on, jingling or rattling. The large deer [horses] bellowed, and there was much neighing and they sweated a great deal. Their hooves made holes, and they dug holes in the ground wherever they placed them. . . .

In the third file or rank were those who had iron crossbows, the crossbowmen. As they came, the iron crossbows sat in their arms. They came along testing them out, pointing and aiming them. . . . Their quivers went hanging at their sides under their arms, well packed with iron bolts.

The fourth file were likewise horsemen whose garb was the same as stated before.

The fifth group were those with firearms, the harquebusiers, who shouldered their harquebuses [a sixteenth-century primitive type of matchlock gun supported on a hooked wooden support]. . . .

And when they went into the great palace, the residence of the ruler, they repeatedly shot off their harquebuses. They exploded, sputtered, discharged them, and they thundered and smoke spread, it grew dark with the smoke, everywhere was filled with smoke. People grew dizzy and fainted from the fetid smell.

---

*The Spanish version ends abruptly and states simply "All of that remaining in this chapter does not say anything else except the order in which the Spaniards and their Indian allies came when they entered into Mexico" (folio 22r). The remainder of the description translated here comes from the extensive Nahuatl descriptive prose dismissed and abbreviated by the Spanish translator in this chapter.

And last, bringing up the rear, went the war leader, thought to be the ruler and director in battle, like our war leader, a *Tlacateccatl.*[†]

Gathered and massed about him, going at his side, accompanying him, enclosing him were his warriors. . . . All those from the various *altepetl* [city-states] on the other side of the mountains [allies of the Spaniards], the Tlaxcalans, the people of Tliliuhquitepec, [those] of Huexotzinco, [they all] came following behind. They came outfitted for war with their cotton armor [*imiichcahuipil*], their shields [*inchichimal*] and with their bows and quivers full with arrows. . . .

Some bore burdens and provisions on their backs, some used bands around their forehead [to carry their burdens], some wore bands around their chests, others carrying wooden frames . . . and some baskets.

. . . Some dragged the large cannons, which went resting on wooden wheeled carriages, making a great noise as they came.

And when the Spaniards had come as far as Xoluco, when they had stopped there, Moctezuma dressed and prepared himself for a meeting, along with other great rulers and high nobles, his rulers and nobles, to receive in peace and with great honor Don Hernando Cortés and his other captains, and they took with them many beautiful flowers.

Then they went to the meeting. On gourd bases they set out different precious flowers. . . . And they carried golden necklaces, necklaces with pendants, wide necklaces.

And when Moctezuma went out to meet them, he arrived at the place they call Huitzillan. . . . and here Moctezuma gave various things to the Captain Hernan Cortés; he placed a golden collar with inlaid stones, and he gave him flowers, he put flower necklaces on him, he girded him with flowers, he put flower wreaths on his head. Then he laid before him the golden necklaces, all the different things used for greeting people.

Then [Cortés] asked Moctezuma "Is it not you? Is it not you then? Moctezuma?" Moctezuma said, "Yes, it is me."

Thereupon he stood up straight, he stood up with their faces meeting. He bowed down deeply to him. He stretched as far as he could, standing stiffly.

Addressing him, he said to him:

"Oh our lord, be doubly welcomed on your arrival in this land to your city; your home Mexico [Tenochtitlan], you have come to sit on your throne, your royal seat, which I have kept for many days for you. . . .

For a time I have been concerned, looking toward the mysterious place from which you have come, among clouds and mist. It is so that the [former] rulers on departing said that you would come in order to acquaint yourself with your *altepetl* [city-state/kingdom] and sit upon your royal seat . . .

[†]A *Tlacateccatl* was a Mexica (Aztec) military rank roughly equivalent to general. During wars and battles he was the second-in-command under the Aztec ruler (Tlatoani).

And now it has come true, you have come to rule over these kingdoms, and to seat yourself on your throne. Now I see that it is true what our leaders have told us. You are very welcome, great labors you have passed traveling a long way along the road.

Rest now here in your house, in your palaces: Take them and rest in them with all of your captains and companions who have come with you."

Once Moctezuma finished his speech, Marina [the translator] related it to Don Hernando Cortés. Then Cortés responded when he had understood what Moctezuma had said:

"Let Moctezuma be at ease, let him be not afraid, for we greatly esteem him. Now we are truly satisfied to see him in person and hear him, for until now we have greatly desired to see him and look upon his face. Well, now we have seen him, we have come to his homeland of Mexico. Bit by bit he will hear what we have to say."

Then Don Hernando Cortés took Moctezuma by the hand, and they went together side by side to the royal palace.

And the Spaniards looked at him, each of them looking at him closely. They would start along walking, then mount, then dismount again in order to see him.

Source: Fray Bernardino de Sahagún, *The Florentine Codex,* Book XII, "On the Conquest," folios 21v–25v. Translated by John Chuchiak.

■ ■ ■

SOURCE 4.3   Images of Encounter

Source 4.3A presents another Mesoamerican view of the first epic encounter between Cortés and Moctezuma, drawn from the Lienzo de Tlaxcala, a series of paintings completed by 1560. Created by Tlaxcalan artists, who had absorbed some elements of European styles, these paintings highlighted the role of the Tlaxcalan people as valued allies of the Spanish.

1. How does this painting present the relationship between Cortés and Moctezuma? Are they meeting as equals, as enemies, as allies, or as ruler and subject? Notice that both sit on European-style chairs, which had come to suggest authority in the decades following Spanish conquest. Is it significant that Cortés is seated on a platform?

2. Does this image support or challenge the perception that the Aztecs viewed the Spanish newcomers, at least initially, in religious terms as gods?

3. What does this painting add to the written accounts of this initial encounter in Sources 4.1 and 4.2?

SOURCE 4.3A

Moctezuma and Cortés | 1560

The Granger Collection

Whatever the character of their initial meeting, the relationship of the Spanish and Aztecs soon deteriorated amid mutual suspicion. Within a week, Cortés had seized Moctezuma, holding him under a kind of house arrest in his own palaces. For reasons not entirely clear, this hostile act did not immediately trigger a violent Aztec response. Perhaps Aztec authorities were concerned for the life of their ruler, or possibly their factional divisions inhibited coordinated resistance.

But in May 1520, while Cortés was temporarily away at the coast, an incident occurred that set in motion the most violent phase of the encounter. During a religious ceremony in honor of Huitzilopochtli, the Aztec patron deity of Tenochtitlán, the local Spanish commander, apparently fearing an uprising, launched a surprise attack on the unarmed participants in the celebration, killing hundreds of the leading warriors and nobles. An Aztec account from *The Florentine Codex* described the scene:

> When the dance was loveliest and when song was linked to song, the Spaniards were seized with an urge to kill the celebrants. They all ran forward, armed as if for battle. They closed the entrances and passageways ... then [they] rushed into the Sacred Patio to slaughter the inhabitants. ... They attacked the man who was drumming and cut off his arms. Then they cut off his head, and it rolled across the floor. They attacked all the celebrants stabbing them, spearing them, striking them with swords. ... Others they beheaded ... or split their heads to pieces. ... The blood of the warriors flowed like water and gathered into pools. ... [T]hey invaded every room, hunting and killing.[1]

Source 4.3B shows a vivid Aztec depiction of this "massacre of the nobles," drawn from the *Codex Duran*, first published in 1581.

1. What elements of the preceding description are reflected in this painting?

2. What image of the Spanish does this painting reflect?

3. What do the drums in the center of the image represent?

The Massacre of the Nobles | 1581

Bridgeman-Giraudon/Art Resource, NY

■ ■ ■

SOURCE 4.4 Conquest and Victory: The Fall of Tenochtitlán from a Spanish Perspective

The massacre of the nobles prompted a citywide uprising against the hated Spanish, who were forced to flee Tenochtitlán on June 30, 1520, across a causeway in Lake Texcoco amid ferocious fighting. Some six hundred Spaniards and several thousand of their Tlaxcalan allies perished in the escape, many of them laden with gold they had collected in Tenochtitlán. For the Spaniards, it was La Noche Triste (the night of sorrow); for the Aztecs, it was no doubt a fitting revenge and a great triumph.

While the Aztecs may have thought themselves permanently rid of the Spanish, La Noche Triste offered only a temporary respite from the European invaders. Cortés and his now-diminished forces found refuge among their Tlaxcalan allies, where they regrouped and planned for yet another assault on Tenochtitlán. In mid-1521, Cortés returned, strengthened with yet more Mesoamerican allies, and laid siege to the Aztec capital. Bitter fighting ensued for several months, often in the form of house-to-house combat, ending with the surrender of the last Aztec emperor on August 13, 1521.

A Spanish account of this event comes from Francisco de Aguilar, a conquistador who took part in the siege of Tenochtitlán, though he subsequently regretted his action and became a priest. Much later in life, around 1560, he wrote an account of his experiences, including this description of the final battle of the Spanish conquest.

1. How does Aguilar account for the Spanish victory?

2. How does he portray the Spanish and their Aztec adversaries?

FRANCISCO DE AGUILAR | *Brief Record of the Conquest of New Spain* | ca. 1560

[W]ith [Spanish] forces encircling the city and with the brigantines [warships], which were a great help on the lake, the city [Tenochtitlán] began to be battered by land and water. In addition great trouble was taken to cut off the fresh water from the springs, which reached the city by conduits. . . .

The Christians wounded some of the Indians, and great numbers of Indians were killed in the assaults on horseback and by the guns, harquebuses and crossbows. In spite of all this, they put up their strong barricades, and opened causeways and canals and defended themselves courageously. . . . They also killed some of the Spaniards and captured alive one of them called Guzman, who was Cortés's aide.

The war was sustained fiercely by both sides, since on our side we had the help of many Tlaxcalan warriors, while the Mexicans [had the advantage of] their rooftops and high buildings from which they battered us. . . . As soon as the Spaniards took any of the houses, which were all on the water, they had the Tlaxcalan Indians demolish and level them, for this gave more freedom to maneuver.

When some of the Indian lords inside the city began to see the danger they were in . . . , they decided to escape by night . . . [and] came over to our side. . . . In addition to this, when the Christians were exhausted from the war, God saw fit to send the Indians smallpox and there was a great pestilence in the city, because there were so many people there, especially women, and they had nothing more to eat. . . . Also for these reasons they began to slacken in their fighting.

The Mexicans, almost vanquished, withdrew to their fortresses on the water, and since a great number of women were left among them, they armed them all and stationed them on the rooftops. The Spaniards were alarmed at seeing so many of the enemy again, whooping and shouting at them, and when they began killing them and saw they were women, there was dismay on both sides.

[*Twice the last Aztec ruler, Cuauhtemoc, refused Spanish offers to surrender in return for a "pardon and many privileges." He was finally captured.*]

This done, the Spaniards seized the house that had been Cuauhtemoc's stronghold, where they found a great quantity of gold and jewels and other plunder. The Tlaxcalans, who were assisting us in the war . . . , knew [the city's] ins and outs, so that when they went home again, they were rich with the spoils they took.

Source: *The Conquistadors: First-Person Accounts of the Conquest of Mexico*, edited by Patricia de Fuentes, translated by Patricia de Fuentes, translation copyright © 1963 by Penguin Random House LLC, 158–60. Used by permission of Viking Books, an imprint of Penguin Publishing Group, a division of Penguin Random House LLC. All rights reserved.

■ ■ ■

SOURCE 4.5 Defeat: The Fall of Tenochtitlán from an Aztec Perspective

From *The Florentine Codex* (see Source 4.2) comes an Aztec account of what was, to the Aztecs, a devastating defeat.

1. To what extent does this document confirm, contradict, or supplement Aguilar's account of the fall of Tenochtitlán?

2. How does this account explain the terrible defeat?

3. What posture toward the Spanish does this document reflect?

FRAY BERNARDINO DE SAHAGÚN | *The Florentine Codex* | mid-16th century

---

Before the Spaniards who were in Tlaxcala returned to conquer Mexico, there appeared a great pestilence of smallpox in all of the Indians in the month they call *Tepeihuitl*, which is at the end of September.[*] And from this pestilence a great many of the Indians died, and they had their entire bodies, their faces, and all of their limbs so full of the smallpox sores and painful, that they could not get up or move from one side to the other, nor turn over from one side to another. And if one moved about, they cried out in pain.

This pestilence killed an innumerable number of people, and many of them died of hunger because there was no one who could make food.

And those who survived this pestilence remained with their faces marked and filled with holes by the pox. This pestilence lasted sixty days. . . . The Mexica warriors were greatly weakened by it.

When the pestilence was ending in Mexico the Spaniards, who were already in Tetzcoco, arrived.

They came down into the lagoon and they entered from Quauhtitlan, until they arrived at Tacuba and from there they divided themselves up into captaincies setting up in various places…

The warriors fought them in boats; the warriors in the boats shot at the Spaniards, and their arrows sprinkled down on them. Many times they skirmished, and the Mexica went out to face them. . . .

Before leaving Tlaxcala, the Spaniards had built twelve brigantines[†] which the Indian [allies] brought in pieces to Tetzcoco and there they built them, placing the artillery in them and with the Spaniards on them they went into the lagoon . . . with the determination to destroy the Mexicans. . . .

---

[*]The Aztec month *Tepeihuitl* was the thirteenth month of their calendar and it was known as the "month of the mountains" dedicated to the rain-god Tlaloc and the twin volcanos Popocatepetl and Iztaccihuatl. In Sahagún's time this month fell in the Spanish Calendar dates of September 30–October 19.

[†]A brigantine was a small Spanish boat with one mast equipped both for sailing and rowing.

And as the war began on the water, many of the Mexicans [Mexica] who had their houses close to the water began to run away with their children, and their women, some of them carrying their children on their backs and others in canoes. . . .

And the Indians that aided the Spaniards entered into their houses that they left and they robbed them of whatever they found. . . .

A gun went in the prow of each of their boats, and where the Mexica boats were thickest they fired on them and many people died from it. . . .

But when the Mexica had been able to see and judge how the guns fired and hit, or the iron bolts flew, they no longer went straight, but they went back and forth, going from one side to the other, zigzagging. . . .

When the Spanish adjusted the aim of their guns, they shot at the wall. The wall then ripped and broke open.

The second time it was hit, the wall went to the ground; it was knocked down in places, perforated, holes were blown in it. . . .

The warriors who had been lying at the wall dispersed and came fleeing; everyone escaped in fear, and then the Indian allies of the Spaniards quickly went filling in the canals with stones, adobe, earth, and timbers in order to be able to go forward. . . .

And when the canals were stopped up, and filled, the horsemen came and entered into the city, lancing the Indians that they could, and then they went out, and other horsemen came and did the same. . . .

And the Spaniards did not move at all; when they fired the cannon, it grew very dark, and smoke spread. . . .

During the fighting, the Mexica captured many Spaniards, according to their count they took fifty-three Spanish captives, as well as many of the Tlaxcalans and people from Tetzcoco, Chalco, and Xochimilco [allies of the Spaniards].

Then they [the Mexica] took the captives to Yacacolco, hurrying them along, herding their captives together.

Some went weeping, some singing, some went shouting while hitting their hands against their mouths.

When they got to Yacacolco, they lined them all up. Each one went to the altar platform, where the sacrifice was performed. The Spaniards went first, going in the lead, and the people of the other cities just followed coming last.

And when the sacrifice was over, they strung the Spaniards' heads on poles; they also strung up the horses' heads. They placed them below, and the Spaniards heads were placed above, facing the east. . . .

And the common people suffered greatly and there was great hunger among the Mexica, and much sickness, because they drank salty water from the lake and they ate vermin, lizards, maize straw, and the grass that grew along the lake.

And they gnawed at wood, flowers, plaster, leather and deerskin, which they roasted, baked and toasted so that they could eat them, and they ground up medicinal herbs and adobe bricks. . . .

There had never been the like of such suffering. The siege was frightening and a great number died of hunger. . . .

Along every stretch of road, the Spaniards took things from people by force. . . . They were looking for gold; they cared nothing for green stone, feathers, or turquoise. They looked everywhere with the women, on their abdomens, under their skirts. And they looked everywhere with the men, under their loincloths and in their mouths.

They took, picked out, the most beautiful women, with yellow bodies. And some of the women got away because they covered their faces with mud and they clothed themselves in rags.

And some men were picked out, those who were strong and in their prime, and those who were barely youths, to run errands for them.

They then burned some of them on the mouth [branded them] and some they branded on the cheeks, some on the mouth.

And when the weapons were laid down and we collapsed, the year was *Three House* and the day count was *One Serpent*.

Source: Fray Bernardino de Sahagún, *The Florentine Codex,* Book XII, "On the Conquest," folios 53r–56v, 67r–68r, 82r–83v. Translated by John Chuchiak.

■ ■ ■

SOURCE 4.6 Depicting the Seizure of the Aztec Capital

The seizure of Tenochtitlán was a formative event in the creation of colonial Mexico and represented the starting point for the profound transformations of Mexican society that accompanied the conquest. In the centuries that followed, the drama of this event attracted the interest of artists, writers, and others in this new society. One particularly impressive late seventeenth-century effort to depict the siege was painted by an unknown artist in Mexico on a large folding screen, which was most likely given by a local member of the Spanish elite to the new viceroy, Conde de Galve. On one side, the conquest of the city in 1521 unfolds in a series of scenes from the top left—where Cortés, bathed in sunshine, lands in Mexico and meets Moctezuma—to the bottom right—where in darker tones the Spanish are driven from the city on the "sad night" and Native American refugees flee into the surrounding forests to escape the violence. In between, scenes depicting critical moments in the conquest take place in different parts of an imagined cityscape. While key elements of the conquest story are present, the overall scene is most striking for its depiction of what one critic has called the "motley banquet of violence," which contrasts sharply with the serene, peaceful, and idealized cityscape of seventeenth-century Mexico City depicted on the other side of the screen.[2]

The scene reproduced here chronicles a dramatic moment from a central panel in the screen, in which Aztecs battle the Spanish near the Temple Mayor in the central plaza of Tenochtitlán. The building labeled D is the temple itself, depicted here as a hollowed-out octagon rather than in its true form, a towering pyramid. While violent scenes of battle swirl around the temple, in the background one can see the remains of ritually sacrificed Spanish soldiers and those of a horse, which had also been sacrificed.

1. What elements of the struggle described in Sources 4.4 and 4.5 can you identify?

2. Does this painting have a point of view? Was it created more from a European or an Indigenous perspective?

3. Why might the artist have included the gruesome depiction of the executed Spaniards in this painting?

The Conquest of Tenochtitlán | 17th century

Clashes between Aztecs and Spaniards in Mexico City, detail of folding screen with Conquest of Mexico, by an unknown artist, oil on canvas, 16th century/DE AGOSTINI EDITORE/Bridgeman Images

■ ■ ■

SOURCE 4.7 Lamentation: The Aftermath of Defeat

In the aftermath of their agonizing defeat by Cortés and his men, the Aztec survivors composed a number of songs or poems, lamenting their terrible loss. These selections are part of a larger collection of Aztec poetry known as the *Cantares Mexicanos* (Songs of the Aztecs), compiled in the late sixteenth century.

1. What do the poems of lamentation suggest about Aztec efforts to come to terms with their enormous loss?

2. To what extent do these lamentations represent universal expressions of loss and defeat? In what ways might they be considered uniquely and distinctly Aztec?

Cantares Mexicanos | late 16th century

The Fall of Tenochtitlán

Our cries of grief rise up / and our tears rain down, / for Tlatelolco [an Aztec city] is lost.
The Aztecs are fleeing across the lake; / they are running away like women.
How can we save our homes, my people? / The Aztecs are deserting the city: the city is
   in flames, and all / is darkness and destruction . . .
Weep, my people: / know that with these disasters / we have lost the Mexican nation.
The water has turned bitter, / our food is bitter! / These are the acts of the Giver of Life . . .
The Aztecs are besieged in the city; / the Tlatelolcas are besieged in the city!
The walls are black, / the air is black with smoke, / the guns flash in the darkness.
They have captured Cuauhtemoc; / they have captured the princes of Mexico . . . /
The kings are prisoners now. / They are bound with chains.

Flowers and Songs of Sorrow

Nothing but flowers and songs of sorrow / are left in Mexico and Tlatelolco,
   where once we saw warriors and wise men.
We know it is true / that we must perish, / for we are mortal men.
You, the Giver of Life, / you have ordained it.
We wander here / and there in our desolate poverty. / We are mortal men.
We have seen bloodshed and pain / where once we saw beauty and valor.
We are crushed to the ground; / we lie in ruins.
There is nothing but grief and suffering / In Mexico and Tlatelolco, /
   where once we saw beauty and valor.
Have you grown weary of your servants? / Are you angry with your servants, / O Giver
   of Life?

Source: From *The Broken Spears* by Miguel León-Portilla, 146–49. Copyright © 1962, 1990 by Miguel León-Portilla. Expanded and updated edition Copyright © 1992 by Miguel León-Portilla. Reprinted by permission of Beacon Press, Boston.

DOING HISTORY

1. **Evaluating evidence and objectivity:** Based on these sources, how might a historian compose a history of the conquest of Mexico, seeking to be as objective as possible? What information from these sources might be reliably used, and what might be discarded? Is it actually possible to be wholly objective about these events? How would such an account differ if it were written from a distinctly Aztec or Spanish point of view?

2. **Considering morality:** What moral or ethical issues arose for the participants in these events? Should historians take a position on such questions? Is it possible to avoid doing so?

3. **Considering outcomes:** Was Spanish victory inevitable? Under what circumstances might the outcome have been different?

4. **Assessing perspective:** What differences in outlook can you identify between the Spanish and the Aztec sources?

HISTORIANS' VOICES

Conquest, Disease, and Demographic Collapse in the Aztec Empire

Historians agree that diseases endemic in Africa and Eurasia but new to the Americas played a significant role in the demographic collapse of the Native American population in central Mexico. However, the relative importance of new pandemic diseases as opposed to other factors in both the initial conquest of the Aztecs by the Spanish and the "Great Dying" that followed this event has sparked considerable scholarly debate, which is reflected in the two selections that follow. In Voice 4.1, the historian Alfred Crosby, who coined the term "Columbian Exchange," makes the case that disease played an important role both at the time of conquest and over the longer term. In Voice 4.2, Philip Hoffman, an historian and economist, offers a skeptical view of the relative importance of new epidemic diseases in the conquest and the demographic collapse that followed.

1. Do Crosby and Hoffman offer opposing interpretations, or can you find some common ground between them?

2. How does Hoffman's longer time frame, which incorporates the post-conquest period, affect his account?

3. **Integrating primary and secondary sources:** How might you construct an account of the role of disease in the Spanish conquest of the Aztecs that integrates both primary and secondary sources?

VOICE 4.1

Alfred Crosby on the Impact of Disease on the Conquest of the Aztec Empire | 1972

The melodrama of Cortés and the conquest of Mexico needs no retelling. After occupying Tenochtitlán ... he and his troops had to fight their way out of the city to sanctuary. ... Even as the Spanish withdrew, an ally more formidable than the Tlacala [a Native American group allied with the Spanish] appeared. Years later Francisco de Aguillar, a former follower of Cortés. . . . recalled the terrible retreat. . . . "When the Christians were exhausted from war, God saw fit to send the Indians smallpox, and there was a great pestilence in the city." . . .

The sixty days during which the epidemic lasted in the city ... gave Cortés and his troops desperately needed respite to reorganize and prepare a counterattack. When the epidemic subsided, the siege of the Aztec capital began. Had there been no epidemic, the Aztecs. . . . could have pursued the Spaniards. . . . Clearly the epidemic sapped the endurance of Tenochtitlán. . . .

The impact of the smallpox pandemic on the Aztec [Empire] . . . is easy for the twentieth-century reader to underestimate. We have so long been hypnotized by the daring of the conquistador that we have overlooked the importance of biological allies. Because of the achievements of modern medical science we find it hard to accept statements from the conquest period that the pandemics killed one-third to one-half of the populations struck by it. . . . The proportion may be exaggerated but perhaps not by as much as we might think. The Mexicans had no resistance to the disease at all. Other diseases were probably operating quietly and efficiently behind the screen of smallpox. Add the factors of food shortage and the lack of even minimal care for the sick. . . .

Source: Alfred Crosby, *The Columbian Exchange: Biological and Cultural Consequences of 1492* (Westport, CT: Greenwood, 1972), 48–49, 52–53.

VOICE 4.2

Philip Hoffman on the Roles of Disease, Social Disruption, and Technology in the Conquest of the Aztecs | 2015

The trouble, though, is that the demographic catastrophe in the Aztec and Inca Empires had multiple causes—and not just smallpox and measles—for otherwise the native population would have recovered even if the epidemics returned repeatedly. That at least is the conclusion of a demographic analysis that takes into account how populations react after being ravaged by new diseases like smallpox. And what kept the Native American population from recovering was the conquest itself, by wreaking havoc with their domestic life. Indians fled from warfare, and survivors were forced to work for the Europeans, often away from home, so that they could not provide their families with food. Indian women were also drawn into the conquerors' households often as their sexual partners. In short, it became much harder for the Native Americans to have children, making much of the population decline the result, not of disease, but of brutal conquest itself. . . .

How could the Europeans triumph against such numbers? As an answer disease alone fails. . . . For some military historians, the answer is clear: the Europeans simply had better technology. Epidemics and divisions among the natives helped in the Americas . . . but technology gave the Europeans the edge, particularly against the centralized empires of the Aztecs and Incas.

Source: Philip T. Hoffman, *Why Did Europe Conquer the World* (Princeton, NJ: Princeton University Press, 2015), 5–7.

NOTES

1. Stuart B. Schwartz, *Victors and Vanquished* (Boston, MA: Bedford/St. Martin's, 2000), 164.

2. Much of this interpretation is taken from Anna More, *Baroque Sovereignty: Carlos de Sigüenza y Góngora and the Creole Archive of Colonial Mexico* (Philadelphia, PA: University of Pennsylvania Press, 2012).

5 Voices from the Slave Trade

By any measure, the Atlantic slave trade was an enormous enterprise and enormously significant in modern world history. Its geographical scope encompassed four continents; it endured for almost four centuries; its victims numbered in the many millions; its commercial operation was global, complex, and highly competitive; and its consequences echo still in both public and private life. The sources that follow allow us to hear several individual voices from this vast historical process and to sample the evidence available to historians as they seek to chart this painful chapter of the human story.

SOURCE 5.1 The Journey to Slavery

We begin with the voice of an individual victim of the slave trade—Olaudah Equiano. Born in what is now the Igbo-speaking region of southern Nigeria around 1745, Equiano was seized from his home at the age of eleven and sold into the Atlantic slave trade at the high point of that infamous commerce. In service to three different owners, his experience as an enslaved person in the Americas was quite unusual. He learned to read and write, traveled extensively as a seaman aboard one of his enslavers' ships, and was allowed to buy his freedom in 1766. Settling in England, he became a prominent voice in the emerging abolitionist movement of the late eighteenth century and wrote a widely read account of his life, addressed largely to European Christians: "O, ye nominal Christians! Might not an African ask you, Learned you this from your God, who says unto you, Do unto all men as you would men should do unto you?" His book was published in 1789 as abolitionism was gaining wider acceptance.

Despite some controversy about his birthplace and birth date, most historians accept Equiano's autobiography as broadly accurate. Source 5.1 presents Equiano's account of his capture, his journey to the coast, his experience on a slave ship, and his arrival in the Americas. It was a journey forcibly undertaken by millions of others as well.

1. How does Equiano describe the kind of slavery he knew in Africa? How does it compare with the plantation slavery of the Americas?

2. What part did Africans play in the slave trade, according to this account?

3. What aspects of the shipboard experience contributed to the enslaved people's despair?

OLAUDAH EQUIANO │ *The Interesting Narrative of the Life of Olaudah Equiano* │ 1789

As we live in a country where nature is prodigal of her favours, our wants are few and easily supplied; of course we have few manufactures. They consist for the most part of calicoes, earthen ware, ornaments, and instruments of war and husbandry. . . . We have also markets, at which I have been frequently with my mother. These are sometimes visited by stout mahogany-coloured men from the south west of us: . . . They generally bring us fire-arms, gunpowder, hats, beads, and dried fish. . . . They always carry slaves through our land; . . . Sometimes indeed we sold slaves to them, but they were only prisoners of war, or such among us as had been convicted of kidnapping or adultery, and some other crimes, which we esteemed heinous. . . .

My father, besides many slaves, had a numerous family, of which seven lived to grow up, including myself and a sister, who was the only daughter. . . . I was trained up from my earliest years in the art of war; my daily exercise was shooting and throwing javelins; and my mother adorned me with emblems, after the manner of our greatest warriors. In this way I grew up till I was turned the age of eleven, when an end was put to my happiness in the following manner. . . .

One day, when all our people were gone out to their works as usual, and only I and my dear sister were left to mind the house, two men and a woman got over our walls and in a moment seized us both, and, without giving us time to cry out, or make resistance, they stopped our mouths, and ran off with us into the nearest wood. Here they tied our hands, and continued to carry us as far as they could, till night came on. . . . The next morning we left the house, and continued travelling all the day. For a long time we had kept [to] the woods, but at last we came into a road which I believed I knew. I had now some hopes of being delivered; for we had advanced but a little way before I discovered some people at a distance, on which I began to cry out for their assistance: but my cries had no other effect than to make them tie me faster and stop my mouth, and then they put me into a large sack. . . .

The next day proved a day of greater sorrow than I had yet experienced; for my sister and I were then separated, while we lay clasped in each other's arms. It was in vain that we besought them not to part us; she was torn from me, and immediately carried away. . . .

At length, after many days traveling, during which I had often changed masters, I got into the hands of a chieftain, in a very pleasant country. This man had two wives and some children, and they all used me extremely well, and did all they could to comfort me; particularly the first wife, who was something like my mother. Although I was a great many days journey from my father's house, yet these people spoke exactly the same language with us. . . .

[After about a month], I was again sold. . . . The people I was sold to used to carry me very often, when I was tired, either on their shoulders or on their backs. I saw many convenient well-built sheds along the roads, at proper distances, to accommodate the merchants and travelers, who lay in those buildings along with their wives, who often accompany them; and they always go well armed.

I was again sold, and carried through a number of places, till, after traveling a considerable time, I came to a town called Tinmah, in the most beautiful country I had yet seen in Africa. . . . Their money consisted of little white shells, the size of the finger nail. I was sold here for one hundred and seventy-two of them by a merchant who lived and brought me there. I had been about two or three days at his house, when a wealthy widow, a neighbor of his, came there one evening, and brought with her an only son, a young gentleman about my own age and size. Here they saw me; and, having taken a fancy to me, I was bought of the merchant, and went home with them. . . . The next day I was washed and perfumed, and when meal-time came I was led into the presence of my mistress, and ate and drank before her with her son. This filled me with astonishment; and I could scarce help expressing my surprise that the young gentleman should suffer me, who was bound, to eat with him who was free; and not only so, but that he would not at any time either eat or drink till I had taken first, because I was the eldest, which was agreeable to our custom. Indeed everything here, and all their treatment of me, made me forget that I was a slave. The language of these people resembled ours so nearly, that we understood each other perfectly. . . . In this resemblance to my former happy state I passed about two months; and I now began to think I was to be adopted into the family, and was beginning to be reconciled to my situation, and to forget by degrees my misfortunes when all at once the delusion vanished; for, without the least previous knowledge, one morning early, while my dear master and companion was still asleep, I was wakened out of my reverie to fresh sorrow, and hurried away. . . .

Thus I continued to travel, sometimes by land, sometimes by water, through different countries and various nations, till, at the end of six or seven months after I had been kidnapped, I arrived at the sea coast. . . . The first object which saluted my eyes when I arrived on the coast was the sea, and a slave ship, which was then riding at anchor, and waiting for its cargo. These filled me with astonishment, which was soon converted into terror when I was carried on board. I was immediately handled and tossed up to see if I were sound by some of the crew; and I was now persuaded that I had gotten into a world of bad spirits, and that they were going to kill me. Their complexions too differing so much from ours, their long hair, and the language they spoke . . . united to confirm me in this belief. . . . When I looked round the ship too and saw a large furnace or copper boiling, and a multitude of black people of every description chained together, every one of their countenances expressing dejection and sorrow, I no longer doubted of my fate; and quite overpowered with horror and anguish, I fell motionless on the deck and fainted. . . .

I was soon put down under the decks, and there I received such a salutation in my nostrils as I had never experienced in my life: so that, with the loathsomeness of the stench and crying together, I became so sick and low that I was not able to eat, nor had I the least desire to taste anything. I now wished for the last friend, death, to relieve me; but soon, to my grief, two of the white men offered me eatables; and on my refusing to eat, one of them held me fast by the hands, and laid me across I think the windlass and tied my feet, while the other flogged me severely. . . .

I had never seen among any people such instances of brutal cruelty; and this not only shewn towards us blacks, but also to some of the whites themselves. One white man in particular I saw, when we were permitted to be on deck, flogged so unmercifully with a large rope near the foremast that he died in consequence of it; and they tossed him over the side as they would have done a brute. . . .

The closeness of the place, and the heat of the climate, added to the number in the ship, which was so crowded that each had scarcely room to turn himself, almost suffocated us. This produced copious perspirations, so that the air soon became unfit for respiration, from a variety of loathsome smells, and brought on a sickness among the slaves, of which many died, thus falling victims to the improvident avarice, as I may call it, of their purchasers. This wretched situation was again aggravated by the galling of the chains, now become insupportable; and the filth of the necessary tubs, into which the children often fell, and were almost suffocated. The shrieks of the women, and the groans of the dying, rendered the whole a scene of horror almost inconceivable. . . .

At last we came in sight of the island of Barbados, at which the whites on board gave a great shout, and made many signs of joy to us. . . . Many merchants and planters now came on board, though it was in the evening. They put us in separate parcels, and examined us attentively. They also made us jump, and pointed to the land, signifying we were to go there. We thought by this we should be eaten by those ugly men, as they appeared to us; . . . at last the white people got some old slaves from the land to pacify us. They told us we were not to be eaten, but to work, and were soon to go on land, where we should see many of our country people. This report eased us much; and sure enough, soon after we were landed, there came to us Africans of all languages. We were conducted immediately to the merchant's yard, where we were all pent up together like so many sheep in a fold, without regard to sex or age.

Source: Olaudah Equiano, *The Interesting Narrative of the Life of Olaudah Equiano, or Gustavus Vassa, the African*, vol. 1 (London, 1789), chaps. 1, 2.

■ ■ ■

SOURCE 5.2 The Business of the Slave Trade

For its African victims like Equiano, the slave trade was a horror beyond imagination; for kings and merchants—both European and African—it was a business. Source 5.2 explains how that business was conducted. This account comes from the journal of an

English merchant, Thomas Phillips, who undertook a voyage to the kingdom of Whydah in what is now the West African country of Benin in 1693–1694.

1. How would you describe the economic transactions described in the document? To what extent were they conducted between equal parties? Who, if anyone, held the upper hand in these dealings?

2. How might an African merchant have described the same transaction? How might Equiano have described it?

3. Notice the outcomes of Phillips's voyage to Barbados in the last two paragraphs. What does this tell you about European preferences for enslaved people, about the Middle Passage, and about the profitability of the enterprise?

THOMAS PHILLIPS │ *A Journal of a Voyage Made in the* Hannibal *of London* │ **1694**

As soon as the king understood of our landing, he sent two of his cappasheirs, or noble-men, to compliment us at our factory, where we design'd to continue that night, and pay our [respects] to his majesty next day . . . whereupon he sent two more of his grandees to invite us there that night, saying he waited for us, and that all former captains used to attend him the first night: whereupon being unwilling to infringe the custom, or give his majesty any offence, we took our hamocks, and Mr. Peirson, myself, Capt. Clay, our surgeons, pursers, and about 12 men, arm'd for our guard, were carry'd to the king's town, which contains about 50 houses. . . .

We returned him thanks by his interpreter, and assur'd him how great affection our masters, the royal African company of England, bore to him, for his civility and fair and just dealings with their captains; and that notwithstanding there were many other places, more plenty of negro slaves that begg'd their custom, yet they had rejected all the advantageous offers made them out of their good will to him, and therefore had sent us to trade with him, to support his country with necessaries, and that we hop'd he would endeavour to continue their favour by his kind usage and fair dealing with us in our trade, that we may have our slaves with all expedition. . . . He answer'd that we should be fairly dealt with, and not impos'd upon; But he did not prove as good as his word . . . so after having examin'd us about our cargoe, what sort of goods we had, and what quantity of slaves we wanted, etc., we took our leaves and return'd to the factory. . . .

According to promise we attended his majesty with samples of our goods, and made our agreement about the prices, tho' not without much difficulty; . . . next day we paid our customs to the king and cappasheirs, . . . then the bell was order'd to go about to give notice to all people to bring their slaves to the trunk to sell us. . . .

Capt. Clay and I had agreed to go to the trunk to buy the slaves by turns, each his day, that we might have no distractions or disagreement in our trade, as often happens when there are here more ships than one, and . . . their disagreements create animosities, underminings, and out-bidding each other, whereby they enhance the prices to their general loss and detriment, the blacks well knowing how to make the best use of such opportunities, and as we found make it their business, and endeavour to create and foment misunderstandings and jealousies between commanders, it turning to their great account in the disposal of their slaves.

When we were at the trunk, the king's slaves, if he had any, were the first offer'd to sale, . . . and we must not refuse them, tho' as I observ'd they were generally the worst slaves in the trunk, and we paid more for them than any others, which we could not remedy, it being one of his majesty's prerogatives: then the cappasheirs each brought out his slaves according to his degree and quality, the greatest first, etc. and our surgeon examin'd them well in all kinds, to see that they were sound wind and limb, making them jump, stretch out their arms swiftly, looking in their mouths to judge of their age; for the cappasheirs are so cunning, that they shave them all close before we see them, so that let them be never so old we can see no grey hairs in their heads or beards; and then having liquor'd them well and sleek with palm oil, 'tis no easy matter to know an old one from a middle-age one. . . .

When we had selected from the rest such as we liked, we agreed in what goods to pay for them, the prices being already stated before the king, how much of each sort of merchandize we were to give for a man, woman, and child, which gave us much ease, and saved abundance of disputes and wranglings. . . . [T]hen we mark'd the slaves we had bought in the breast, or shoulder, with a hot iron, having the letter of the ship's name on it, the place being before anointed with a little palm oil, which caus'd but little pain, the mark being usually well in four or five days, appearing very plain and white after. . . .

After we are come to an agreement for the prices of our slaves, . . . we are oblig'd to pay our customs to the king and cappasheirs for leave to trade, protection and justice; which for every ship are as follow, viz.

To the king six slaves value in cowries, or what other goods we can perswade him to take, but cowries are most esteem'd and desir'd; all which are measur'd in his presence, and he would wrangle with us stoutly about heaping up the measure.

To the cappasheirs in all two slaves value, as above. . . .

The best goods to purchase slaves here are cowries, the smaller the more esteem'd. . . .

The next in demand are brass neptunes or basons, very large, thin, and flat; for after they have bought them they cut them in pieces to make . . . bracelets, and collars for their arms legs and necks. . . .

[I]f they can discover that you have good store of cowries and brass aboard, then no other goods will serve their turn, till they have got as much as you have; and after, for the rest of the goods they will be indifferent, and make you come to their own terms, or else lie a long time for your slaves, so that those you have on board are dying while you are buying others ashore. . . .

Having bought my compliment of 700 slaves, viz. 480 men and 220 women, and finish'd all my business at Whidaw, I took my leave of the old king, and his cappasheirs, and parted, with many affectionate expressions on both sides, being forced to promise him that I would return again the next year, with several things he desired me to bring him from England; and having sign'd bills of lading . . . for the negroes aboard, I set sail the 27th of July in the morning. . . .

I deliver'd alive at Barbadoes to the company's factors 372, which being sold, came out at about nineteen pounds per head.

Source: Thomas Phillips, "A Journal of a Voyage Made in the *Hannibal* of London in 1694," in *Documents Illustrative of the History of the Slave Trade to America*, edited by Elizabeth Donnan (Washington, DC: Carnegie Institute, 1930), 399–405, 408, 410.

■ ■ ■

SOURCE 5.3 The Slave Trade and the Kingdom of Kongo

While African elites often eagerly facilitated the traffic in enslaved people and benefited from doing so, in one well-known case, quite early in the slave-trade era, an African ruler sought to curtail it. This effort occurred in the Kingdom of Kongo, in what is now Angola. That state had welcomed Portuguese traders as early as the 1480s, as its rulers imagined that an alliance with Portugal could strengthen their regime. The royal family converted to Christianity and encouraged the importation of European guns, cattle, and horses. Several Kongolese were sent to Portugal for education, while Portuguese priests, artisans, merchants, and soldiers found a place in the kingdom. This relationship did not work out as planned, however, and by the early sixteenth century, Kongo was in disarray and the authority of its ruler greatly undermined. This was the context in which its monarch Nzinga Mbemba, whose Christian name was Affonso I, wrote a series of letters to King João of Portugal in 1526, extracts of which are presented here.

1. What did Affonso seek from Portugal? What kind of relationship did he envisage with the Portuguese?

2. To what extent did Affonso seek the end of the slave trade? What was the basis for his opposition to it? Do you think he was opposed to slavery itself?

3. How did the operation of the slave trade in Kongo differ from that of Whydah as described in Source 5.2? How did the rulers of these two states differ in their relationship to Europeans?

KING AFFONSO I │ *Letters to King João of Portugal* │ 1526

Sir, Your Highness [of Portugal] should know how our Kingdom is being lost in so many ways that it is convenient to provide for the necessary remedy, since this is caused by the excessive freedom given by your factors and officials to the men and merchants who are allowed to come to this Kingdom to set up shops with goods and many things which have been prohibited by us, and which they spread throughout our Kingdoms and Domains in such an abundance that many of our vassals, whom we had in obedience, do not comply because they have the things in greater abundance than we ourselves; and it was with these things that we had them content and subjected under our vassalage and jurisdiction, so it is doing a great harm not only to the service of God, but to the security and peace of our Kingdoms and State as well.

And we cannot reckon how great the damage is, since the mentioned merchants are taking every day our natives, sons of the land and the sons of our noblemen and vassals and our relatives, because the thieves and men of bad conscience grab them wishing to have the things and wares of this Kingdom which they are ambitious of; they grab them and get them to be sold; and so great, Sir, is the corruption and licentiousness that our country is being completely depopulated, and Your Highness should not agree with this nor accept it as in your service. And to avoid it we need from those [your] Kingdoms no more than some priests and a few people to teach in schools, and no other goods except wine and flour for the holy sacrament. That is why we beg of Your Highness to help and assist us in this matter, commanding your factors that they should not send here either merchants or wares, because it is our will that in these Kingdoms there should not be any trade of slaves nor outlet for them. Concerning what is referred above, again we beg of Your Highness to agree with it, since otherwise we cannot remedy such an obvious damage. . . .

Moreover, Sir, in our Kingdoms there is another great inconvenience which is of little service to God, and this is that many of our people, keenly desirous as they are of the wares and things of your Kingdoms, which are brought here by your people, and in order to satisfy their voracious appetite, seize many of our people, freed and exempt men; and very often it happens that they kidnap even noblemen and the sons of noblemen, and our relatives, and take them to be sold to the white men who are in our Kingdoms; and for this purpose they have concealed them; and others are brought during the night so that they might not be recognized.

And as soon as they are taken by the white men they are immediately ironed and branded with fire, and when they are carried to be embarked, if they are caught by our guards' men the whites allege that they have bought them but they cannot say from whom, so that it is our duty to do justice and to restore to the freemen their freedom, but it cannot be done if your subjects feel offended, as they claim to be.

And to avoid such a great evil we passed a law so that any white man living in our Kingdoms and wanting to purchase goods in any way should first inform three of our noblemen and officials of our court . . . who should investigate if the mentioned goods are captives or free men, and if cleared by them there will be no further doubt nor embargo for them to be taken and embarked. But if the white men do not comply with it they will lose the aforementioned goods. . . .

Sir, Your Highness has been kind enough to write to us saying that we should ask in our letters for anything we need, and that we shall be provided with everything, and as the peace and the health of our Kingdom depend on us, and as there are among us old folks and people who have lived for many days, it happens that we have continuously many and different diseases which put us very often in such a weakness that we reach almost the last extreme; and the same happens to our children, relatives, and natives owing to the lack in this country of physicians and surgeons who might know how to cure properly such diseases. And as we have got neither dispensaries nor drugs which might help us in this forlornness, many of those who had been already confirmed and instructed in the holy faith of Our Lord Jesus Christ perish and die; and the rest of the people in their majority cure themselves with herbs and breads and other ancient methods, so that they put all their faith in the mentioned herbs and ceremonies if they live, and believe that they are saved if they die; and this is not much in the service of God.

And to avoid such a great error and inconvenience, since it is from God in the first place and then from your Kingdoms and from Your Highness that all the goods and drugs and medicines have come to save us, we beg of you to be agreeable and kind enough to send us two physicians and two apothecaries and one surgeon, so that they may come with their drugstores and all the necessary things to stay in our kingdoms, because we are in extreme need of them all and each of them.

Source: Basil Davidson, *The African Past* (Boston, MA: Little, Brown, 1964), 191–94.

■ ■ ■

SOURCE 5.4 The Slave Trade and the Kingdom of Asante

The slave trade did not always have such politically destabilizing effects as it did in Kongo. In the region known as the Gold Coast (now the modern state of Ghana), the Kingdom of Asante (uh-SAWN-tay) arose in the eighteenth century, occupying perhaps 100,000 square miles and encompassing some 3 million people. It was a powerful conquest state, heavily invested in the slave trade, from which much of its wealth derived. Many enslaved people from Asante's wars of expansion and from the tribute of its subject people were funneled into Atlantic commerce, while still others were used as labor in the goldmines and on the plantations within Asante itself. No wonder, then, that the ruler (or Asante-hene) Osei Bonsu was dismayed in the early nineteenth century when, in reaction to the expanding abolitionist movement, the British stopped buying enslaved people. A conversation between Osei Bonsu and a British diplomat in 1820 highlights the role of the slave trade in Asante and in the thinking of its monarch.

1. How did Osei Bonsu understand the slave trade and its significance for his kingdom?

2. Some scholars have argued that the slave trade increased the incidence of warfare in West Africa, as various states deliberately sought captives whom they could exchange for desired goods from Europe. How might Osei Bonsu respond to that idea? What was his understanding of the relationship between war and the slave trade?

3. In what ways did Osei Bonsu compare Muslim traders from the north with European merchants from the sea?

OSEI BONSU | *Conversation with Joseph Dupuis* | 1820

"Now," said the king, after a pause, "I have another palaver, and you must help me to talk it. A long time ago the great king [of England] liked plenty of trade, more than now; then many ships came, and they bought ivory, gold, and slaves; but now he will not let the ships come as before, and the people buy gold and ivory only. This is what I have in my head, so now tell me truly, like a friend, why does the king do so?" "His majesty's question," I replied, "was connected with a great palaver, which my instructions did not authorise me to discuss. I had nothing to say regarding the slave trade." "I know that too," retorted the king; "because, if my master liked that trade, you would have told me so before. I only want to hear what you think as a friend: this is not like the other palavers." I was confessedly at a loss for an argument that might pass as a satisfactory reason, and the sequel proved that my doubts were not groundless. The king did not deem it plausible, that this obnoxious traffic should have been abolished from motives of humanity alone; neither would he admit that it lessened the number either of domestic or foreign wars.

Taking up one of my observations, he remarked, "[T]he white men who go to council with your master, and pray to the great God for him, do not understand my country, or they would not say the slave trade was bad. But if they think it bad now, why did they think it good before? Is not your law an old law, the same as the Crammo [Muslim] law? Do you not both serve the same God, only you have different fashions and customs? Crammos are strong people in fetische [magical powers], and they say the law is good, because the great God made the book [Quran]; so they buy slaves, and teach them good things, which they knew not before. This makes everybody love the Crammos, and they go everywhere up and down, and the people give them food when they want it. Then these men come all the way from the great water [Niger River], and from Manding, and Dagomba, and Killinga; they stop and trade for slaves, and then go home. If the great king would like to restore this trade, it would be good for the white men and for me too, because Ashantee is a country for war, and the people are strong; so if you talk that palaver for me properly, in the white country, if you go there, I will give you plenty of gold, and I will make you richer than all the white men."

I urged the impossibility of the king's request, promising, however, to record his sentiments faithfully. "Well then," said the king, "you must put down in my master's book all I shall say, and then he will look to it, now he is my friend. And when he sees what is true, he will surely restore that trade. I cannot make war to catch slaves in the bush, like a thief. My ancestors never did so. But if I fight a king, and kill him when he is insolent, then certainly I must have his gold, and his slaves, and the people are mine too. Do not the white kings act like this? Because I hear the old men say, that before I conquered Fantee and killed the Braffoes and the kings, that white men came in great ships, and fought and killed many people; and then they took the gold and slaves to the white country: and sometimes they fought together. That is all the same as these black countries. The great God and the fetische made war for strong men every where, because then they can pay plenty of gold and proper sacrifice. When I fought Gaman, I did not make war for slaves, but because Dinkera (the king) sent me an arrogant message and killed my people, and refused to pay me gold as his father did. Then my fetische made me strong like my ancestors, and I killed Dinkera, and took his gold, and brought more than 20,000 slaves to Coomassy. Some of these people being bad men, I washed my stool in their blood for the fetische. But then some were good people, and these I sold or gave to my captains: many, moreover, died, because this country does not grow too much corn like Sarem, and what can I do? Unless I kill or sell them, they will grow strong and kill my people. Now you must tell my master that these slaves can work for him, and if he wants 10,000 he can have them. And if he wants fine handsome girls and women to give his captains, I can send him great numbers."

Source: Joseph Dupuis, *Journal of a Residence in Ashantee* (London, UK: Henry Colburn, 1824), 162–64.

■ ■ ■

SOURCE 5.5 Images of the Slave Trade

Images of the slave trade abound, offering another perspective on the journey from freedom to slavery. Source 5.5A, a French engraving published in 1796 as part of an encyclopedic travel book, shows the sale of enslaved people at Gorée, a major slave-trading port in what is now Dakar, Senegal. A European merchant and an African slave trader negotiate the arrangement, while the shackled victims wait for their fate to be decided. Based on an early photograph, Source 5.5B is an engraving published in the popular American periodical *Harper's Weekly* in 1860. It illustrates the Middle Passage by recording the enormously crowded conditions aboard a slave ship, which was captured before it could land its human cargo in Cuba. Source 5.5C, a handbill advertising a slave auction in South Carolina in 1769, indicates what lay ahead for those who survived the Middle Passage.

1. What aspects of the documents in Sources 5.1 through 5.4 do these images illustrate?

2. In what ways do images such as these provide an understanding of the slave trade beyond what written sources can convey? What are their limitations as sources useful to historians?

SOURCE 5.5A

Sale of Enslaved Men in West Africa │ 1796

The Slave Ship Wildfire | 1860

THE SLAVE DECK OF THE BARK "WILDFIRE," BROUGHT INTO KEY WEST ON APRIL 30, 1860.—[FROM A DAGUERREOTYPE.]

The Slave Deck of the Bark *Wildfire*, Brought into Key West on April 30, 1860, illustration from *Harper's Weekly*, June 2, 1860 (engraving from a daguerreotype) (b&w photo)/ American School (19th century)/Private Collection/Bridgeman Images

Advertisement for a Slave Auction in Charleston, South Carolina | 1769

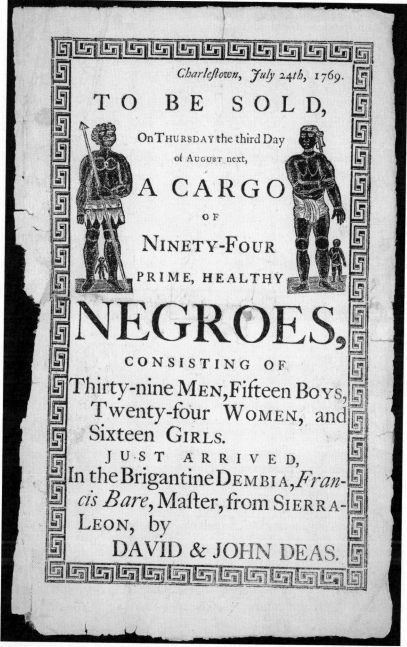

Broadside from Charlestown, South Carolina, advertising the sale of a new shipment of slaves, 24th July, 1769 (print)/American School (18th century)/
AMERICAN ANTIQUARIAN SOCIETY/American Antiquarian Society, Worcester, Massachusetts, USA/Bridgeman Images

■ ■ ■

SOURCE 5.6 Data: Patterns of the Slave Trade

Numbers, or quantitative data, may not convey the same immediacy or emotional impact that images or first-person accounts often carry. Nevertheless, they have an important role in informing historians' efforts to understand the slave trade. Here are two tables and an aggregate statistic that provide information on various aspects of the slave trade. They are derived from the *Trans-Atlantic Slave Trade Database* (slavevoyages.org), a huge collection of searchable information culled from almost 35,000 individual slave voyages.

1. What kind of understandings can be obtained from data such as this that are not available from the other sources in this feature? What are the limitations of this information?

2. In what ways did the slave trade change over time, according to this data? How might you account for these changes?

3. What might you find surprising in this data?

SOURCE 5.6A

Voyages and Slave Rebellion: An Aggregate Statistic

Overall percentage of voyages (1501–1866) that experienced a major slave rebellion: 10 percent

SOURCE 5.6B

Changing Patterns of the Slave Trade

Century	Total Taken from Africa	Total Landed at Destination	% Died during Middle Passage	Avg. Days in Middle Passage	Avg. % Enslaved People = Children	Avg. % Enslaved People = Male
1501–1600	227,506	199,285	12.0	—	0	58
1601–1700	1,875,631	1,522,677	23.3	76.1	11.6	58.4
1701–1800	6,494,619	5,609,869	11.9	70	18.4	64.2
1801–1866	3,873,580	3,370,825	10.3	45.9	29.4	67.6
Total or Average	12,521,336 (Total)	10,702,656 (Total)	11.9 (Avg.)	60 (Avg.)	20.9 (Avg.)	64.7 (Avg.)

Data from *Voyages: The Trans-Atlantic Slave Trade Database,* 2009, http://www.slavevoyages.org (accessed June 8, 2015).

SOURCE 5.6C

Percentage of Enslaved People Brought to Each Region

Century	Europe	North America	Caribbean	Spanish American Mainland	Brazil	Africa	Other
1501–1600	1.1	—	8	66.7	1.9	0.3	22
1601–1700	0.6	1.5	56.4	22.7	17	0.1	1.6
1701–1800	0.1	5.2	64.4	1.2	29	0.1	0.1
1801–1866	—	2.0	31.9	0.9	60	4.8	0
Average of Total	0.1	3.8	51.9	3.3	38.9	1.8	0.3

Data from *Voyages: The Trans-Atlantic Slave Trade Database,* 2009, http://www.slavevoyages.org (accessed June 8, 2015).

DOING HISTORY

1. **Noticing what is missing:** What perspectives are missing that might add other dimensions to our understanding of this trade in people?

2. **Understanding the operation of the transatlantic slave system:** To what extent was that system based on conquest and coercion? In what ways was it a negotiated arrangement?

3. **Assessing historical responsibility:** What light do these sources shed on the much-debated question about who should be held responsible for the tragedy of the Atlantic slave trade?

HISTORIANS' VOICES

Describing the Middle Passage

The sources used and questions asked by historians can lead to accounts of the same event or process that differ significantly in tone or emphasis. This is the case with the two Voices that follow, both of which describe the Middle Passage—the harrowing sea journey across the Atlantic taken by millions of enslaved people. In Voice 5.1, Lisa Lindsay, a specialist in West African history, draws upon eyewitness accounts of the voyages to describe the conditions on board slave ships during the Middle Passage. Note in particular Lindsay's use of a passage from Equiano that is reproduced in Source 5.1. In Voice 5.2, Johannes Postma, a specialist in the Atlantic slave trade, summarizes the recent scholarship on mortality rates during the Middle Passage, which draws heavily on slave-ship logbooks.

1. How do the two accounts differ in tone and coverage?

2. What does each voice add to your understanding of the Middle Passage?

3. **Integrating primary and secondary sources:** Write a description of the Middle Passage using both the primary sources and historians' voices in this feature.

VOICE 5.1

Lisa Lindsay on Conditions above and below Deck during the Middle Passage | 2008

Between the large numbers of people crammed into unventilated spaces and the intestinal diseases that ravaged them, the holds of slave vessels became filthy cesspools. "The closeness of the place, and the heat of the climate," Equiano wrote, "added to the number in the ship, which was so crowded that each had scarcely room to turn himself, almost suffocated us. This produced copious perspirations, so that the air soon became unfit for respiration, from a variety of loathsome smells, and brought on a sickness among the slaves, of which many died." The French slave trader Jean Barbot noted that sometimes the heat and lack of oxygen on the lower decks of slave ships were so intense that the surgeons would faint away and the candles would not burn." . . . Below decks, the muck and stench from blood, sweat, urine, feces, and vomit overwhelmed any attempts at cleanliness. Crews were ordered to mop up the mess, scrub down the ship, and clear the air below decks with vinegar, whitewash or tar. . . .

Women and children frequently were allowed to move freely on deck, but slave traders brought out adult men only at specific times, including for exercise. With the prodding of a whip and occasionally a drum, accordion, or fiddle for accompaniment, they forced slaves to "dance": on deck. . . . Sometimes ships' crews took sadistic delight in such spectacles. In 1792, for instance, Capitan John Kimber was tried in the British Court of Admiralty over the death of a 15-year-old female slave. . . . According to the prosecution, Kimber tortured the young woman to death because she had refused to dance naked on the deck of his ship. He was ultimately acquitted. . . .

Source: Lisa A. Lindsay, *Captives as Commodities: The Transatlantic Slave Trade* (Upper Saddle River, NJ: Pearson/Prentice Hall, 2008), 91–92.

Johannes Postma on Mortality during the Middle Passage | 2003

One of the much debated issues concerning the Atlantic slave trade is the death rate for slaves during the Middle Passage. . . . Abolitionists cited extremely high mortality figures for slaves and sailors, and used them to denounce the slave trade as both immoral and wasteful. Because slaves were valuable investment property, ship captains kept careful records in logbooks and mortality lists of the dates and causes of death, as well as the gender and age of the deceased. These records survive for about one-fifth of the documented slave voyages and are now accessible through the Cambridge University Press Database. They show that on average 12 percent of the enslaved did not survive the ocean crossing, though there was considerable variation from one transport to another. Before 1700, death rates tended to be higher, averaging more than 22 percent. They decreased to about 10 percent by the end of the eighteenth century, but rose again to nearly 12 percent during the years of illegal trading in the mid-nineteenth century. . . .

High mortality rates during the Middle Passage were usually blamed on conditions aboard the slave ships, and there is no doubt that crowding spread contagious diseases quickly. Intestinal disorders such as dysentery were the most common killers, often appearing in epidemic proportions. These ailments, along with tropical diseases such as malaria and yellow fever were responsible for about 70 percent of the casualties. Smallpox and scurvy also killed slaves, particularly before the mid-eighteenth century. Respiratory illnesses, heart attacks, suicide (jumping overboard or refusing to eat), revolts, storms, shipwrecks, attacks by pirates, and fights among slaves were also listed as causes of death.

Source: Johannes Postma, *The Atlantic Slave Trade* (Westport, CT: Greenwood Press, 2003), 43–45.

CHAPTER 6

Renewal and Reform in the Early Modern World

Cultural and religious traditions change over time in various ways and for various reasons. Some of these changes occur as a result of internal tensions or criticisms within these traditions or in response to social and economic transformations in the larger society. The Protestant Reformation, for example, grew out of deep dissatisfaction with the prevailing teachings and practices of the Roman Catholic Church and drew support from a growing middle class and a disaffected peasantry. At other times, cultural change has occurred by incorporating or reacting against new ideas drawn from contact with outsiders. Chinese Confucianism took on a distinctive tone and flavor as it drew on the insights of Buddhism, and a new South Asian religion called Sikhism sought to combine elements of Hindu and Muslim beliefs. Whatever the stimulus for cultural change, departures from accepted ways of thinking have sometimes been expressed as a return to a purer and more authentic past, even if that past is largely imaginary. In other cases, however, change was presented as a necessary break from an outmoded past, even if many elements from earlier times were retained.

All across the Eurasian world of the early modern era—in Western Europe, India, and the Middle East—significant protests against established ways of thinking were brewing. In each of the sources that follow, we are listening in on just one side of extended debates or controversies, focusing on those seeking change. To what extent were these changes moving in the same direction? How did they differ? What were the sources of these changes, and how were they expressed? How might those who opposed these changes respond?

SOURCE 6.1 Luther's Protest

Europe was home to perhaps the most substantial cultural transformations during the early modern centuries. In that region, the Protestant Reformation sharply challenged both the doctrines and the authority of the Roman Catholic Church, ending the near monopoly on religion that the church had exercised in Western Europe for many centuries and introducing a bitter and often-violent divide into the religious and political life of the region. Later, the practitioners of the Scientific Revolution, and the Enlightenment that followed from it, introduced a revolutionary new understanding of both the physical world and human society while urging novel means of obtaining knowledge.

The Protestant Reformation and the Scientific Revolution/Enlightenment shared a common hostility to established authority, and both represented a clear departure from previous patterns of thought and behavior. But they differed sharply in how they represented the changes they sought. Reformation leaders looked to the past, seeking to restore or renew what they believed was an earlier and more authentic version of Christianity. Leaders of the Scientific Revolution and the Enlightenment, by contrast, foresaw and embraced an altogether new world in the making. They were the "moderns" combating the "ancients."

The most prominent figure in the Protestant Reformation was Martin Luther (1483–1546), a German monk, priest, and theologian. A prolific scholar and writer, Luther translated the Bible into German and composed many theological treatises and hymns. The excerpts in Source 6.1, however, come from conversations with his students, friends, and colleagues, which they carefully recorded. After Luther's death, these recollections of the reformer's thoughts were compiled and published under the title *Table Talk*.

1. Based on this source, what issues drove the Protestant Reformation?

2. What theological questions are addressed in these excerpts? How does Luther understand the concepts of law, good works, grace, and faith?

3. In what ways is Luther critical of the papacy, monks, and the monastic orders of the Catholic Church? What do you make of the tone of Luther's remarks?

MARTIN LUTHER | *Table Talk* | early 16th century

On the Bible

No greater mischief can happen to a Christian people, than to have God's Word taken from them, or falsified, so that they no longer have it pure and clear. The ungodly papists prefer the authority of the church far above God's Word; a blasphemy abominable and not to be endured; wherewith, void of all shame and piety, they spit in God's face.

Pope, cardinals, bishops, not a soul of them has read the Bible; 'tis a book unknown to them. They are a pack of guzzling, stuffing wretches, rich, wallowing in wealth and laziness, resting secure in their power, and never, for a moment, thinking of accomplishing God's will.

On Salvation

He that goes from the gospel to the law, thinking to be saved by good works, falls as uneasily as he who falls from the true service of God to idolatry; for, without Christ, all is idolatry and fictitious imaginings of God, whether of the Turkish Koran [Quran], of the pope's decrees, or Moses' law.

The Gospel preaches nothing of the merit of works; he that says the Gospel requires works for salvation, I say, flat and plain, is a liar. Nothing that is properly good proceeds out of the works of the law, unless grace be present; for what we are forced to do, goes not from the heart, nor is acceptable.

But a true Christian says: I am justified and saved only by faith in Christ, without any works or merits of my own. . . .

Prayer in popedom is mere tongue-threshing . . . ; not prayer but a work of obedience.

On the Pope and the Church Hierarchy

The great prelates, the puffed-up saints, the rich usurers, the ox drovers that seek unconscionable gain, etc., these are not God's servants. . . .

Our dealing and proceeding against the pope is altogether excommunication, which is simply the public declaration that a person is disobedient to Christ's Word. Now we affirm in public, that the pope and his retinue believe not; therefore we conclude that he shall not be saved, but be damned. . . .

Antichrist is the pope and the Turk together; a beast full of life must have a body and soul; the spirit or soul of antichrist is the pope, his flesh or body the Turk. . . . Kings and princes coin money only out of metals, but the pope coins money out of every thing—indulgences, ceremonies, dispensations, pardons; 'tis all fish comes to his net. . . .

The pope and his crew are mere worshippers of idols, and servants of the devil. . . . He pretends great holiness, under color of the outward service of God, for he has instituted orders with hoods, with shavings, fasting, eating of fish, saying mass, and such like. . . . [F]or his doctrine he gets money and wealth, honor and power, and is so great a monarch, that he can bring emperors under his girdle.

The chief cause that I fell out with the pope was this: the pope boasted that he was the head of the church, and condemned all that would not be under his power and authority. . . .

The fasting of the friars is more easy to them than our eating to us. For one day of fasting there are three of feasting. Every friar for his supper has two quarts of beer, a quart of wine, and spice-cakes, or bread prepared with spice and salt, the better to relish their drink. Thus go on these poor fasting brethren; getting so pale and wan, they are like the fiery angels.

The state of celibacy is great hypocrisy and wickedness. . . . Christ with one sentence confutes all their arguments: God created them male and female. . . . Now eating, drinking, marrying, etc., are of God's making, therefore they are good. . . .

A Christian's worshipping is not the external, hypocritical mask that our spiritual friars wear, when they chastise their bodies, torment and make themselves faint, with ostentatious fasting, watching, singing, wearing hair shirts, scourging themselves, etc. Such worshipping God desires not.

Source: William Hazlitt, ed. and trans., *The Table Talk of Martin Luther* (London, UK: H. G. Bohn, 1857).

■ ■ ■

SOURCE 6.2 Calvinism and Catholicism

Protestant opposition to Roman Catholic practice was not limited to matters of theology, liturgy, and church corruption, but came to include the physical appearance of churches as well. Martin Luther was suspicious of the many sculptures and paintings that served as objects of devotion to the Catholic faithful, but John Calvin, the prominent French-born Protestant theologian, went even further, declaring that "God forbade . . . the making of any images representing him."

Perhaps the most dramatic expression of these ideas took place in regions of Europe where Protestants took over formerly Roman Catholic churches for their new forms of worship. During the 1560s, waves of Protestant image smashing, sometimes called the Iconoclastic Fury, took place in England, France, Switzerland, the Netherlands, and elsewhere. This engraving, produced in 1566 at the height of these religious conflicts, depicts Protestants "cleansing" a Catholic church in Antwerp, in what is now Belgium, of what they viewed as idolatrous decorations but Catholics revered as objects of devotion.

An English Catholic observer described this event and others like it with horror: "These fresh followers of this new preaching [Protestantism] threw down the graven and defaced the painted images. . . . They tore the curtains, dashed in pieces the carved work of brass and stone, . . . pulled up the brass of the gravestones. . . . [T]he Blessed Sacrament of the altar . . . they trod under their feet and (horrible it is to say!) shed their stinking piss upon it. . . . [T]hese false brethren burned and rent not only all kind of Church books, but, moreover, destroyed whole libraries of books of all sciences and tongues, yea the Holy Scriptures and the ancient fathers, and tore in pieces the maps and charts of the descriptions of countries."[1]

These often-dramatic attacks on churches served a practical purpose in preparing the site for Protestant worship. But they also reflected the new beliefs of the Protestants, or, as one scholar has put it, expressed "theology in stone." These churches were stripped of visual distractions and altars where the miracle of the mass took place. Instead there emerged a church, frequently without any images or other diversions like organs or other musical instruments, whose main focal point was the pulpit where the word of God was preached.

1. What elements of the Catholic description of this attack can you identify in the image? What other acts of destruction can you notice?

2. What differences in religious understanding lay behind such attacks?

3. What accounts for the passion displayed in these attacks? Is this kind of religious violence a thing of the past or does it have contemporary counterparts today?

Engraving of Calvinists Destroying Statues in a Catholic Church | 1566

Photo 12/Getty Images

■ ■ ■

SOURCE 6.3 Progress and Enlightenment

If the Protestant Reformation represented a major change within the framework of the Christian faith, the Scientific Revolution and the European Enlightenment came to be seen by many as a challenge to all Christian understandings of the world. After all, these two movements celebrated the powers of human reason to unlock the mysteries of the universe and proclaimed the possibility of a new human society shaped by human reason. Among the most prominent spokesmen for the Enlightenment was the Marquis de Condorcet (1743–1794), a French mathematician, philosopher, and active participant in the French Revolution. In his *Sketch of the Progress of the Human Mind*, Condorcet described ten stages of human development. Source 6.3 contains excerpts from "The Ninth Epoch," whose title refers to the era in which Condorcet was living, and "The Tenth Epoch," referring to the age to come. Condorcet's optimism about that future was not borne out in his own life, for he fell afoul of the radicalism of the French Revolution and died in prison in 1794.

1. What is Condorcet's view of the relationship between the Scientific Revolution and the Enlightenment?

2. How, precisely, does Condorcet imagine the future of humankind?

3. How might Martin Luther respond to Condorcet's vision of the future? How do their understandings of human potential differ?

MARQUIS DE CONDORCET | *Sketch of the Progress of the Human Mind* | 1793–1794

The Ninth Epoch: From Descartes to the Formation of the French Republic

[T]he progress of philosophy ... destroyed within the general mass of people the prejudices that have afflicted and corrupted the human race for so long a time.

Humanity was finally permitted to boldly proclaim the long ignored right to submit every opinion to reason, that is to utilize the only instrument given to us for grasping and recognizing the truth. Each human learned with a sort of pride that nature had never destined him to believe the word of others. The superstitions of antiquity and the abasement of reason before the madness of supernatural religion disappeared from society just as they had disappeared from philosophy....

If we were to limit ourselves to showing the benefits derived from the immediate applications of the sciences, or in their applications to man-made devices for the well-being of individuals and the prosperity of nations, we would be making known only a slim part of their benefits. The most important, perhaps, is having destroyed prejudices, and reestablished human intelligence, which until then had been forced to bend down to false instructions instilled in it by absurd beliefs passed on to the children of each generation by the terrors of superstition and the fear of tyranny....

The advances of scientific knowledge are all the more deadly to these errors because they destroy them without appearing to attack them, while lavishing on those who stubbornly defend them the degrading taunt of ignorance....

Finally this progress of scientific knowledge ... results in a belief that not birth, professional status, or social standing gives anyone the right to judge something he does not understand. This unstoppable progress cannot be observed without having enlightened men search unceasingly for ways to make the other branches of learning follow the same path....

The Tenth Epoch: The Future Progress of the Human Mind

Our hopes for the future of the human species may be reduced to three important points: the destruction of inequality among nations; the progress of equality within nations themselves; and finally, the real improvement of humanity. Should not all the nations of the world approach one day the state of civilization reached by the most enlightened peoples such as the French and the Anglo-Americans? Will not the slavery of nations subjected to kings, the barbarity of African tribes, and the ignorance of savages gradually disappear? ...

If we cast an eye at the existing state of the globe, we will see right away that in Europe the principles of the French constitution are already those of all enlightened men.

We will see that they are too widely disseminated and too openly professed for the efforts of tyrants and priests to prevent them from penetrating into the hovels of their slaves. . . .

Can it be doubted that either wisdom or the senseless feuds of the European nations themselves, working with the slow but certain effects of progress in their colonies, will not soon produce the independence of the new world; and that then the European population, spreading rapidly across that immense land, must either civilize or make disappear the savage peoples that now inhabit these vast continents? . . .

Thus the day will come when the sun will shine only on free men born knowing no other master but their reason; where tyrants and their slaves, priests and their ignorant, hypocritical writings will exist only in the history books and theaters. . . . If we consider the human creations based on scientific theories, we shall see that their progress can have no limits; . . . that new tools, machines, and looms will add every day to the capabilities and skill of humans; they will improve and perfect the precision of their products while decreasing the amount of time and labor needed to produce them. . . .

A smaller piece of land will be able to produce commodities of greater usefulness and value than before; greater benefits will be obtained with less waste; the production of the same industrial product will result in less destruction of raw materials and greater durability. . . . [E]ach individual will work less but more productively and will be able to better satisfy his needs. . . .

Among the advances of the human mind we should reckon as most important for the general welfare is the complete destruction of those prejudices that have established an inequality of rights between the sexes, an inequality damaging even to the party it favors. . . .

The most enlightened people . . . will slowly come to perceive war as the deadliest plague and the most monstrous of crimes. . . . They will understand that they cannot become conquerors without losing their liberty; that perpetual alliances are the only way to preserve independence; and that they should seek their security, not power. . . .

We may conclude then that the perfectibility of humanity is indefinite.

Finally, can we not also extend the same hopes to the intellectual and moral faculties? . . . Is it not also probable that education, while perfecting these qualities, will also influence, modify, and improve that bodily nature itself? . . .

Source: Marquis de Condorcet, *Sketch of the Progress of the Human Mind* (Paris: Firmin Didot Frères, 1847), Epoch 9 and Epoch 10.

■ ■ ■

SOURCE 6.4 Art and Enlightenment

Public lectures on scientific topics became widespread in Europe during the eighteenth century, serving to spread the new knowledge and to bring "enlightenment" to a wider circle of people. The following painting, titled *A Philosopher Giving a Lecture on the Orrery*, by English artist Joseph Wright (1734–1797), illustrates such a presentation.

The central figure in a red robe—modeled, some suggest, on the famous scientist Isaac Newton—is demonstrating the movements of the planets around the sun, using an "orrery," a mechanical device that shows their orbits and their relationship to one another. His captivated audience includes three men, two small boys, and two girls or young women. The light source is an oil lamp, which represents the sun at the center of the solar system.

1. The kind of fascination or awe that characterizes the spectators had previously been reserved largely for witnesses to religious events. What is stimulating that sense of wonderment in this painting? Is there something quasi-religious about the scene?

2. What metaphorical or symbolic meaning might be attached to the illuminated faces, which contrast sharply with the surrounding darkness?

3. In what ways does this painting illustrate Condorcet's vision of the role that science and reason will play in the coming age of progress and enlightenment?

JOSEPH WRIGHT | *A Philosopher Giving a Lecture on the Orrery* | ca. 1766

The Orrery, ca. 1766 (oil on canvas), Joseph Wright of Derby (1734–1797)/Derby Museum and Art Gallery, UK/Bridgeman Images

■ ■ ■

SOURCE 6.5 The Wahhabi Perspective on Islam

Within the Islamic world, the major cultural movements of the early modern era were those of religious renewal. Such movements sought to eliminate the "deviations" that had crept into Islamic practice over the centuries and to return to a purer version of the faith that presumably had prevailed during the foundational period of the religion. The most influential of these movements was associated with Muhammad Ibn Abd al-Wahhab, whose revivalist movement spread widely in Arabia during the second half of the eighteenth century. Source 6.5, written by the grandson of al-Wahhab shortly after the capture of Mecca in 1803, provides a window into the outlook of Wahhabi Islam.

1. What specific objections did the Wahhabis have to the prevailing practice of Islam in eighteenth-century Arabia?

2. How did the Wahhabis put their ideas into practice once they had seized control of Mecca?

3. What similarities do you see between the outlook of the Wahhabis and that of Martin Luther? What differences can you identify?

ABDULLAH WAHHAB │ *History and Doctrines of the Wahhabis* │ 1803

Now I was engaged in the holy war . . . , when God, praised be He, graciously permitted us to enter Mecca. . . . Now, though we were more numerous, better armed and disciplined than the people of Mecca, yet we did not cut down their trees, neither did we hunt, nor shed any blood except the blood of victims, and of those four-footed beasts which the Lord has made lawful by his commands.

When our pilgrimage was over . . . our leader, whom the Lord saves, explained to the divines what we required of the people, . . . namely, a pure belief in the Unity of God Almighty. He pointed out to them that there was no dispute between us and them except on two points, and that one of these was a sincere belief in the Unity of God, and a knowledge of the different kinds of prayer. . . .

They then acknowledged our belief, and there was not one among them who doubted. . . . And they swore a binding oath, although we had not asked them, that their hearts had been opened and their doubts removed, and that they were convinced whoever said, "Oh prophet of God!" or "Oh Ibn 'Abbes!" or "Oh 'Abdul Qadir!" or called on any other created being, thus entreating him to turn away evil or grant what is good (where the power belongs to God alone), such as recovery from sickness, or victory over enemies, or protection from temptation, etc.; he is a Mushrik, guilty of the most heinous form of shirk [unbelief], his blood shall be shed and property confiscated. . . . Again, the tombs which had been erected over the remains of the pious, had become in these times as it were idols where the people went to pray for what they required; they humbled themselves before them, and called upon those lying in them, in their distress, just as did those who were in darkness before the coming of Muhammad. . . .

We razed all the large tombs in the city which the people generally worshipped and believed in, and by which they hoped to obtain benefits or ward off evil, so that there did not remain an idol to be adored in that pure city, for which God be praised. Then the taxes and customs we abolished, all the different kinds of instruments for using tobacco we destroyed, and tobacco itself we proclaimed forbidden. Next we burned the dwellings of those selling hashish, and living in open wickedness, and issued a proclamation, directing the people to constantly exercise themselves in prayer. They were not to pray in separate groups ..., but all were directed to arrange themselves at each time of prayer behind any Imam who is a follower of any of the four Imams [founders of major schools of Islamic law].... For in this way the Lord would be worshiped by as it were one voice, the faithful of all sects would become friendly disposed towards each other, and all dissensions would cease....

[W]e do not reject anyone who follows any of the four Imams, as do the Shias.... We do not claim to exercise our reason in all matters of religion, and of our faith, save that we follow our judgment where a point is clearly demonstrated to us in either the Quran or the Sunnah [traditions of Muhammad's actions].... We do not command the destruction of any writings except such as tend to cast people into infidelity to injure their faith, such as those on Logic, which have been prohibited by all Divines. But we are not very exacting with regard to books or documents of this nature; if they appear to assist our opponents, we destroy them.... We do not consider it proper to make Arabs prisoners of war, nor have we done so, neither do we fight with other nations. Finally, we do not consider it lawful to kill women or children....

We consider pilgrimage is supported by legal custom, but it should not be undertaken except to a mosque, and for the purpose of praying in it. Therefore, whoever performs pilgrimage for this purpose, is not wrong, and doubtless those who spend the precious moments of their existence in invoking the Prophet, shall ... obtain happiness in this world and the next.... We do not deny miraculous powers to the saints, but on the contrary allow them.... But whether alive or dead, they must not be made the object of any form of worship....

We prohibit those forms of Bidah [innovation or heresy] that affect religion or pious works. Thus drinking coffee, reciting poetry, praising kings, do not affect religion or pious works and are not prohibited....

All games are lawful. Our prophet allowed play in his mosque. So it is lawful to chide and punish persons in various ways; to train them in the use of different weapons; or to use anything which tends to encourage warriors in battle, such as a war-drum. But it must not be accompanied with musical instruments. These are forbidden, and indeed the difference between them and a war drum is clear.

Source: J. O'Kinealy, "Translation of an Arabic Pamphlet on the History and Doctrines of the Wahhabis," *Journal of the Asiatic Society of Bengal* 43 (1874): 68–82.

■ ■ ■

SOURCE 6.6 **The Poetry of Kabir**

Early modern India was a place of much religious creativity and the interaction of various traditions. The majority of India's people practiced one or another of the many forms of Hinduism, while its Mughal rulers and perhaps 20 percent of the population were Muslims. And a new religion—Sikhism—took shape in the sixteenth century as well. Certainly there was tension and sometimes conflict among these religious communities, but not all was hostility across religious boundaries. In the writings of Kabir (1440–1518), perhaps India's most beloved poet, the sectarian differences among these religions dissolved into a mystical and transcendent love of the Divine in all of its many forms. Born into a family of Muslim weavers, Kabir as a young man became a student of a famous Hindu ascetic, Ramananda. Kabir's own poetry was and remains revered among Hindus, Muslims, and Sikhs alike. Source 6.6 contains selections from his poetry, translated by the famous Indian writer Rabindranath Tagore in the early twentieth century.

1. In what ways was Kabir critical of conventional religious practice—both Muslim and Hindu?

2. How would you describe Kabir's religious vision?

3. How might more orthodox Hindus and Muslims respond to Kabir? How would the Wahhabis, in particular, take issue with Kabir's religious outlook?

KABIR | *Poetry* | ca. late 15th century

O servant, where dost thou seek Me? Lo! I am beside thee.

I am neither in temple nor in mosque: I am neither in Kaaba [central shrine of Islam] nor in Kailash [a mountain sacred to Hindus]
Neither am I in rites and ceremonies, nor in Yoga and renunciation.
If thou art a true seeker, thou shalt at once see Me: . . . Kabir says, "O Sadhu! [a Hindu ascetic seeker] God is the breath of all breath."

It is needless to ask of a saint the caste to which he belongs;
For the priest, the warrior, the tradesman, and all the thirty-six castes, alike are seeking for God.
The barber has sought God, the washerwoman, and the carpenter —
Even Raidas [a low-caste poet] was a seeker after God.
The Rishi Swapacha was a tanner by caste [an untouchable].
Hindus and Moslems alike have achieved that End, where remains no mark of distinction.

Within this earthen vessel [the human body] are bowers and groves, and within it is the Creator:
Within this vessel are the seven oceans and the unnumbered stars.

The touchstone and the jewel-appraiser are within;
And within this vessel the Eternal soundeth, and the spring wells up.
Kabir says: "Listen to me, my Friend! My beloved Lord is within."

Your Lord is near: yet you are climbing the palm-tree to seek Him.
The Brâhman priest goes from house to house and initiates people into faith:
Alas! the true fountain of life is beside you, and you have set up a stone to worship.
Kabir says: "I may never express how sweet my Lord is.
Yoga and the telling of beads, virtue and vice—these are naught to Him."

I do not ring the temple bell:
I do not set the idol on its throne:
I do not worship the image with flowers.
It is not the austerities that mortify the flesh which are pleasing to the Lord,
When you leave off your clothes and kill your senses, you do not please the Lord.
The man who is kind and who practices righteousness, who remains passive amidst the
    affairs of the world, who considers all creatures on earth as his own self,
He attains the Immortal Being, the true God is ever with him.

There is nothing but water at the holy bathing places;
And I know that they are useless, for I have bathed in them.
The images are all lifeless, they cannot speak; I know, for I have cried aloud to them.
The Purana [Hindu religious texts] and the Koran [Quran] are mere words; lifting up
    the curtain, I have seen.

Kabir gives utterance to the words of experience; and he knows very well that all other
    things are untrue.

Source: Rabindranath Tagore, trans., *The Songs of Kabir* (New York, NY: Macmillan, 1915).

■ ■ ■

SOURCE 6.7 Religious Syncretism in Indian Art

Another site of religious blending in early modern India took shape at the court of the Mughal emperor. There, Akbar presided over what we might now call interfaith gatherings and created a blended religious cult for Mughal elites. European-style religious art, painted by Mughal artists, appeared prominently at court, featuring scenes including Jesus, Mary, and various Christian saints.

The Muslim rulers of the Mughal Empire were also taking a growing interest in the ancient Hindu mind–body practice known as yoga. Some of the sultans seemed persuaded that such postures and practices conveyed great power that might well benefit themselves. Around 1550, a Muslim Sufi master closely connected to the Mughal court, Muhammad Gwaliyari, compiled systematic descriptions of twenty-two yoga postures, hoping to incorporate them into Sufi spiritual practice. Somewhat later, the Muslim prince Salim, who subsequently became the emperor Jahangir, commissioned a Hindu artist to illustrate this text, known as *The Ocean of Life*. In some of these illustrations, such as the one reproduced here, the yogi's face is painted to resemble that of Jesus, as depicted in the European religious literature then circulating in the Mughal court. Such images represented a remarkable cultural blending of Islamic patrons, Hindu practice, and Christian traditions.

1. Why might Muslim rulers and Sufi masters want to incorporate Hindu-based yoga techniques into their own practices?

2. What does the painting of a yogi with the face of Christ suggest about Indian views of Jesus?

Kumbhaka (breathing exercises) | ca. 1600

DOING HISTORY

1. **Comparing views of human potential:** What different understandings of human potential might you infer from these sources? What do the people who created them believe is necessary to realize or fulfill that potential?

2. **Comparing religious reformers:** Consider the religious outlooks of Luther, al-Wahhab, and Kabir. What similarities and differences can you identify?

3. **Imagining a conversation:** Construct an imaginary debate or conversation between Condorcet and one or more of the religious or spiritually inclined authors of these sources.

Reform and Renewal in the Christian and Islamic Worlds

Both the Christian and Islamic worlds experienced vibrant reform movements in the early modern period that were expressed through commitments to do away with human corruptions of the faith that had accrued over centuries and to return to the "pure" and uncorrupted original message of each faith's holy text. The two selections that follow offer an opportunity to compare the goals and principles of two of the most prominent movements of the period—the Protestant Reformation in Christian Europe and Wahhabism in Islamic Arabia. Voice 6.1 is that of Robert W. Scribner, a leading British historian of the early Protestant Reformation in Germany, while Voice 6.2 belongs to Natana DeLong-Bas, a theologian and historian based in Canada who has written extensively on the founder of the Wahhabi movement.

1. For Scribner in Voice 6.1, what were the positive and negative elements of the Protestant Reform agenda, and what does he mean by "positive" and "negative"?

2. In what ways are the reform agendas of German Protestants and al-Wahhab similar?

3. **Integrating primary and secondary sources:** Using these two Voices and Sources 6.1, 6.2, and 6.5, compare and contrast the agendas of the Protestant Reformation and the Wahhabi movement.

VOICE 6.1

R. W. Scribner on the Evangelical Agenda in Protestant Germany | 1986

For some time now it has been common for scholars of the Reformation to speak of it as an 'evangelical movement'. The term captures the tone of the upsurge of religious enthusiasm that swept through Germany in the early 1520s. In its broadest manifestations, it was a movement of biblical renewal. Many felt that the genuine Christian message, the 'pure word of God' as it was recorded in the Bible, had been rediscovered after it had lain hidden or obscured for many generations. . . .

Beyond its catchwords, what was the message of this movement? It is traditional to associate it with the doctrines of Luther, and these certainly played a prominent role. . . . However, the evangelical message was far more complex than the ideas of one man. It had both positive and negative elements. The negative elements drew on an endemic anticlericalism, the product of a long disillusionment with the clergy. . . . Priests and monks were stigmatised as 'enemies of the Gospel'. . . . who were likely to lead people to damnation rather than to salvation.

The positive message stood in counterpoint to the negative: the laity no longer needed the clergy for salvation, since each Christian was free to find salvation through a direct encounter with God in the Bible. This encounter occurred in two ways: through reading the Bible, and through hearing the Word preached. . . . The Word was seen not just as a way to salvation, but as a guide for life in the world.

Source: R. W. Scribner, *The German Reformation* (Basingstoke, UK: Macmillan, 1986), 17–18.

VOICE 6.2

Natana DeLong-Bas on the Teachings of Ibn Abd al-Wahhab | 2004

Ibn Abd al-Wahhab's dissatisfaction with and ultimate rejection of adherence to past interpretations of Islam (*taqlid*) grew out of his encounter with *hadith* criticism [the writings of earlier scholars on the *hadith*, sayings traditionally attributed to Muhammad]. Recognizing the importance of returning directly to scripture rather than relying on secondhand interpretations, led him to call for the rejuvenation of the practice of independent reasoning (*ijtihad*). His rejuvenation of *ijtihad* involved the clear and unequivocal assertion of the Quran and *hadith* alone as authoritative sources of revelation, taking precedence over human interpretation. . . .

His rejection of *taqlid*, therefore, was not so much a matter of rejecting the past as it was a desire to break away from a mentality insisting that only people who had lived in the past were capable of correct interpretation of the scripture. . . . [H]e sought to push Muslims into their own personal encounters with God by direct reading and interpretation of scripture.

Source: Natana J. DeLong-Bas, *Wahhabi Islam: From Revival and Reform to Global Jihad* (Oxford, UK: Oxford University Press, 2004), 282.

NOTE

1. Robert S. Miola, ed., *Early Modern Catholicism: An Anthology of Primary Sources* (Oxford: Oxford University Press, 2007), 59.

CHAPTER 7

Debating Rights

In 1948, the United Nations General Assembly adopted a "Universal Declaration of Human Rights," which subsequently inspired over seventy human rights treaties, including those dealing with the rights of children, prisoners, and disabled persons. Political discourse today frequently articulates the notion of rights—LGBTQ rights, minority rights, national rights, civil rights, religious rights, property rights, and many others. These recent developments mark the globalization of ideas and values that derived from the European Enlightenment and first found concrete expression in the era of the Atlantic revolutions (1750–1900). At that time, three questions in particular generated intense controversy: the right to revolution, the rights of enslaved persons, and the rights of women. Each of these issues had fervent advocates and equally passionate opponents. The documents and images that follow illustrate these controversies as they played out during the century and a half when the ongoing debate about "rights" was initially taking shape.

SOURCE 7.1 The Right to Revolution

Before the French Revolution, most European governments were grounded in the notion of the "divine right of kings," the idea that rulers governed by the will of God. This meant, of course, that rebellion against such sacred authority was wholly illegitimate and even sinful. The Declaration of the Rights of Man and Citizen, created in 1789 at the outset of the French Revolution, affirmed a very different basis of political authority: the consent of the governed. That document enumerated a series of "rights" that governments should protect. These included political liberty, participation in political life, freedom of opinion and speech even in religious matters, and freedom from arbitrary arrest and punishment.

Perhaps the most iconic representation of the declaration to appear in the months following its promulgation was a painting created by Jean-Jacques Le Barbier (1738–1826). Like many other artists who have sought to publicize and assert the legitimacy of radically new ideas, he drew heavily on older, established symbols and artistic conventions to convey his message. Thus Le Barbier reproduced the text of the declaration on tablets similar to those used in religious paintings to represent the Ten Commandments brought down by Moses from Mount Sinai. The two easily identifiable symbolic female figures—the winged allegorical figure representing Fame and the other personifying France—conveyed the virtue of and the audience for the declaration's articles. Throughout the painting, Le Barbier used common classical symbols to provide visual cues to help his audience interpret its message, like the snake biting its tail representing eternity, the broken chains in the hands of France representing victory over oppression, and the laurel bunting, long associated with glory, draped over the tablets. One symbol in particular, the red bonnet or "Phrygian," would have resonated with Le Barbier's audience. It was of ancient Greek origin but had become a popular symbol of the new French nation. Engravings of Le Barbier's painting were printed in large numbers and circulated across the kingdom, spreading the declaration's ideas and Le Barbier's visual tribute to them to a broad audience.

1. Why do you think that Le Barbier used well-known figures, symbols, and imagery in his painting? Why did the artist adorn the image with only female figures?

2. What message is conveyed by placing the Declaration of the Rights of Man and Citizen on tablets evoking the Ten Commandments?

3. The whole composition is overseen by the eye of God the Creator radiating from a triangle, which by the late eighteenth century had both biblical and Masonic connotations. What does this symbol add to the composition? How does it compare to the religious justification for the "divine right of kings"?

JEAN-JACQUES LE BARBIER │ *Declaration of the Rights of Man and Citizen* │ ca. 1789

Declaration of the Rights of Man and Citizen, 1789 (oil on canvas)/French School (18th century)/Musée de la Ville de Paris, Musée Carnavalet, Paris, France/ Bridgeman Images

■ ■ ■

SOURCE 7.2 **Contesting the Right to Revolution**

To many others, the language of "rights" opened the door to violence and chaos because it disregarded tradition, encouraged excessive individualism, and promoted selfishness and political ambition. Such a viewpoint found justification as the French Revolution became more radical and violent, culminating in the Reign of Terror (1793–1794), during which thousands of political opponents of the revolutionary regime were executed. An important step in this descent into violence was the execution of Louis XVI in January 1793. Source 7.2, a British political cartoon, conveys a highly critical, indeed horrified, outlook on the violence that accompanied the French Revolution. Captioned *Hell Broke Loose*, it depicts the execution of Louis XVI and was printed shortly after his death. The flying demonic figures in the image are repeating popular slogans of the revolution: "*Vive la nation*" ("Long live the nation") and "*Ça ira*" ("That will go well," or more loosely, "We will win").

1. What is the significance of the demons and dragons in the cartoon? How are the soldiers at the bottom of the image portrayed?

2. What meaning would you attribute to the caption, *Hell Broke Loose*? What disasters might critics of the revolution have imagined coming in its wake?

3. How do you understand the beam of light from heaven that falls on Louis XVI?

Hell Broke Loose, or, The Murder of Louis │ 1793

■ ■ ■

SOURCE 7.3 Rights and Slavery: Confronting a Contradiction

The language of "rights," derived from the French Revolution, had profound implications for the long-established practice of slavery. If "rights" were universal, did they not also apply to enslaved persons? Or were enslaved people not regarded as fully human? The contradiction between the "rights of man," racial inequality, and, by implication, slavery was addressed in an engraving produced in 1793, the year before France temporarily abolished slavery in its colonies. It was titled *All Mortals Are Equal, It Is Not Birth but Virtue That Makes the Difference.* The allegorical figure at the center of the image is Reason, with the sacred flame of "love of the fatherland" emerging from her head. She places a level on a white man and a Black man, behind whom is a cornucopia of abundance. The Black man holds in one hand the Declaration of the Rights of Man and Citizen (1789) and in the other the Decree of May 15, 1791, which granted free Blacks and multiracial people political rights. Reason is pushed by the allegorical figure of Nature, who is seated on a sack out of which flee the demons labeled Aristocracy, Selfishness, Injustice, and Insurrection. While this image celebrates political rights granted to free Blacks and multiracial people, it could also be read as advocating the same rights for enslaved people at a time when France was edging toward emancipation legislation.

1. What role do the allegorical figures of Reason and Nature play in this scene?

2. What does the level symbolize in this image? What meaning might you derive from the fact that the Black man is depicted in a loincloth, while the white man is fully clothed?

3. How might a supporter of slave emancipation interpret this scene? How might an opponent?

All Mortals Are Equal, It Is Not Birth but Virtue That Makes the Difference | 1793

"All Mortals are Equal, It Is not Birth but Virtue That Makes the Difference," 1793 (colored engraving)/French School (18th century)/Bibliothèque Nationale, Paris, France/Bridgeman Images

■ ■ ■

SOURCE 7.4 Rights and Slavery in the United States Constitution

Delegates meeting to draft a constitution for the fledgling United States of America in 1787 faced the difficult task of reconciling the lofty principles espoused early in the revolution with the brutal realities of slavery and the strong support for its continuation among political elites in some states. At the outset of the revolution, the American Declaration of Independence had boldly declared "liberty, and the pursuit of Happiness" as divinely sanctioned universal rights, and the same year the Continental Congress had declared that "no slave shall be imported into any of the thirteen United Colonies." But delegates representing several southern colonies at the Constitutional Convention threatened to go their own way if the new constitution prohibited the continuation of slavery in their states. Desire to keep the union together meant that the final version of the Constitution contained several compromises between abolitionist and proslavery positions and other provisions that simply upheld slavery. Reproduced here are the articles in the Constitution that most directly address the issue of slavery; note that the drafters carefully avoided using terms like "slave," "enslaved person," or "slavery" in the document.

1. Which provisions in these articles provide evidence of compromise between pro-slavery and abolitionist positions? Which simply uphold slavery?

2. How did the drafters of the Constitution avoid referring directly to slavery or enslaved people? Why do you think that they did this?

3. What does this source reveal about the thinking of American revolutionaries concerning universal rights and slavery?

U.S. Constitution | 1787

Article I, Section 2: . . . Representatives and direct Taxes shall be apportioned among the several States which may be included within this Union, according to their respective Numbers, which shall be determined by adding to the whole Number of free Persons, including those bound to Service for a Term of Years, and excluding Indians not taxed, three fifths of all other persons.

Article I, Section 9: The Migration or Importation of such Persons as any of the States now existing shall think proper to admit, shall not be prohibited by the Congress prior to the Year one thousand eight hundred and eight, but a Tax or duty may be imposed on such Importation, not exceeding ten dollars for each Person.

Article IV, Section 2: . . . No Person held to Service or Labour in one State, under the Laws thereof, escaping into another, shall, in Consequence of any Law or Regulation therein, be discharged from such Service or Labour, but shall be delivered up on Claim of the Party to whom such Service or Labour may be due.

■ ■ ■

SOURCE 7.5 The Rights of Women Asserted

Alongside the right to revolution and the rights of enslaved persons, the rights of women became a topic of intense debate during the era of the Atlantic revolutions, with some advocates in the United States and Europe asserting that everyone enjoyed universal rights regardless of gender. An important moment in this movement occurred on July 19 and 20, 1848, in Seneca Falls, New York, when the first major meeting of women's rights advocates drafted the *Declaration of Sentiments*, an early and influential statement of women's rights. Consciously drawing on wording from the American Declaration of Independence, the *Declaration of Sentiments* included many controversial resolutions, none more so than the ninth resolution, which asserted that men had unjustly deprived women of their right to vote. The wide-ranging declaration was radical for its time, reflected by the fact that only about a third of the attendees signed it. Nonetheless, over the coming decades advocates had some success in rallying support in the wider society and implementing some of the *Declaration of Sentiments'* resolutions, as when the United

States Congress ratified the Nineteenth Amendment in 1920, enshrining in the Constitution the right for women to vote.

1. What are the primary demands made in the *Declaration of Sentiments*? How are these demands justified?

2. To what extent does the *Declaration of Sentiments* see denial of the franchise (right to vote) as the reason that other injustices and inequalities suffered by women had taken root or persisted in society?

3. Why do you think that the drafters of the *Declaration of Sentiments* modeled its opening passages on the Declaration of Independence?

Declaration of Sentiments | 1848

We hold these truths to be self-evident; that all men and women are created equal; that they are endowed by their Creator with certain inalienable rights; that among these are life, liberty, and the pursuit of happiness; that to secure these rights governments are instituted, deriving their just powers from the consent of the governed. Whenever any form of Government becomes destructive of these ends, it is the right of those who suffer from it to refuse allegiance to it, and to insist upon the institution of a new government. . . .

The history of mankind is a history of repeated injuries and usurpations on the part of man toward woman, having in direct object the establishment of an absolute tyranny over her. . . .

He has never permitted her to exercise her inalienable right to the elective franchise [the right to vote].

He has compelled her to submit to laws, in the formation of which she had no voice.

He has withheld from her rights which are given to the most ignorant and degraded men — both natives and foreigners.

Having deprived her of this first right of a citizen, the elective franchise . . . he has oppressed her on all sides.

He has made her, if married, in the eye of the law, civilly dead.

He has taken from her all right in property, even to the wages she earns. . . .

In the covenant of marriage, she is compelled to promise obedience to her husband, he becoming, to all intents and purposes, her master — the law giving him power to deprive her of her liberty, and to administer chastisement.

He has so framed the laws of divorce, as to what shall be the proper causes of divorce; in case of separation, to whom the guardianship of the children shall be given, as to be wholly regardless of the happiness of women — the law, in all cases, going upon the false supposition of the supremacy of man, and giving all power into his hands. . . .

He has monopolized nearly all the profitable employments, and from those she is permitted to follow, she receives but a scanty remuneration.

He closes against her all the avenues to wealth and distinction, which he considers most honorable to himself. As a teacher of theology, medicine, or law, she is not known.

He has denied her the facilities for obtaining a thorough education—all colleges being closed against her.

He allows her in Church as well as State, but a subordinate position, claiming Apostolic authority for her exclusion from the ministry, and with some exceptions, from any public participation in the affairs of the Church.

He has created a false public sentiment, by giving to the world a different code of morals for men and women. . . .

He has usurped the prerogative of Jehovah [God] himself, claiming it as his right to assign for her a sphere of action, when that belongs to her conscience and her God.

He has endeavored, in every way that he could to destroy her confidence in her own powers, to lessen her self-respect, and to make her willing to lead a dependent and abject life.

Now, in view of this entire disfranchisement of one-half the people of this country . . . , we insist that they have immediate admission to all the rights and privileges which belong to them as citizens of these United States.

■ ■ ■

SOURCE 7.6 Imagining Women's Suffrage

Of all the demands made at Seneca Falls, the right to vote, known as suffrage, brought the fiercest negative reaction. Critics frequently made their cases against women's suffrage by imagining a world that might be created if the suffragettes, as women who advocated for the right to vote were labeled, won the rights that they sought. In this 1897 cartoon entitled "An Inauguration of the Future," the artist offers a vision of what America would become if women were granted the right to vote. It depicts the inauguration of a female president, who is surrounded on the stage by other women in positions of power. To the bottom right on the sidelines of the inauguration, a man is depicted in a distinctly domestic role holding a crying baby.

1. Note the women in military uniforms on the stage and in the crowd. Why do you think that the artist included these figures in the image?

2. What potential implications of granting women the right to vote does this artist want the viewer to consider?

3. While not so far-fetched today, how might this image have been viewed during the late nineteenth century?

An Inauguration of the Future | 1897

DOING HISTORY

1. **Making comparisons:** What common elements can you find in the sources that celebrate and advocate for "human rights"?

2. **Making comparisons:** What common elements can you find in those sources that fear the consequences of "human rights"?

3. **Identifying supporters and opponents:** Based on these sources, which groups of people supported the Atlantic revolutions, and which opposed them?

4. **Finding common ground:** Is there any common ground between the advocates and opponents of human rights as expressed in these sources?

5. **Making connections between past and present:** In what ways do these sources resonate with current debates about human rights? And in what ways do they differ? Are you more impressed with the continuities or the changes in the ongoing controversies about "human rights"?

Debating the Lessons of the French Revolution

Generations of observers have drawn a remarkable variety of often contradictory lessons from the French Revolution, and debates over its meaning and legacy continue even today. The two Voices reproduced here explore these debates from different perspectives. In Voice 7.1, the historians Jack R. Censer and Lynn Hunt examine disagreements over when the French Revolution concluded and lessons about the legitimacy of revolution as a mode of political action. In Voice 7.2, the historian Bailey Stone contextualizes the French Revolution by exploring why it differed both from earlier revolutions, including the American Revolution, and the Russian and Chinese revolutions that followed it.

1. How would you describe the spectrum of attitudes toward the right to revolution that Censer and Hunt identify in Voice 7.1?

2. According to Stone in Voice 7.2, what makes the French Revolution a pivotal moment in "the world history of revolutions"?

3. What lasting legacies of the French Revolution are identified in Voices 7.1 and 7.2?

4. **Integrating primary and secondary sources:** Using Voice 7.1 and Sources 7.1 and 7.2, describe the debate over the right to revolution sparked by the French Revolution.

VOICE 7.1

Jack R. Censer and Lynn Hunt on the Contradictory Lessons Taken from the French Revolution | 2001

Until Napoleon fell from power, Europeans could not be sure that the French Revolution was over. For some, Napoleon represented a natural continuation of the French Revolution because he brought its principles of legal equality and religious toleration to other peoples. For others, Napoleon, turning a fledgling democracy into an authoritarian state dependent on military conquest, represented a perversion or distortion of those principles. Still others condemned the French Revolution and Napoleon alike. Whatever their response to the events, most contemporaries agreed . . . that the French Revolution had fundamentally changed the course of world history. . . .

Communists, radical democrats, liberals, and conservatives drew contradictory lessons from the French Revolution because they held contradictory opinions about revolution as a mode of political action. Communists viewed revolution as the best instrument for fashioning a fundamentally new world; radical democrats considered revolution an occasional necessity to be entered upon only in times of extremity; liberals accepted revolutions only when they were made for constitutional guarantees; and conservatives considered revolution a sign of human pride, a fundamentally mistaken activity that could only bring in its train political disaster and attacks on religion and morals. Because revolution still generates controversy in the present day, the French Revolution, as the first modern revolution and as the model for communist revolution, has lost none of its ability to provoke discussion and debate.

Source: Jack R. Censer and Lynn Hunt, *Liberty Equality, Fraternity: Exploring the French Revolution* (University Park: Pennsylvania University Press, 2001), 172 and 178.

VOICE 7.2

Bailey Stone on the French Revolution's Pivotal Place in the Global History of Revolution | 2002

If . . . we situate [the French Revolution] within a global-historical context, we cannot help but see it as a "transitional upheaval" in the history of modern sociopolitical revolutions. The transition referred to here was one from revolutions, such as those in mid-seventeenth-century England and late-eighteenth-century British North America, which took place in essentially insular societies under minimal pressure from the outside world, to revolutions of the twentieth century, such as those in Russia and China, which have occurred in societies under extreme exogenous [outside] pressures. . . . [T]he French in 1789, unlike their revolutionary forerunners [in England and British North America], were attempting to live up to a very old tradition of greatness . . . in the teeth of the armed opposition of much of Europe. Is it at all astonishing, in the light of these realities, that the Terror of 1793–94 had no real equivalent in either of the earlier revolutions? On the other hand, the upheaval in France was less brutal and involved less thoroughgoing sociopolitical change than either the Russian or the Chinese Revolution. This was so for a number of reasons, of course; but foremost among them was the fact that the Russians and the Chinese in the first half of the twentieth century faced, in Germany and Japan respectively, much greater external threats to their existence than the French confronted in the 1790s. . . .

So the winds of change that gusted across the picturesque French landscape during 1789–99 were pivotal in what we might call the world history of revolution.

Source: Bailey Stone, *Reinterpreting the French Revolution: A Global Perspective* (Cambridge: Cambridge University Press, 2002), 266–67.

CHAPTER 8

Experiencing the Early Industrial Revolution

WORKING WITH EVIDENCE

The immense economic and social changes of the Industrial Revolution left almost no one untouched in the societies that experienced it most fully. Especially in its early phases (roughly 1780–1875), that immense transformation generated a traumatic upheaval in ways of living for many people. For others, it brought new opportunities, wealth, and comfort. In seeking to understand how individuals experienced this unprecedented revolutionary process, historians have at their disposal a wealth of evidence, both documentary and visual. Each of the sources that follow provides just a glimpse into what living through those early decades of the Industrial Revolution may have meant to those who experienced it, mostly in England where it all began.

SOURCE 8.1 The Experience of an English Factory Worker

The early Industrial Revolution represented not only a technological breakthrough of epic proportions, but also a transformation in the organization of work, expressed most fully in the factory. Unlike the artisan's workshop, which it increasingly replaced, the factory concentrated human labor in a single space and separated workers from the final product by assigning them highly specialized and repetitive tasks. In the name of efficiency and productivity, owners and managers imposed strict discipline in their factories and regulated workers' lives according to clock time. Finally, workers were wage earners, dependent for their economic survival on a very modest income and highly uncertain employment, both of which were subject to the vagaries of the market.

One such worker was Elizabeth Bentley, who had worked in a factory since the age of six. In 1831, when she was twenty-three years old, Bentley testified before a British parliamentary committee investigating conditions in textile mills. A subsequent inquiry elicited testimony from William Harter, a mill owner. As a result of these investigations, legislation in 1833 limited the hours of employment for women and children.

1. Child labor was nothing new, as children had long worked in the fields and work-shops of preindustrial Europe. What was different about the conditions under which children worked in early industrial factories?

2. Why do you think the investigator queried Elizabeth Bentley specifically about the treatment of girls?

3. How does William Harter's testimony explain the willingness of factory owners to impose these conditions on their workers? How might he respond to Elizabeth Bentley's testimony?

SOURCE 8.1A

ELIZABETH BENTLEY, FACTORY WORKER | *Testimony* | 1831

What age are you?—Twenty-three.

Where do you live?—At Leeds.

What time did you begin to work at a factory?—When I was six years old.

What kind of mill is it?—Flax-mill.

What was your business in that mill?—I was a little doffer [cleaner of the machines].

What were your hours of labour in that mill?—From 5 in the morning till 9 at night, when they were thronged [busy].

For how long a time together have you worked that excessive length of time?—For about half a year.

What were your usual hours when you were not so thronged?—From 6 in the morning till 7 at night.

What time was allowed for your meals?—Forty minutes at noon.

Had you any time to get your breakfast or drinking?—No, we got it as we could.

Explain what it is you had to do?—When the frames are full, they have to stop the frames, and take the flyers off, and take the full bobbins off, and carry them to the roller; and then put empty ones on, and set the frame going again.

Does that keep you constantly on your feet?—Yes, there are so many frames, and they run so quick.

Suppose you flagged a little, or were too late, what would they do?—Strap us.

Are they in the habit of strapping those who are last in doffing?—Yes.

Constantly?—Yes.

Girls as well as boys?—Yes.

Have you ever been strapped?—Yes.

Severely?—Yes.

Were the girls struck so as to leave marks upon their skin?—Yes, they have had black marks many times, and their parents dare not come to him about it, they were afraid of losing their work.

Could you eat your food well in that factory?—No, indeed I had not much to eat, and the little I had I could not eat it, my appetite was so poor, and being covered with dust; and it was no use to take it home, I could not eat it, and the overlooker took it, and gave it to the pigs.

How far had you to go for dinner?—We could not go home to dinner.

Where did you dine?—In the mill.

Did you live far from the mill?—Yes, two miles.

Supposing you had not been in time enough in the morning at these mills, what would have been the consequence?—We should have been quartered. If we were a quarter of an hour too late, they would take off half an hour; we only got a penny an hour, and they would take a halfpenny more.

Were you also beaten for being too late?—No, I was never beaten myself, I have seen the boys beaten for being too late.

Were you generally there in time?—Yes; my mother had been up at 4 o'clock in the morning, and at 2 o'clock in the morning; the colliers used to go to their work about 3 or 4 o'clock, and when she heard them stirring she has got up out of her warm bed, and gone out and asked them the time; and I have sometimes been at Hunslet Car at 2 o'clock in the morning, when it was streaming down with rain, and we have had to stay until the mill was opened.

SOURCE 8.1B

WILLIAM HARTER, MILL OWNER | *Testimony* | 1832

What effect would it have on your manufacture to reduce the hours of labor to ten?—It would instantly much reduce the value of my mill and machinery, and consequently far prejudice my manufacture. . . . To produce the same quantity of work under a ten-hours bill will require an additional outlay of 3,000 or 4,000 pounds; therefore a ten-hours bill would impose upon me the necessity of this additional outlay in such perishable property as buildings and machinery, or I must be content to relinquish one-sixth portion of my business.

Source: *British Sessional Papers*, vol. 15 (London, 1832), 195–196; vol. 21, pt. D-3 (London, 1833), 26–28.

■ ■ ■

SOURCE 8.2 Urban Living Conditions

If factory working conditions were deplorable in the early decades of the English Industrial Revolution, the urban living conditions for many of those workers were no less horrific. In a classic description of industrial Manchester in the early 1840s, a twenty-four-year-old Friedrich Engels, who later became a close collaborator with Karl Marx, provided a vivid portrait of urban working-class life in England's premier industrial city. By the time his German-language account was translated into English in 1886, Engels acknowledged that "the most crying abuses described in this book have either disappeared or have been made less conspicuous." He added, however, that broadly similar conditions were prevalent in later-industrializing countries such as France, Germany, and the United States.

1. How does Engels describe working-class life in Manchester in the early 1840s?

2. What implied contrasts does Engels make with the earlier rural life of poor peasants?

3. To what does he attribute these conditions?

FRIEDRICH ENGELS │ *The Condition of the Working Class in England* │ *1844*

Manchester contains about four hundred thousand inhabitants. . . . The town itself is peculiarly built, so that a person may live in it for years, and go in and out daily without coming into contact with a working-people's quarter or even with workers, that is, so long as he confines himself to his business or to pleasure walks. This arises chiefly from the fact, that by unconscious tacit agreement, as well as with outspoken conscious determination, the working people's quarters are sharply separated from the sections of the city reserved for the middle-class. . . .

Here [in Old Town Manchester] one is in an almost undisguised working-men's quarter, for even the shops and beer houses hardly take the trouble to exhibit a trifling degree of cleanliness. But all this is nothing in comparison with the courts and lanes which lie behind, to which access can be gained only through covered passages, in which no two human beings can pass at the same time. Of the irregular cramming together of dwellings in ways which defy all rational plan, of the tangle in which they are crowded literally one upon the other, it is impossible to convey an idea. Right and left a multitude of covered passages lead from the main street into numerous courts, and he who turns in thither gets into a filth and disgusting grime, the equal of which is not to be found. . . .

In one of these courts there stands directly at the entrance, at the end of the covered passage, a privy without a door, so dirty that the inhabitants can pass into and out of the court only by passing through foul pools of stagnant urine and excrement. . . . Below it on the river there are several tanneries which fill the whole neighbourhood with the stench of animal putrefaction. Below Ducie Bridge the only entrance to most of the houses is by means of narrow, dirty stairs and over heaps of refuse and filth. The first court below Ducie Bridge, known as Allen's Court, was in such a state at the time of the cholera that the sanitary police ordered it evacuated, swept, and disinfected with chloride of lime. . . . At the bottom flows, or rather stagnates, the Irk [River], a narrow, coal-black, foul-smelling stream, full of debris and refuse. . . .

In dry weather, a long string of the most disgusting, blackish-green, slime pools are left standing on this bank, from the depths of which bubbles of miasmatic gas constantly arise and give forth a stench. . . . Above the bridge are tanneries, bone mills, and gasworks, from which all drains and refuse find their way into the Irk, which receives further the contents of all the neighbouring sewers and privies. It may be easily imagined, therefore, what sort of residue the stream deposits. Here the background embraces the pauper burial-ground, the station of the Liverpool and Leeds railway, and, in the rear of this, the Workhouse [where the desperately poor found shelter and employment], . . . which, like a citadel, looks threateningly down from behind its high walls and parapets on the hilltop, upon the working-people's quarter below.

Passing along a rough bank, among stakes and washing-lines, one penetrates into this chaos of small one-storied, one-roomed huts, in most of which there is no artificial floor; kitchen, living and sleeping-room all in one. In such a hole, scarcely five feet long by six broad, I found two beds—and such bedsteads and beds!—which, with a staircase and chimney-place, exactly filled the room. In several others I found absolutely nothing, while the door stood open, and the inhabitants leaned against it. Everywhere before the doors refuse and offal; that any sort of pavement lay underneath could not be seen but only felt, here and there, with the feet. This whole collection of cattle-sheds for human beings was surrounded on two sides by houses and a factory, and on the third by the river. . . .

In almost every court one or even several such pens [of pigs] may be found, into which the inhabitants of the court throw all refuse and offal, whence the swine grow fat; and the atmosphere, confined on all four sides, is utterly corrupted by putrefying animal and vegetable substances. . . .

Such is the Old Town of Manchester. . . . Everything which here arouses horror and indignation is of recent origin, belongs to the *industrial epoch*.

Source: Friedrich Engels, *The Condition of the Working Class in England in 1844* (London, UK: Swan Sonnenschein & Co., 1892), 45, 48–53.

■ ■ ■

SOURCE 8.3 Another View of Factory Life

As Engels admitted, early working and living conditions in industrial England had improved by the later nineteenth century, though the debate about factory life had hardly ended. Source 8.3, an 1874 painting by English artist Eyre Crowe, provides a more benevolent view of an industrial factory as it portrays a number of young women workers during their dinner hour outside the cotton textile mill in the industrial town of Wigan.

1. How does this depiction of factory life compare with that of Source 8.1? How might you account for the differences?

2. How do you respond to Crowe's painting? Do you think it was an honest portrayal of factory life for women? What might be missing?

3. Notice the details of the painting—the young women's relationship to one another, the hairnets on their heads, their clothing, their activities during this break from work. What marks them as working-class women? What impression of factory life did Crowe seek to convey? Was he trying to highlight or minimize the class differences of industrial Britain?

EYRE CROWE | *Outside the Factory* | 1874

The Dinner Hour, Wigan, 1874 (oil on canvas)/by Eyre Crowe (1824-1910)/Manchester Art Gallery, UK/Bridgeman Images

■ ■ ■

SOURCE 8.4 A Weaver's Lament

As industrialization generated new work in the factories, it also destroyed older means of livelihood, particularly that of skilled artisans. By the early 1860s, the silk weavers of Coventry, England, a long-established and previously thriving group of artisans, were in desperate straits, owing in part to a decline in the fashion of wearing silk ribbons. Many individual weavers had to sell their looms to the larger manufacturers, who were organizing more efficient production in factories. The song that follows was sung by unemployed weavers as they paraded through the streets of Coventry on their way to relief work, often in stone quarries. It reflects the costs of the Industrial Revolution for a body of proud and skilled artisans and their distress at an economic system that seemed to cast them adrift.

1. Who or what does the song blame for the plight of the weavers?

2. What does the song mean by mentioning the "commercial plan" and "political economy"? And how do you understand the line "He's only a weaver whom nobody owns"?

3. How might you compare the life of an unemployed weaver with that of a factory worker like Elizabeth Bentley?

The Weaver | 1860s

Who is that man coming up the street,
With wearied manner and shuffling feet,
With a face that tells of care and grief,
And in hope seems to have lost belief ? . . .
    For wickedness past he now atones;
    He's only a weaver whom nobody owns.
He's coming no doubt from breaking stones,
With saddened heart and aching bones;
But why should he grumble? he gets good pay,
A loaf and sixpence every day. . . .
He thought if he worked both night and day
He ought to receive equivalent pay.
He's evidently an inconsistent man,
Who don't understand the commercial plan. . . .
Political economy now must sway,
And say when a man shall work or play.
If he's wanted, his wages may be high;
If he isn't, why then he may starve and die. . . .
And if you employ him, don't mend the price;

He's starving, you know, and has no choice;
And give him to weave the worst of silk,
For it's only a weaver's time you bilk. . . .
     But take no heed of his sighs and groans,
     His careworn face and agony moans,
     For wickedness past he now atones;
He's only a weaver whom nobody owns.

Source: Joseph Gutteridge, *Light and Shadows in the Life of an Artisan* (Coventry: Coventry, Curtis and Beamish, 1893), 153–55.

■ ■ ■

SOURCE 8.5 Poetry from the Factory Floor

Born around 1835 to a working-class family in an industrializing Scotland, Ellen Johnston worked in a variety of textile mills throughout her life, lived as a single mother, and, most unusually, became a published poet with a modest local reputation under her pseudonym "the factory girl." Johnston had hoped to make her living as a poet, thereby escaping the poverty to which factory wages condemned her. She did receive occasional financial support from upper-class benefactors, including a small gift from Queen Victoria, and a published collection of her work appeared in 1867. Nevertheless, she was aware that both class and gender made it difficult for her to win acceptance among middle- and upper-class members of the literary establishment, a recognition expressed in her writing: "I am so small I cannot shine / Amidst the great that read my rhyme." In 1870, only a year after the publication of the second edition of her book of poetry, Johnston had to apply for "poor relief." In 1874, she died in a Scottish poorhouse, not yet forty years of age.

In her poetry, Johnston did not advocate for socialism or revolutionary upheaval; rather, her poems reflected on the joys and struggles of working people and called for better working conditions, often by appealing to the "master" of the mill to behave in a benevolent fashion toward his employees. Her own experience in working for a caring factory owner is expressed in *Kennedy's Dear Mill*. Nonetheless, Johnston was fully aware of the inequalities and exploitation endemic in industrial life and the need for workers to take action to secure better wages. In *Lines on Behalf of the Boatbuilders and Boilermakers of Great Britain and Ireland*, she highlights the poor treatment of workers in the shipbuilding industry that was so central to Scotland's economy.

1. How can one explain the contrasting attitudes toward industrialists in these two poems?

2. How might Ellen Johnston have responded to the parliamentary testimony in Source 8.1?

3. How would you describe Ellen Johnston's outlook on industrial Britain?

ELLEN JOHNSTON | *Poetry* | 1867

Kennedy's Dear Mill

OH! Kennedy's dear mill!
To you I'll sing a song
For winter dark and dull;
    For another season's gone,
And summer's bright sunshine
    Thy little shed doth fill.
Prosperity is thine,
    Oh, Kennedy's dear mill!

. . .

Thou hast a secret spell
    For all as well as me;
Each girl loves thee well
    That ever wrought in thee.
They may leave thy blessed toil;
    But, find work they will,
They return back in a while
    To Kennedy's dear mill.

. . .

And freedom's glorious shrine
    Is center'd in thy walls;
No tyrant knave to bind,
    No slavish chain enthrals.
The workers are as free
    As the sunshine on the hill;
Thy breath is liberty
    Oh! Kennedy's dear mill.

We feel no coward fear
When our dear master comes;
    And when he's standing near,
And gazing on our looms,
He hails us with a smile
    That is a brother's still,
No haughty lord of toil
    Owns Kennedy's dear mill.

. . .

When his workers are in grief,
    It is against his will;
He's the first to send relief
    From Kennedy's dear mill.

. . .

Now, Kennedy's dear mill,
    The best wish of my heart
Shall linger near you still,
    When from you I depart.
Whate'er my fate may be,
    Let me wander where I will,
Peace and prosperity
To Kennedy's dear mill.

Source: Ellen Johnston, *Autobiography, Poems, and Songs*, 2nd ed. (Glasgow: William Love, 1869), 19–21.

Lines on Behalf of the Boatbuilders and Boilermakers of Great Britain and Ireland

O that I could rob fortune of her gold as she has robbed the poor man of his rights,
I would give each worthy man his share, and then would thousands live who die for want
of that which some of those who are less worthy have too much.— *The Factory Girl*

O gather hay while the sun shines
All ye who wish to be free;
Nip, ere too late, the chain that binds
    The gems of sweet liberty.

Why will ye hesitate longer
    While cruel despotic power
Is working the chain still stronger
    That draws on the evil hour.

Our brothers in prison were cast
    Because like brave men they spoke,
When crushed in the powerful grasp
    of slavery's galling yoke.

Shall our democrats still be slaves —
    Still unknown to fortune's smile —
And drop into premature graves
    The victims of ill paid toil.

Shall their children cry out for bread,
    And mothers have none to give,
And die — but ere they are dead
    Curse the hour that saw them live?

Shall tyrants exalt o'er the spoil
    Of gold that was ne'er their own —
Gold obtained by the poor man's toil
    which to his children belong?

. . .

Shall the rich man behold his ship
    With her gallant mast and bow,
Moistened with sweat on the slip
    Wrung out from the poor man's brow?

. . .

Yet still ye would trample him down;
    Yes down to sixpence a day,
For work that is well worth a pound,
    Were justice dealt his pay.

. . .

But now ye'll not spare him a groat
    That he might drink your good health,
And wish speed to the gallant boat,
    to return again with wealth.

. . .

All ye who toil by the river,
    Now is the day and the hour.
Be your watchword—'Union for ever,'
    Till union has gold in its power.

So gather ye hay while the sun shines,
    The Union's harvest secure;
Reap well while yet there's no fierce winds,
'Prevention is better than cure.'

Source: Ellen Johnston, *Autobiography, Poems, and Songs,* 2nd ed. (Glasgow: William Love, 1869), 83–86.

■ ■ ■

SOURCE 8.6 **Railroads and the Middle Class**

Among the new experiences of the early industrial era for many people was railroad travel, made possible by the steam locomotive during the early nineteenth century. By 1850, Great Britain had almost 10,000 kilometers of railroad lines and Germany almost 6,000. To Industrial Age enthusiasts, the railroad was a thing of wonder, power, and speed. Samuel Smiles, the nineteenth-century British advocate of self-help, thrift, and individualism, wrote rhapsodically of the railroad's beneficent effects:

> The iron rail proved a magicians' road. The locomotive gave a new celerity to time. It virtually reduced England to a sixth of its size. It brought the country nearer to the town and the town to the country. . . . It energized punctuality, discipline, and attention; and proved a moral teacher by the influence of example.[1]

Like almost everything else, railroads and railway travel were shaped by the social changes of the early industrial era, including the growth of a more numerous and prosperous middle class of industrialists, bankers, and educated professionals of various kinds. Such people invested heavily in railroads, spurring the rapid expansion of railways in Britain. Moreover, travel on the new trains was segregated by class. First-class passengers occupied luxurious compartments with upholstered seats, while second-class travelers enjoyed rather less comfortable accommodations. Third-class travel, which was designed for the poor or working classes, originally took place in uncovered freight wagons, often with standing room only and located closest to the locomotive, where noise and the danger of fire were the greatest. In 1844, regulations required that third-class carriages be roofed.

Source 8.6, dating from the 1870s, illustrates this intersection of an emerging middle class and railway travel, showing a family in a railroad compartment, returning home from a vacation.

1. What attitude toward the railroad in particular and the Industrial Age in general does this image suggest?

2. What marks this family as middle class and their compartment as "first class"?

3. What does the poem at the top of the image suggest about the place of "home" in industrial Britain? How does the image itself present the railway car as a home away from home?

The Railroad as a Symbol of the Industrial Era │ 1870s

And Papa and Mamma took them home the same day,— They were glad to go home, and yet wanted to stay; But the train went quite fast, and it seemed a nice change To be back in their own home, where nothing was strange:

And always they reckon'd that seeing these sights Was a thing to remember—a week of delights; And, though they may see them all many times more, They'll never enjoy them so much, I am sure.

Chronicle/Alamy Stock Photo

■ ■ ■

SOURCE 8.7 Inequality

In the early industrial era, almost everyone became acutely aware of the sharp class inequalities of social life. Of course, such differences in status and wealth had characterized all civilizations since ancient Egypt and Mesopotamia. Now, however, those inequalities were experienced within the confined space of city life; they found expression in two relatively new social groups — the urban working class and the growing middle class; and they occurred as democratic ideas and socialist movements challenged the ancient legitimacy of such inequalities. These features of the early industrial era are illustrated in Source 8.7, an image by British artist John Leech, published in 1843 in *Punch*, a magazine of humor and social satire.

1. How are the class differences of early industrial Britain represented in this image? Notice the depiction of the life of miners in the bottom panel.

2. How does this source connect the Industrial Revolution with Britain's colonial empire? Notice the figure in the upper right reclining in exotic splendor, perhaps in India.

3. To what extent does the image correspond to Friedrich Engels's description of industrial society in Source 8.2?

JOHN LEECH | *Capital and Labour* | **1843**

CAPITAL AND LABOUR.

The Granger Collection, New York

DOING HISTORY

1. **Celebrating industrialization:** Based on these sources, construct an argument in celebration of the Industrial Revolution.

2. **Criticizing industrialization:** Construct an argument based on these sources criticizing the Industrial Revolution.

3. **Considering images and written documents as evidence:** What are the strengths and limitations of visual sources, as compared to written documents, in helping historians understand the Industrial Revolution?

4. **Distinguishing capitalism and industrialization:** To what extent are these sources actually dealing with the Industrial Revolution itself, and in what ways are they addressing the economic system known as capitalism? How useful is this distinction for understanding the early Industrial Age?

HISTORIANS' VOICES

Children and Family during the Industrial Revolution

Few developments in world history have had a greater influence on society and culture than the Industrial Revolution. The two Voices that follow explore the impact of industrialization on that most basic of social relationships — the one between parents and their children. In Voice 8.1, Elinor Accampo examines how industrialization altered the role of the family in preparing children for the world of work. In Voice 8.2, Louise A. Tilly and Joan W. Scott explore how the wages earned by children engaged in industrial work changed the relationship between parents and their offspring.

1. What specific changes to family life were the result of industrialization?

2. Why were children who worked in factories less reliant on their parents than other children?

3. **Integrating primary and secondary sources:** Use the sources and voices in this feature to assess the impact on the family life of those who worked in factories during the Industrial Revolution.

VOICE 8.1

Elinor Accampo on Migration, Industry, and the Loosening of Parental Control | 1989

Migration [to urban areas] also created a gap between generations that mechanization deepened. . . . Even when the older generation did work in industry of some kind, they could no longer transmit useful skills to their offspring. Children ceased adopting the same occupations as their parents; parents stopped teaching children work skills and passing on traditions associated with work. Certainly, in some cases industrial change opened new doors to the children of these workers, and the break in generational bonds meant upward mobility. . . .

Whether or not the working-class father lost status among his children, the authority and power of the family vis-à-vis employers did decline. Mechanization of work gave employers, the owners of machines, a greater measure of control over the workplace as well as over the worker. The workplace became an arena for discipline and training. . . .

Source: Elinor Accampo, *Industrialization, Family Life and Class Relations: Saint Chamond, 1815–1914* (Berkeley, CA: University of California Press, 1989), 214.

VOICE 8.2

Louise Tilly and Joan Scott on Daughters and Industrial Work | 1978

A teen-aged child's ability to earn wages and, particularly in textiles, the importance of those wages for the family meant that children were no longer as dependent as they once had been on their parents. In fact, the roles might sometimes reverse, with parents depending increasingly on their children. In textile towns, for example, where work was most plentiful and most remunerative for young people in their late teens and early twenties, according to Michael Anderson "children's high wages allowed them to enter into relational bargains with their parents on terms of more or less precise equality." "The children that frequent the factories make almost the purse of the family," observed a contemporary, "and by making the purse of the family, they share in the ruling of it." In France, an observer at a later period bemoaned the decline of apprenticeship training and the easy availability of wage labor for children. As their wages increased and sometimes surpassed their parents', he wrote, children assumed they had the right to a say in family matters. "When the father earns more than his children, he still has the right to his authority; from the day they earn as much as he does, they no longer recognize his right to command." Furthermore, by earning wages a child established a measure of potential independence. She could move elsewhere and still earn her keep. Hence, while the ability to earn wages increased the importance to a family of a daughter's labor, it also created the potential for a daughter to leave home at an early age.

Source: Louise A. Tilly and Joan W. Scott, *Women, Work, and Family* (New York, NY: Holt, Rinehart and Winston, 1978), 120–21.

NOTE

1.   Quoted in Francis D. Klingender, *Art and the Industrial Revolution* (New York, NY: Augustus M. Kelley, 1968), 139.

Colonial India: Experience and Response

India was Britain's "jewel in the crown," the centerpiece of its expanding empire in Asia and Africa. Until the late 1850s, Britain's growing involvement with South Asia was organized and led by the British East India Company, a private trading firm that had acquired a charter from the Crown allowing it to exercise military, political, and administrative functions in India as well as its own commercial operations. But after the explosive upheaval of the Indian Rebellion of 1857–1858, the British government itself assumed control of the region until India's independence in 1947.

Throughout the colonial era, the British relied heavily on alliances with established elite groups in Indian society—landowners; the "princes" who governed large parts of the region; and the Brahmins, the highest-ranking segment of India's caste-based society. These alliances strengthened or hardened elements of "traditional" India and brought them under British control. At the same time, colonial rule changed India in a hundred ways. Its schools gave rise to a class of Western-educated and English-speaking Indians; its economic and cultural policies fostered rebellion in the rural areas; its railroads, telegraphs, and postal services linked India more closely together; its racism provoked a growing sense of an all-Indian identity; its efforts to define, and thus control, India's enormously diverse population contributed to a growing divide between its Hindu and Muslim communities.

This collection begins with a group of images that evoke familiar features of British colonial rule in India, followed by a series of documents that present a range of Indian responses to the colonial experience.

SOURCE 9.1 Images of Colonial Rule

The British colonial presence in India has been recorded in a plethora of artistic representations. The four images that follow provide a highly selective glimpse at several features of that experience.

1. What information does each of these images convey to you about colonial India?

2. How might each of these scenes have been experienced by both British and Indian participants?

3. What kinds of interactions between rulers and ruled are suggested in these images?

SOURCE 9.1A

J. BOUVIER │ *A British Breakfast in India* │ **1842**

British officials and their families sought to re-create as much of English life as possible in the very different environment of India and to maintain a sharp separation between themselves and Indians. In what ways does this engraving, published in 1842, suggest that effort?

The Breakfast, plate 3 from "Anglo Indians," engraving by J. Bouvier, 1842/The Stapleton Collection/Bridgeman Images

Tiger Hunting in Colonial India | 1860s

A favorite sport among British colonial elites and tourists, tiger hunting served to display Victorian era "manliness," "a virile, muscular, patriotic sense of endurance." It also suggested the invincibility of the colonial state in triumphing over such a savage beast as well as its benevolence in ridding villages of their "man-eating tigers."[1]

British Officers Tiger Shooting in India, 1860s (color litho)/English School (19th century)/PETER NEWARK'S PICTURES/Private Collection/Bridgeman Images

The British and Indian Princes | ca. 1820

In many parts of colonial India, the British governed indirectly, through traditional authorities known as "princes." Here Prince Mahadaji Sindhia entertains two British military officers at a traditional Indian nautch, or dance concert, performed by professional Indian dancing girls around 1820. Stylistically, this illustration differs from the other images in this selection because it was created by an Indian artist rather than a British one. What does this image suggest about British efforts to relate to Indian elites and Indian culture?

Prince Mahadaji Sindhia Entertaining a British army Officer and a naval officer to a Nautch, ca. 1820 (gouache on paper)/Indian School (19th century)/BRITISH LIBRARY/ British Library, London, UK/Bridgeman Images

Blowing from a Gun | 1858

Following Mughal precedents, the British frequently employed a particularly horrific form of public execution for rebels—namely, they tied the victim, or sometimes several victims, to the mouth of a cannon and then fired it. This practice was used quite extensively during the Indian uprising of 1857–1858, as illustrated in this image. The British argued that it served as a deterrent to rebellion, was more humane than the earlier Mughal practice of "flogging to death," and allowed high-caste rebels to avoid the disgrace of being polluted by contact with the untouchables who often conducted hangings. For the families of the victims, both Muslim and Hindu, it proved almost impossible to perform proper funeral and burial rites. The practice was used as late as 1871, but then was discontinued.

Blowing Mutinous Sepoys from the Guns, from "The History of the Indian Mutiny," published in 1858 (engraving)/English School (19th century)/KEN WELSH/Private Collection/ Bridgeman Images

■ ■ ■

SOURCE 9.2   Seeking Western Education

Indian understanding of and responses to British rule varied widely and changed over time, involving gratitude, acceptance, disappointment with unfulfilled promise, active resistance, and sharp criticism of many kinds. Sources 9.2 through 9.5 provide four examples, covering almost a hundred years, from the early nineteenth century to the early twentieth century.

The first comes from Ram Mohan Roy (1772–1833). Born and highly educated within a Brahmin Hindu family, Roy subsequently studied both Arabic and Persian, learned English, came into contact with British Christian missionaries, and found employment with the British East India Company. He emerged in the early nineteenth century as a leading advocate for religious and social reform within India, with a particular interest in ending *sati*, the practice in which widows burned themselves on their husbands' funeral pyres. In 1823, Roy learned about a British plan to establish a school in Calcutta that was to focus on Sanskrit texts and traditional Hindu learning. Source 9.2 records his response to that school, and to British colonial rule, in a letter to the British governor-general of India.

1. Why was Roy opposed to the creation of this school?

2. What does this letter reveal about Roy's attitude toward Indian and European cultures?

3. How would you describe Roy's attitude toward British colonial rule in India?

RAM MOHAN ROY | *Letter to Lord Amherst* | **1823**

The establishment of a new Sanskrit School in Calcutta evinces the laudable desire of Government to improve the natives of India by education, a blessing for which they must ever be grateful. . . . When this seminary of learning was proposed . . . we were filled with sanguine hopes that [it would employ] European gentlemen of talent and education to instruct the natives of India in Mathematics, Natural Philosophy, Chemistry, Anatomy, and other useful sciences, which the natives of Europe have carried to a degree of perfection that has raised them above the inhabitants of other parts of the world. . . . Our hearts were filled with mingled feelings of delight and gratitude; we already offered up thanks to Providence for inspiring the most generous and enlightened nations of the West with the glorious ambition of planting in Asia the arts and sciences of Modern Europe.

We find [however] that the Government are establishing a Sanskrit school under Hindu Pandits [scholars] to impart such knowledge as is already current in India. This seminary can only be expected to load the minds of youth with grammatical niceties and metaphysical distinctions of little or no practical use to the possessors or to society.

The pupils will there acquire what was known two thousand years ago with the addition of vain and empty subtleties since then produced by speculative men, such as is already commonly taught in all parts of India. . . .

Neither can much improvement arise from such speculations as the following which are the themes suggested by the Vedanta [a branch of Hindu philosophy]: in what manner is the soul absorbed in the Deity? What relation does it bear to the Divine Essence? Nor will youths be fitted to be better members of society by the Vedantic doctrines which teach them to believe that all visible things have no real existence, that as father, brother, etc., have no actual entity, they consequently deserve no real affection, and therefore the sooner we escape from them and leave the world the better. . . .

[T]he Sanskrit system of education would be the best calculated to keep this country in darkness, if such had been the policy of the British legislature. But as the improvement of the native population is the object of the Government, it will consequently promote a more liberal and enlightened system of instruction, embracing Mathematics, Natural Philosophy, Chemistry, Anatomy, with other useful sciences, which may be accomplished with the sums proposed by employing a few gentlemen of talent and learning educated in Europe and providing a College furnished with necessary books, instruments, and other apparatus. In presenting this subject to your Lordship, I conceive myself discharging a solemn duty which I owe to my country-men, and also to that enlightened sovereign and legislature which have extended their benevolent care to this distant land, actuated by a desire to improve the inhabitants, and therefore humbly trust you will excuse the liberty I have taken in thus expressing my sentiments to your Lordship.

Source: Rammohun Roy, *The English Works of Raja Rammohun Roy* (Allahabad, India: Panini Office, 1906), 471–74.

■ ■ ■

SOURCE 9.3 The Indian Rebellion

In 1857–1858, British-ruled India erupted in violent rebellion. Some among the rebels imagined that the Mughal Empire might be restored to its former power and glory. Such was the hope that animated the Azamgarh Proclamation, issued in the summer of 1857, allegedly by the grandson of the last and largely powerless Mughal emperor, Bahadur Shah.

1. What grievances against British rule does this document disclose?

2. How does the proclamation imagine the future of India, should the rebellion succeed? How does this compare to Ram Mohan Roy's vision of India's future in Source 9.2?

3. To what groups or classes of people was the proclamation directed? What groups were left out in the call to rebellion? Why might they have been omitted?

PRINCE FEROZE SHAH | *The Azamgarh Proclamation* | 1857

It is well known to all that in this age the people of Hindustan, both Hindus and Muslims, are being ruined under the tyranny and oppression of the infidel and the treacherous English. It is therefore the bounden duty of all the wealthy people of India, especially of those who have any sort of connection with any of the Muslim royal families and are considered the pastors and masters of their people, to stake their lives and property for the well-being of the public.... I, who am the grandson of Bahadur Shah, have ... come here to extirpate the infidels residing in the eastern part of the country, and to liberate and protect the poor helpless people now groaning under their iron rule....

Section I: Regarding Zamindars [large landowners]

It is evident the British government, in making [land] settlements, have imposed exorbitant jummas [taxes], and have disgraced and ruined several zamindars, by putting up their estates to public auction for arrears of rent, insomuch, that on the institution of a suit by a common ryot [peasant farmer] yet, a maidservant, or a slave, the respectable zamindars are summoned into court, arrested, put in gaol, and disgraced.... Besides this, the coffers of the zamindars are annually taxed with subscriptions for schools, hospitals, roads, etc. Such extortions will have no manner of existence in the Badshahi [restored Mughal] government; but, on the contrary, the jummas will be light, the dignity and honour of the zamindars safe, and every zamindar will have absolute rule in his own zamindary.

Section II: Regarding Merchants

It is plain that the infidel and treacherous British government have monopolized the trade of all the fine and valuable merchandise such as indigo, cloth, and other articles of shipping, leaving only the trade of trifles to the people, and even in this they are not without their share of the profits, which they secure by means of customs and stamp fees, etc., in money suits, so that the people have merely a trade in name. Besides this, the profits of the traders are taxed with postages, tolls, and subscriptions for schools. Notwithstanding all these concessions, the merchants are liable to imprisonment and disgrace at the instance or complaint of a worthless man. When the Badshahi government is established, all these aforesaid fraudulent practices shall be dispensed with, and the trade of every article, without exception both by land and water, shall be open to the native merchants of India, who will have the benefit of the government steam-vessels and steam carriages for the conveyance of their merchandise gratis....

Section III: Regarding Public Servants

It is not a secret thing, that under the British government, natives employed in the civil and military services have little respect, low pay, and no manner of influence; and all the posts of dignity and emolument in both the departments are exclusively bestowed upon

Englishmen. . . . But under the Badshahi government, [these] posts . . . will be given to the natives. . . . Natives, whether Hindus or Muslims, who fall fighting against the English, are sure to go to heaven; and those killed fighting for the English, will, doubtless, go to hell; therefore, all the natives in the British service ought to be alive to their religion and interest, and, abjuring their loyalty to the English, side with the Badshahi government and obtain salaries of 200 or 300 rupees per month for the present, and be entitled to high posts in future.

Section IV: Regarding Artisans

It is evident that the Europeans, by the introduction of English articles into India, have thrown the weavers, the cotton-dressers, the carpenters, the blacksmiths, and the shoe-makers, etc., out of employ, and have engrossed their occupations, so that every description of native artisan has been reduced to beggary. But under the Badshahi government the native artisan will exclusively be employed in the services of the kings, the rajahs, and the rich; and this will no doubt insure their prosperity.

Section V: Regarding Pundits [scholars], Fakirs [religious mystics], and Other Learned Persons

The pundits and fakirs being the guardians of the Hindu and Muslim religions, respectively, and the European being the enemies of both the religions, and as at present a war is raging against the English on account of religion, the pundits and fakirs are bound to present themselves to me and take their share in the holy war, otherwise they will stand condemned . . . but if they come, they will, when the Badshahi government is well established, receive rent-free lands.

Lastly, be it known to all, that whoever out of the above-named classes, shall . . . still cling to the British government, all his estates shall be confiscated, and his property plundered, and he himself, with his whole family, shall be imprisoned, and ultimately put to death.

Source: "The Azamgarh Proclamation," *Delhi Gazette*, September 29, 1857.

■ ■ ■

SOURCE 9.4 The Credits and Debits of British Rule in India

Dadabhai Naoroji (1825–1917) was a well-educated Indian intellectual, a cotton trader in London, and a founding member of the Indian National Congress, an elite organization established in 1885 to press for a wider range of opportunities for educated Indians within the colonial system. He was also the first Indian to serve in the British Parliament.

In 1871, while addressing an English audience in London, Naoroji was asked about the impact of British rule in India. Representing a "moderate" view within Indian political circles at the time, he organized his response in terms of "credits" and "debits."

1. According to Naoroji, what are the chief advantages and drawbacks of British rule?

2. What is Naoroji seeking from Britain?

3. How does Naoroji's posture toward British rule compare to that of Ram Mohan Roy in Source 9.2 or the Azamgarh Proclamation in Source 9.3?

DADABHAI NAOROJI | *Speech to a London Audience* | **1871**

Credit

In the Cause of Humanity: Abolition of *suttee* and infanticide. Destruction of *Dacoits, Thugs, Pindarees* [various criminal groups] and other such pests of Indian society. Allowing remarriage of Hindu widows, and charitable aid in time of famine. Glorious work all this, of which any nation may well be proud. . . .

In the Cause of Civilization: Education, both male and female. Though yet only partial, an inestimable blessing as far as it has gone, and leading gradually to the destruction of superstition, and many moral and social evils. Resuscitation of India's own noble literature, modified and refined by the enlightenment of the West.

Politically: Peace and order. Freedom of speech and liberty of the press. Higher political knowledge and aspirations. Improvement of government in the native states. Security of life and property. Freedom from oppression caused by the caprice or greed of despotic rulers, and from devastation by war. Equal justice between man and man (sometimes vitiated by partiality to Europeans). Services of highly educated administrators, who have achieved the abovementioned results.

Materially: Loans for railways and irrigation. Development of a few valuable products, such as indigo, tea, coffee, silk, etc. Increase of exports. Telegraphs.

Generally: A slowly growing desire of late to treat India equitably, and as a country held in trust. Good intentions. No nation on the face of the earth has ever had the opportunity of achieving such a glorious work as this. . . . I appreciate, and so do my countrymen, what England has done for India, and I know that it is only in British hands that her regeneration can be accomplished. Now for the debit side.

Debit

In the Cause of Humanity: Nothing. Everything, therefore, is in your favor under this heading.

In the Cause of Civilization: As I have said already, there has been a failure to do as much as might have been done, but I put nothing to the debit. Much has been done, though.

Politically: Repeated breach of pledges to give the natives a fair and reasonable share in the higher administration of their own country, which has much shaken confidence in the good faith of the British word. Political aspirations and the legitimate claim to have a reasonable voice in the legislation and the imposition and disbursement of taxes, met to a very slight degree, thus treating the natives of India not as British subjects, in whom representation is a birthright. Consequent on the above, an utter disregard of the feelings and views of the natives. . . .

Financially: All attention is engrossed in devising new modes of taxation, without any adequate effort to increase the means of the people to pay; and the consequent vexation and oppressiveness of the taxes imposed, imperial and local. Inequitable financial relations between England and India, i.e., the political debt of £100,000,000 clapped on India's shoulders, and all home charges also, though the British Exchequer contributes nearly £3,000,000 to the expense of the colonies.

Materially: The political drain, up to this time, from India to England, of above £500,000,000, at the lowest computation, in principal alone, which with interest would be some thousands of millions. The further continuation of this drain at the rate, at present, of above £12,000,000 per annum, with a tendency to increase. The consequent continuous impoverishment and exhaustion of the country, except so far as it has been very partially relieved and replenished by the railway and irrigation loans, and the windfall of the consequences of the American war, since 1850. Even with this relief, the material condition of India is such that the great mass of the poor have hardly tuppence a day and a few rags, or a scanty subsistence. The famines that were in their power to prevent, if they had done their duty, as a good and intelligent government. The policy adopted during the last fifteen years of building railways, irrigation works, etc., is hopeful, has already resulted in much good to your credit, and if persevered in, gratitude and contentment will follow. An increase of exports without adequate compensation; loss of manufacturing industry and skill. Here I end the debit side.

Summary

To sum up the whole, the British rule has been: morally, a great blessing; politically, peace and order on one hand, blunders on the other; materially, impoverishment, relieved as far as the railway and other loans go. The natives call the British system "Sakar ki Churi," the knife of sugar. That is to say, there is no oppression, it is all smooth and sweet, but it is the knife, notwithstanding. I mention this that you should know these feelings. Our great misfortune is that you do not know our wants. When you will know our real wishes, I have not the least doubt that you would do justice. The genius and spirit of the British people is fair play and justice.

Source: Dadabhai Naoroji, *Essays, Speeches, Addresses and Writings* (Bombay: Caxton Printing Works, 1887), 131–36.

■ ■ ■

SOURCE 9.5 Gandhi on Modern Civilization

Mahatma Gandhi (1869–1948), clearly modern India's most beloved leader, is best known for his theories of *satyagraha*. This was an assertive but nonviolent approach to political action that directly challenged and disobeyed unjust laws, while seeking to change the hearts of India's British oppressors. But Gandhi's thinking was distinctive in another way as well: he objected not only to the foreign and exploitative character of British rule, but also, and more fundamentally, to the modern civilization that it carried. In 1909, he spelled out that critique in a pamphlet titled *Hind Swaraj* (*Indian Home Rule*). In this document, Gandhi assumes the role of an "editor," responding to questions from a "reader."

1. What is Gandhi's most fundamental criticism of British rule in India?

2. What is the difference between Gandhi's concept of "civilization" and that which he ascribes to the British?

3. What kind of future does Gandhi seek for his country?

MAHATMA GANDHI | *Indian Home Rule* | *1909*

READER: Now you will have to explain what you mean by civilization.

EDITOR: Let us first consider what state of things is described by the word "civilization." . . . The people of Europe today live in better-built houses than they did a hundred years ago. This is considered an emblem of civilization. . . . If people of a certain country, who have hitherto not been in the habit of wearing much clothing, boots, etc., adopt European clothing, they are supposed to have become civilized out of savagery. Formerly, in Europe, people ploughed their lands mainly by manual labor. Now, one man can plough a vast tract by means of steam engines and can thus amass great wealth. This is called a sign of civilization. Formerly, only a few men wrote valuable books. Now, anybody writes and prints anything he likes and poisons people's minds. Formerly, men traveled in wagons. Now, they fly through the air in trains at the rate of four hundred and more miles per day. This is considered the height of civilization. It has been stated that, as men progress, they shall be able to travel in airship and reach any part of the world in a few hours. . . . Everything will be done by machinery. Formerly, when people wanted to fight with one another, they measured between them their bodily strength; now it is possible to take away thousands of lives by one man working behind a gun from a hill. This is civilization. . . . Formerly, men were made slaves under physical compulsion. Now they are enslaved by temptation of money and of the luxuries that money can buy. . . . This civilization takes note neither of morality nor of religion. Its votaries calmly state that their business is not to teach religion. Some even consider it to be a superstitious growth. . . . This civilization is irreligion, and it has taken such a hold on the people in Europe that those who are in it appear to be half mad. They lack real physical strength or courage. They keep up their energy by intoxication. They can hardly be happy in solitude. Women, who should be the queens of households, wander in the streets or they slave away in factories. For the sake of a pittance, half a million women in England alone are laboring under trying circumstances in factories or similar institutions.

This civilization is such that one has only to be patient and it will be self-destroyed.... I cannot give you an adequate conception of it. It is eating into the vitals of the English nation. It must be shunned.... Civilization is not an incurable disease, but it should never be forgotten that the English are at present afflicted by it.

READER: I now understand why the English hold India. I should like to know your views about the condition of our country.

EDITOR: It is a sad condition. . . . It is my deliberate opinion that India is being ground down, not under the English heel, but under that of modern civilization. It is groaning under the monster's terrible weight. [M]y first complaint is that India is becoming irreligious. . . . We are turning away from God. . . . [W]e should set a limit to our worldly ambition. . . . [O]ur religious ambition should be illimitable. . . .

EDITOR: Railways, lawyers, and doctors have impoverished the country so much so that, if we do not wake up in time, we shall be ruined.

READER: I do now, indeed, fear that we are not likely to agree at all. You are attacking the very institutions which we have hitherto considered to be good.

EDITOR: It must be manifest to you that, but for the railways, the English could not have such a hold on India as they have. The railways, too, have spread the bubonic plague. Without them the masses could not move from place to place. They are the carriers of plague germs. Formerly we had natural segregation. Railways have also increased the frequency of famines because, owing to facility of means of locomotion, people sell out their grain and it is sent to the dearest markets. People become careless and so the pressure of famine increases. Railways accentuate the evil nature of man. Bad men fulfill their evil designs with greater rapidity. . . .

READER: You have denounced railways, lawyers, and doctors. I can see that you will discard all machinery. What, then, is civilization?

EDITOR: The answer to that question is not difficult. I believe that the civilization India has evolved is not to be beaten in the world. . . . India is still, somehow or other, sound at the foundation. . . . India remains immovable and that is her glory. It is a charge against India that her people are so uncivilized, ignorant, and stolid that it is not possible to induce them to adopt any changes. It is a charge really against our merit. What we have tested and found true on the anvil of experience, we dare not change. Many thrust their advice upon India, and she remains steady. This is her beauty: it is the sheet-anchor of our hope.

Civilization is that mode of conduct which points out to man the path of duty. Performance of duty and observance of morality are convertible terms. To observe morality is to attain mastery over our mind and our passions. So doing, we know ourselves. . . . If this definition be correct, then India . . . has nothing to learn from anybody else. . . . Our ancestors, therefore, set a limit to our indulgences. [They] dissuaded us from luxuries and pleasures. We have managed with the same kind of plough as existed thousands of years ago. We have retained the same kind of cottages that we had in former times and our indigenous education remains the same as before. We have had no system of life-corroding competition. Each followed his own occupation or trade and charged a regulation wage. It was not that we did not know how to invent machinery, but our fore-fathers knew that, if we set our hearts after such things, we would become slaves and lose our moral fiber. . . . They were, therefore, satisfied with small villages. . . . A nation with a constitution like this is fitter to teach others than to learn from others. . . .

The tendency of the Indian civilization is to elevate the moral being; that of the Western civilization is to propagate immorality. The latter is godless; the former is based on a belief in God. So understanding and so believing, it behooves every lover of India to cling to the Indian civilization even as a child clings to the mother's breast.

Source: Mohandas Gandhi, *Indian Home Rule* (Madras: Ganesh, 1922), pts. 6, 8, 9, 10, 13.

DOING HISTORY

1. **Describing alternative futures:** What can you infer about the kind of future for India that the authors or creators of these sources anticipate?

2. **Assessing change through time:** In what ways did understandings of British colonial rule change over time? How might you account for these changes?

3. **Considering visual and written sources:** How do these visual and written sources differ in terms of the understanding they convey about British India?

4. **Noticing what's missing:** What voices are not represented in these sources? How might such people have articulated a different understanding of the colonial experience?

5. **Responding to Gandhi:** How might each of the other authors or artists have responded to Gandhi's analysis of British colonial role and his understanding of "civilization"? To what extent do you find Gandhi's views relevant to the conditions of the early twenty-first century?

HISTORIANS' VOICES

The Great Indian Rebellion

The Great Indian Rebellion of 1857–1858, surely a pivotal event in the history of colonial India, came as a stunning surprise to the British and, in its ferocity and extent, perhaps to many Indians as well. (See Sources 9.1D and 9.3.) Historians have long puzzled over its origins, in particular the relationship between the long-term conditions that set the stage for the rebellion and the immediate trigger that sparked it. Voice 9.1 by Stanley Wolpert, a prominent American historian of India, focuses on an array of upsetting changes introduced by the British, providing a larger context for understanding the outbreak of the rebellion. In Voice 9.2, D. R. SarDesai, an Indian-born historian and professor at the University of California, Los Angeles, describes the "immediate cause" of the rebellion in the issues surrounding the "greased cartridges."

1. What do these Voices suggest about the Indian grievances that informed the Great Indian Rebellion of 1857?

2. In what ways might the greased cartridges incident, described in Voice 9.2, have expressed or reinforced the long-term tensions described in Voice 9.1?

3. **Integrating primary and secondary sources:** How does the Azamgarh Proclamation (Source 9.3) provide support for Stanley Wolpert's argument in Voice 9.1?

VOICE 9.1

Stanley Wolpert on British Innovations and Indian Grievances │ 1965

Many were warning that the pace of change was too swift. Important groups within Indian society were being too brashly ignored, too completely alienated. The deposed princes poisoned all ears around with talk of the "faithless" British promises and treaties torn to bits by men without honor. The landed aristocrats, whose estates had always been freeholds, were now assailed by low-born [Indian] tax collectors and bullied by beardless [British] young men in a foreign tongue. Brahmins and Muslim Maulvis [learned teachers of Islamic law] spoke of Christian rulers desirous only of converting all Indians to their English religion. Merchants and craftsmen saw their livelihood undermined by British competition and foreign manufactured goods. Teachers and scholars found the labors of a lifetime no longer valued in a society run in a language they could not understand, according to principles and ideas they feared and hated. Most dangerous of all, the sepoy soldiers [low-ranking Indian troops in Britain's colonial military forces] had grown restive. By 1856 their morale was at an all-time low, just when their number proportionate to British troops in India was at its all-time high.

Source: Stanley Wolpert, *India* (Englewood Cliffs, NJ: Prentice Hall, 1965), 93–94.

D. R. SarDesai on the Greased Cartridges Incident | 2008

The last straw and immediate cause of the army's mutiny centered around the issue of the greased cartridges. More than 90 percent of the troops were Hindu or Muslim. A newly introduced rifle required the user to bite the pouch containing gunpowder before emptying the powder into the barrel. The pouch was coated with grease made from the fat of either pigs, anathema to Muslims, or cows, sacred to Hindus. The British first denied the use of such fat; denial strengthened suspicion of a deliberate conspiracy to have Indian soldiers, Hindus and Muslims, lose their religious affiliation and then convert to the Christian faith. Even though the British stopped using the grease immediately, the damage had been done, and the Indians saw it as another conspiracy by the missionaries and the rulers to convert the troops (and consequently their families) to Christianity. They also believed the withdrawal of the greased cartridges was a sign of weakness and alarm on the part of the British. Many soldiers felt betrayed; they lost respect for their commanders. The effect was more distrust of the rulers on the part of the ruled; every official decision thereafter would be looked upon by the multitudes with palpable suspicion.

Source: D. R. SarDesai, *India: The Definitive History* (Boulder, CO: Westview Press, 2008), 242–43.

NOTE

1. Kevin Hannam and Anya Diekmann, *Tourism and India: A Critical Introduction* (New York, NY: Routledge, 2011), 69–70.

Japan and the West in the Nineteenth Century

CHAPTER

10

During the nineteenth century, Japan's relationship with the West changed profoundly in a pattern that included sharp antagonism, enthusiastic embrace, selective borrowing, and equality on the international stage. At the time, that changing relationship had implications as well for China, Korea, Russia, and elsewhere, even as it laid the foundation for twentieth-century global conflict in World War II.

In the initial decades of the nineteenth century, the Western world was increasingly impinging upon Japan, which had closed itself off from Europe and America 200 years earlier, with the exception of a small Dutch trading port near Nagasaki. Over time, however, a number of Western whaling ships had penetrated Japanese waters, and suspicions rose. Aizawa Seishisai, a prominent Japanese Confucian scholar, gave voice to these worries in 1825:

> The barbarians live ten thousand miles across the sea; when they set off on foreign conquests, they must procure supplies and provisions from the enemy. That is why they trade and fish. Their men of war are self-sufficient away from home. If their only motive for harpooning whales was to obtain whale meat, they could do so in their own waters. Why should they risk long, difficult voyages just to harpoon whales in eastern seas? Their ships can be outfitted for trading, or fishing, or fighting. Can anyone guarantee that their merchant vessels and fishing boats of today will not turn into warships tomorrow?[1]

SOURCE 10.1 Continuing Japanese Isolation

In response to such concerns about Western intervention, the Japanese government, known as the Tokugawa shogunate, issued an edict that reiterated in the strongest possible terms the country's long-standing posture of isolation from the West.

1. What understanding of the West did this edict reflect?

2. What actions did the edict prescribe?

3. Why might Westerners find the policy offensive and unacceptable?

An Edict of Expulsion | **1825**

We have issued instructions on how to deal with foreign ships on numerous occasions up to the present. In the Bunka era [1804–1817] we issued new edicts to deal with Russian ships. But a few years ago a British ship wreaked havoc in Nagasaki, and more recently their rowboats have been landing to procure firewood, water, and provisions. Two years ago they forced their way ashore, stole livestock and extorted rice. Thus they have become steadily more unruly, and moreover seem to be propagating their wicked religion among our people. This situation plainly cannot be left to itself.

All Southern Barbarians and Westerners, not only the English, worship Christianity, that wicked cult prohibited in our land. Henceforth, whenever a foreign ship is sighted approaching any point on our coast, all persons on hand should fire on and drive it off. If the vessel heads for the open sea, you need not pursue it; allow it to escape. If the foreigners force their way ashore, you may capture and incarcerate them, and if their mother ship approaches, you may destroy it as circumstances dictate.

Note that Chinese, Korean, and Ryukyuans [people from a group of islands south of Japan] can be differentiated [from Westerners] by the physiognomy and ship design, but Dutch ships are indistinguishable [from those of other Westerners]. Even so, have no compunctions about firing on [the Dutch] by mistake; when in doubt, drive the ship away without hesitation. Never be caught offguard.

Source: Bob Tadashi Wakabayashi, *Anti-Foreignism and Western Learning in Early-Modern Japan* (Cambridge, MA: Harvard University Press, 1985), 60.

■ ■ ■

SOURCE 10.2 The Debate: Expel the Barbarians

The arrival of U.S. Admiral Matthew Perry in 1853, demanding that the country open to foreign commerce and navigation, brought to a head the question of Japan's isolationist policy and prompted a considerable debate in Japanese circles. Advocating forceful expulsion of the Americans and sharply opposing any treaty with them was Tokugawa Nariaki, the *daimyo*, or ruler, of a domain on the eastern coast of Japan.

1. How does Tokugawa Nariaki characterize Americans?

2. What were his arguments for a policy of war?

3. What did he fear if Japan tried to accommodate Perry's demands?

TOKUGAWA NARIAKI │ *Memorial on the American Demand for a Treaty* │ 1853

[W]e must never choose the policy of peace. . . .

[T]he Americans . . . were arrogant and discourteous, their actions an outrage. . . . The foreigners, having thus ignored our prohibition and penetrated our waters even to the vicinity of the capital, threatening us and making demands upon us, should it happen not only the Bakufu fails to expel them but also that it concludes an agreement in accordance with their requests, then I fear it would be impossible to maintain our national prestige. . . .

[I]f the people of Japan stand firmly united, if we complete our military preparations and return to the state of society that existed before the middle ages [when the emperor ruled the country directly], then we will even be able to go out against foreign countries and spread abroad our fame and prestige. . . . [I]f the Bakufu, now and henceforward, shows itself resolute for expulsion, the immediate effect will be to increase ten-fold the morale of the country . . . only by so doing will the shogun be able to fulfill his "barbarian-expelling" duty and unite the men of every province in carrying out their proper military functions. . . .

Source: *Selected Documents on Japanese Foreign Policy*, translated by William G. Beasley (1955), pp. 102–7.

■ ■ ■

The Debate: A Sumo Wrestler and a Foreigner

The debate about Japan's response to Perry's demands not only engaged political and intellectual elites, but also found expression in the popular media of woodblock prints. In 1861, such a print showed a Japanese sumo wrestler tossing a boastful French competitor. The inscription reads: "Hershan, wrestler without peer, comes from Calais in France, a part of Europe. He has traveled to the countries of the world, and nowhere has he been defeated. He is very boastful and came to our country to Yokohama and asked for a match. To the glory of Japan, a Japanese sumo wrestler threw him to the ground."[2]

1. Why might this image carry considerable appeal in the middle of a national debate about how to deal with the intrusive foreigners?

2. In what ways could it be seen as a visual depiction of Tokugawa Nariaki's point of view?

3. What does the inscription add to your understanding of the image?

YOSHIKU UTAGAWA │ *Throwing a Frenchman* │ **1861**

■ ■ ■

SOURCE 10.4 The Debate: Eastern Ethics and Western Science

The other side of this debate made the case for opening Japan to the West and even embracing aspects of its culture. Ii Naosuke, another *daimyo* and a bitter opponent of Tokugawa Nariaki, wrote in 1853:

> It is impossible in the crisis we now face to ensure the safety and tranquility of our country merely by an insistence on the seclusion laws as we did in former times. . . . The exchange of goods is a universal practice. This we should explain to the spirits of our ancestors. And we should tell the foreigners that we mean in future to send trading vessels to the Dutch company's factory in Batavia to engage in trade. . . . As we increase the number of our ships and our mastery of technique, Japanese will be able to sail the oceans freely and gain direct knowledge of conditions abroad.[3]

More generally and more famously, Sakuma Shozan, a Confucian-educated official in the shogun's government, argued that Japan must combine Eastern Confucian-oriented ethics and Western science. He had been briefly imprisoned in 1854 for encouraging one of his students to stow away on one of Perry's ships in an attempt to learn something of Western ways. Shortly after his release, Sakuma Shozan wrote his famous work, *Reflections on My Errors*. It was not really an apology for his actions, but rather a defense of his position.

1. How do you understand the metaphor in the first paragraph of this excerpt about "giv[ing] the medicine secretly"?

2. What departures from existing practices does Sakuma Shozan advocate? In what ways is he critical of Japan's military and intellectual leaders?

3. On what issues might Sakuma Shozan and Tokugawa Nariaki agree? How would you define their differences?

SAKUMA SHOZAN | *Reflections on My Errors* | mid-1850s

Take, for example, a man who is grieved by the illness of his lord or his father, and who is seeking medicine to cure it. If he is fortunate enough to secure the medicine, and is certain that it will be efficacious, then, certainly, without questioning either its cost or the quality of its name, he will beg his lord or father to take it. Should the latter refuse on the grounds that he dislikes the name, does the younger man make various schemes to give the medicine secretly, or does he simply sit by and wait for his master to die? There is no question about it: . . . the feeling of genuine sincerity and heartfelt grief on the part of the subject or son makes it absolutely impossible for him to sit idly and watch his master's anguish; consequently, even if he knows that he will later have to face his master's anger, he cannot but give the medicine secretly. . . .

The gentleman has five pleasures, but wealth and rank are not among them. That his house understands decorum and righteousness and remains free from family rifts — this is one pleasure. That exercising care in giving to and taking from others, he provides for himself honestly, free, internally, from shame before his wife and children, and externally, from disgrace before the public — this is the second pleasure. That he expounds and glorifies the learning of the sages, knows in his heart the great Way, and in all situations contents himself with his duty, in adversity as well as in prosperity — this is the third pleasure.... That he is born after the opening of the vistas of science by the Westerners, and can therefore understand principles not known to the sages and wise men of old — this is the fourth pleasure. That he employs the ethics of the East and the scientific technique of the West, neglecting neither the spiritual nor material aspects of life, combining subjective and objective, and thus bringing benefit to the people and serving the nation — this is the fifth pleasure....

The principal requisite of national defense is that it prevents the foreign barbarians from holding us in contempt. The existing coastal defense installations all lack method; the pieces of artillery that have been set up are improperly made; and the officials who negotiate with the foreigners are mediocrities who have no understanding of warfare. The situation being such, even though we wish to avoid incurring the scorn of the barbarians, how, in fact, can we do so? ...

Of the men who now hold posts as commanders of the army, those who are not dukes or princes or men of noble rank, are members of wealthy families. As such, they find their daily pleasure in drinking wine, singing, and dancing; and they are ignorant of military strategy and discipline. Should a national emergency arise, there is no one who could command the respect of the warriors and halt the enemy's attack. This is the great sorrow of our times. For this reason, I have wished to follow in substance the Western principles of armament, and, by banding together loyal, valorous, strong men of old, established families not in the military class — men of whom one would be equal to ten ordinary men — to form a voluntary group which would be made to have as its sole aim that of guarding the nation and protecting the people. Anyone wishing to join the society would be tested and his merits examined; and, if he did not shirk hardship, he would then be permitted to join. Men of talent in military strategy, planning, and administration would be advanced to positions of leadership, and then, if the day should come when the country must be defended, this group could be gathered together and organized into an army to await official commands. It is to be hoped that they would drive the enemy away and perform greater service than those who now form the military class....

Mathematics is the basis for all learning. In the Western world after this science was discovered military tactics advanced greatly.... At the present time, if we wish really to complete our military preparations, we must develop this branch of study....

What do the so-called scholars of today actually do? Do they clearly and tacitly understand the way in which the gods and sages established this nation, or the way in which Yao, Shun, and the divine emperors of the three dynasties governed?

Do they, after having learned the rites and music, punishment and administration, the classics and governmental system, go on to discuss and learn the elements of the art of war, of military discipline, of the principles of machinery? Do they make exhaustive studies of conditions in foreign countries? Of effective defense methods? Of strategy in setting up strongholds, defense barriers, and reinforcements? Of the knowledge of computation, gravitation, geometry, and mathematics? If they do, I have not heard of it! Therefore I ask what the so-called scholars of today actually do. . . .

In order to master the barbarians there is nothing so effective as to ascertain in the beginning conditions among them. To do this, there is no better first step than to be familiar with barbarian tongues. Thus, learning a barbarian language is not only a step toward knowing the barbarians, but also the groundwork for mastering them.

Source: *Sources of Japanese Tradition*, Volume 2, compiled by William De Bary et al. Copyright © 2001 Columbia University Press.

■ ■ ■

SOURCE 10.5 **Westernization**

The great debate of the 1850s and 1860s, prompted by Perry's arrival, came to an end with the Meiji Restoration of 1868. The shogunate was replaced by a new government, headed directly by the emperor, and committed to a more thorough transformation of the country than Sakuma Shozan had ever imagined. Particularly among the young, there was an acute awareness of the need to create a new culture that could support a revived Japan. "We have no history," declared one of these students; "our history begins today."[4] In this context, much that was Western was enthusiastically embraced. The technological side of this borrowing, contributing much to Japan's remarkable industrialization, was the most obvious expression of this westernization.

But this borrowing also extended to more purely cultural matters. Eating beef became popular, despite Buddhist objections. Many men adopted Western hairstyles and grew beards, even though the facial hair of Westerners had earlier been portrayed as ugly. In 1872, Western dress was ordered for all official ceremonies. Ballroom dancing became popular among the elite, as did Western instruments like the piano and harpsichord. Women in these circles likewise adopted Western ways, as illustrated in Source 10.5, an 1887 woodblock print titled *Illustration of Singing by the Plum Garden*. At the same time, the image includes many traditional Japanese elements. The flowering trees in the background had long been an important subject of study in Japan's artistic tradition, and the flower arrangement on the right represents a popular Japanese art form. Moreover, the dress of the woman in the middle seems to reflect earlier Japanese court traditions that encouraged women to wear many layers of kimonos.

1. What elements of Western culture can you identify in this visual source?

2. In what ways does this print reflect the continuing appeal of Japanese culture? Pay attention to the scenery, the tree, and the flowers.

3. Why were so many Japanese so enamored of Western culture during this time? Why did the Japanese government actively encourage their interest?

TOYOHARA CHIKANOBU │ *Women and Westernization* │ 1887

Singing by the Plum Garden (Baien shōka zu), Meiji Era, 1887 (ink & colour on paper)/Toyohara Chikanobu (1838–1912)/MUSEUM OF FINE ARTS, BOSTON/Museum of Fine Arts, Boston, Massachusetts, USA/Bridgeman Images

■ ■ ■

SOURCE 10.6 A Critique of Westernization

Not everyone in Japan was so enthusiastic about the adoption of Western culture. Indeed, beginning in the late 1870s and continuing into the next decade, numerous essays and images satirized the apparently indiscriminate fascination with all things European. Source 10.6, drawn by Japanese cartoonist Honda Kinkichiro in 1879, represents that point of view. One caption that accompanied the drawing reads as follows: "Mr. Morse [an American zoologist who introduced Darwin's theory of evolution to Japan in 1877] explains that all human beings were monkeys in the beginning. In the beginning—but even now aren't we still monkeys? When it comes to Western things we think the red beards are the most skillful at everything."[5] A second caption in English below the drawing further develops this theme.

1. What specific aspects of Japan's efforts at westernization is the artist mocking?

2. Why might the artist have used a Western scientific theory (Darwinian evolution) to criticize excessive westernization in Japan?

3. Why do you think a reaction set in against the cultural imitation of Europe?

HONDA KINKICHIRO │ *Critique of Wholesale Westernization* │ **1879**

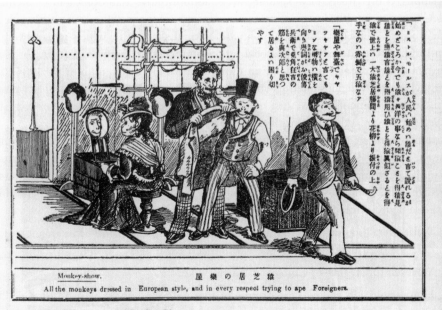

Monkey-show.   猿 芝 居 の 楽 屋

All the monkeys dressed in European style, and in every respect trying to ape Foreigners.

25 猿芝居の楽屋（錦吉郎　明治12年4月）

SOURCE 10.7   War and Empire

Behind Japan's modernization and westernization was the recognition that Western imperialism was surging in Asia and that China was a prime example of what happened to countries that were unable to defend themselves against it. Accordingly, achieving political and military equality with the Great Powers of Europe and the United States became a central aim of Japan's modernization program.

Strengthening Japan against Western aggression increasingly meant "throwing off Asia"—a phrase that implied rejecting many of Japan's own cultural traditions and its habit of imitating China, as well as creating an Asian empire of its own. Fukuzawa Yukichi, a popular advocate of Western knowledge, declared:

> We must not wait for neighboring countries to become civilized so that we can together promote Asia's revival. Rather we should leave their ranks and join forces with the civilized countries of the West. We don't have to give China and Korea any special treatment just because they are neighboring countries. We should deal with them as Western people do. . . . I reject the idea that we must continue to associate with bad friends in East Asia.[6]

Historically the Japanese had borrowed a great deal from China—Buddhism, Confucianism, court rituals, city-planning ideas, administrative traditions, and elements of the Chinese script. But Japan's victory in a war with China in 1894–1895 showed clearly that Japan had emerged from the Chinese cultural shadow in which it had lived for centuries. Furthermore, Japan had begun to acquire an East Asian empire in Korea and Taiwan at the expense of China. Even more dramatically, its triumph in the 1904–1905 Russo-Japanese War illustrated its ability to stand up even to a major European power. This accomplishment was the first modern military victory by an Asian country against a Western power, and its implications resonated widely.

The significance of that victory is expressed in Source 10.7, a 1904 print by Japanese artist Chomatsu Tomisato, created during the Russo-Japanese War. It shows a triumphant Japan, stomping on a Russian battleship and holding aloft a figure representing the Russian czar Nicholas, who carries a white flag of surrender. Korea cowers behind the Japanese figure, while China kneels in submission.

1. What overall message did the artist seek to convey in this print? How might you describe the Japanese view of the world that it expresses?

2. What do the images of China and Korea evoke?

3. How would you describe the posture of Turkey (Tolky), the various European powers, and the United States in this image? Notice that several of them are carrying the Japanese flag.

CHOMATSU TOMISATO │ *Japan, Triumphant* │ 1904

SOURCE 10.8 Japan in the Early Twentieth Century

Early in the new century, a prominent Japanese political figure, Okuma Shigenobu, summed up his view of the country's transformation over the past half century.

1. What were the greatest sources of pride to Okuma?

2. To what did he attribute his country's progress?

3. In his view, what elements of Japanese tradition were maintained amid all the changes?

4. What groups of people might challenge Okuma's description of Japan, and how would they do it?

OKUMA SHIGENOBU │ *Fifty Years of New Japan* │ 1907–1908

By comparing the Japan of fifty years ago with the Japan of today, it will be seen that she has gained considerably in the extent of her territory, as well as in her population, which now numbers nearly fifty million. Her government has become constitutional not only in name, but in fact, and her national education has attained to a high degree of excellence. In commerce and industry, the emblems of peace, she has also made rapid strides, until her import and export trades together amounted in 1907 to the enormous sum of 926,000,000 yen. . . . Her general progress, during the short space of half a century, has been so sudden and swift that it presents a rare spectacle in the history of the world.

This leap forward is the result of the stimulus which the country received on coming into contact with the civilization of Europe and America, and may well, in its broad sense, be regarded as a boon conferred by foreign intercourse. Foreign intercourse it was that animated the national consciousness of our people, who under the feudal system lived localized and disunited, and foreign intercourse it is that has enabled Japan to stand up as a world power. We possess today a powerful army and navy, but it was after Western models that we laid their foundations by establishing a system of conscription in pursuance of the principle "all our sons are soldiers," by promoting military education, and by encouraging the manufacture of arms and the art of shipbuilding. We have reorganized the systems of central and local administration, and effected reforms in the educational system of the empire. All this is nothing but the result of adopting the superior features of Western institutions. That Japan has been enabled to do so is a boon conferred on her by foreign intercourse, and it may be said that the nation has succeeded in this grand metamorphosis through the promptings and the influence of foreign civilization. . . .

For twenty centuries the nation has drunk freely of the civilizations of Korea, China, . . . yet we remain today politically unaltered under one Imperial House and sovereign, that has descended in an unbroken line for a length of time absolutely unexampled in the world. . . . They [the Japanese people] have welcomed Occidental civilization while preserving their old Oriental civilization. They have attached great importance to Bushido [the samurai way of life], and at the same time held in the highest respect the spirit of charity and humanity. They have ever made a point of choosing the middle course in everything, and have aimed at being always well-balanced. . . . We are conservative simultaneously with being progressive; we are aristocratic and at the same time democratic; we are individualistic while also being socialistic. In these respects we may be said to somewhat resemble the Anglo-Saxon race.

Source: Count Shigenobu Okuma, *Fifty Years of New Japan*, English version edited by Marcus Huish, vol. 2 (London, UK: Smith, Elder & Co., 1909), 554–55, 571–72.

DOING HISTORY

1. **Explaining change:** How and why did the Japanese people's perceptions of themselves and their relationship to the West change during the nineteenth and early twentieth centuries? What elements of continuity in Japanese traditions are evident in these sources?

2. **Making comparisons:** Based on these sources and those in Chapter 9 (Colonial India: Experience and Response), how might you compare Japanese and Indian perceptions of the West during the nineteenth century? What accounts for both the similarities and differences?

3. **Distinguishing modernization and westernization:** Based on a careful reading of these sources, do you think that technological borrowing (modernization) requires cultural borrowing (westernization) as well? To what extent was Japan able to modernize while avoiding the incorporation of Western culture at the same time?

HISTORIANS' VOICES

Explaining Japan's Transformation

Historians have long struggled to explain Japan's remarkable economic transformation in the wake of the country's Meiji Restoration of 1868. Why was Japan able to accomplish what no other Afro-Asian or Latin American country could do during the second half of the nineteenth century? In Voice 10.1, James L. Huffman, a specialist in modern Japanese history, looks to the country's recent past for an answer as well as to the character and motivations of the men who led the Meiji regime. To these factors, another historian of Japan, James L. McClain, adds in Voice 10.2 a consideration of the unique international circumstances in which Japan was operating.

1. Do the explanations for Japan's economic transformation identified in these two sources argue with each other, or do they complement one another?

2. To what extent do these two historians argue that long-term developments and international circumstances facilitated Japanese modernization? What role do they define for individual historical actors in the modernization process?

3. **Integrating primary and secondary sources:** How might the primary sources in this feature be used to support or supplement the arguments of these two historians?

VOICE 10.1

James Huffman on Japan's Historical Legacy and Its Meiji Leaders │ 2010

[T]he Meiji rebels did more than survive. They thrived, cobbling together an administration in the name of a shy teen-aged emperor and turning a "restoration" into a revolution of national goals and systems. How did they do it? One answer lies in the Tokugawa legacy. Recall the high literacy rates of that era, the commercial revolution, the bustling cities, and the sophisticated intellectual sphere. Even in its last desperate decade, the *bakufu* [the government of Tokugawa Japan] had engaged Westerners rather than merely resisting them, Chinese style. Big as the problems were, the Meiji innovators inherited a structure with strong foundations.

Another explanation lies in the men who took charge in 1868 . . . The oldest . . . were only in their early forties and none had top-level administrative experience. What they shared, however, was vision, talent, and realism along with commitment to nation-building . . . Their pragmatism was illustrated in their approach to the West . . . [T]hey realistically concluded that expulsion [of the intruding Westerners] was impossible; Japan must compete with the West on its own terms. So when they issued a "charter oath," . . . they promised: "knowledge shall be sought throughout the world," "matters of state shall be decided by public discussion," and "classes high and low shall unite." They issued the proclamation in a formal Shinto ceremony—evidence that they understood the political wisdom of clothing modern policies in comfortable traditional symbols.

Source: James L. Huffman, *Japan in World History* (Oxford, UK: Oxford University Press, 2010), 76.

VOICE 10.2

James L. McClain on the International Context of Japan's Transformation | 2002

There was also a providential, almost serendipitous quality to Japan's economic accomplishments. In some ways the country was fortunate that the West had started down the path of industrialization a few decades before Perry's arrival, for as a late developer, the newly opened island nation could learn from the experiences of Euro-Americans and make use of their technological innovations. At the same time, the West was not so far ahead in the 1870s and 1880s that the Japanese despaired of catching up; indeed the gap between East and West was narrow enough that it inspired determination to bridge it. It was to Japan's benefit, as well, that it began its economic journey when new marketing networks were emerging on an international scale. A revolution in transportation and communication was transforming the world into a global marketplace in the second half of the nineteenth century, and to their delight the Japanese discovered that they already grew and could soon manufacture a variety of goods that people overseas wanted, from raw tea and raw silk to gold leaf and buttons and cotton textiles. The trend lines of growth arched upward in the early Meiji decades, and Japan was able to build on its initial achievements to become one of the world's leading economic powers at the beginning of the twentieth century.

Source: James L. McClain, *A Modern History of Japan* (New York, NY: W. W. Norton and Company, 2002), 243–44.

NOTES

1. Bob Tadashi Wakabayashi, *Anti-Foreignism and Western Learning in Early-Modern Japan* (Cambridge, MA: Harvard University Press, 1985), 208–9.

2. M. William Steele, *Alternative Narratives in Modern Japanese History* (London, UK: Routledge, 2003), 29.

3. Quoted in Peter Duus, *The Japanese Discovery of America* (Boston, MA: Bedford/St. Martin's, 1997), 100–1.

4. Quoted in Marius B. Jansen, *The Making of Modern Japan* (Cambridge, MA: Harvard University Press, 2000), 460.

5. Quoted in Julia Meech-Pekarik, *The World of the Meiji Print: Impressions of a New Civilization* (New York, NY: Weatherhill, 1986), 182.

6. Quoted in Oka Yoshitake, prologue to *The Emergence of Imperial Japan*, edited by Marlene Mayo (Lexington, MA: D. C. Heath, 1970), 7.

Ideologies of the Axis Powers

WORKING WITH EVIDENCE

Even more than the Great War of 1914–1918, the Second World War was a conflict of ideas and ideologies as well as a struggle of nations and armies. The ideas of the losing side in that war, repellant as they were to their enemies and probably to many people today, had for a time attracted considerable support. Described variously as fascist, authoritarian, right-wing, or radically nationalist, the ideologies of the Axis powers — Italy, Germany, and Japan — differed in tone and emphasis. But they shared a repudiation of mainstream Western liberalism and democracy, an intense hatred of Marxist communism, and a desire for imperial expansion. The sources that follow provide a sample of this thinking as it took shape in those three countries.

SOURCE 11.1 Italian Fascism: Creating a New Roman Empire

Empire was central in the thinking of Italy's Benito Mussolini and his understanding of fascism. "For Fascism," he wrote, "the growth of Empire, that is to say the expansion of the nation, is an essential manifestation of vitality, and its opposite a sign of decadence."[1] And for Mussolini, the model for empire was decidedly Roman. Following the conquest of Ethiopia in 1936, he triumphantly celebrated "the reappearance of empire on the fated hills of Rome." "Italy finally has its own empire," he proclaimed. "An empire of civilization and of humanity for all the populations of Ethiopia. This is in the tradition of Rome. . . ."[2] One year later, marking the first anniversary of that victory, the image in Source 11.1 was on the cover of school exercise books. Mussolini appears in the foreground in military uniform including a combat helmet, while in the background looms a famous national monument commemorating the unification of Italy in 1871. Located near the heart of ancient Rome, this monument used classical architectural and sculptural styles to evoke the revival of Italy's glorious past. The golden winged figure, busy inscribing the date of the empire's foundation on a tablet, is Victoria, the Roman goddess of victory, widely revered in Roman armies and worshipped by returning generals. The caption reads: "In the first year of the foundation of the Empire, the Italian people renew the victorious Duce [Mussolini] with fervent testimonies of gratitude and devotion."

1. Why might the artist have chosen to present Mussolini in the context of the ancient Roman Empire?

2. Why might Mussolini want to link his recent conquest of Ethiopia with the nineteenth-century reunification of Italy?

3. What does the arrangement of the image suggest about how Mussolini wanted to be viewed? What attitudes or postures does this portrayal of Mussolini project?

School Exercise Book Celebrating Italy's Victory over Ethiopia | 1937

SOURCE 11.2 | Hitler on Nazism

The ideology of German Nazism found its classic expression in Adolf Hitler's *Mein Kampf* (My Struggle), written while he was briefly imprisoned in 1923 and published a few years later. Armed with these ideas, Hitler assumed the leadership of Germany in 1933.

1. What larger patterns in European thinking do Hitler's ideas reflect, and what elements of European thought does he reject? Consider in particular his use of social Darwinism, then an idea with wide popularity in Europe.

2. How does Hitler distinguish between Aryans and Jews? How does he understand the role of race in human affairs?

3. What kind of political system does Hitler advocate?

ADOLF HITLER │ *Mein Kampf (My Struggle)* │ 1925–1926

There are truths that are so obvious that they are not seen, or at least not recognized, by ordinary people. . . . In the struggle for daily bread the weak and sickly, as well as the less resolute, succumb, while in the struggle of the males for the female only the healthiest is granted the right or opportunity to propagate. . . . However little Nature wishes that the weaker mate with the stronger, even less does she desire the blending of a higher race with a lower. . . . All great cultures of the past collapsed only because the originally creative race died off from the poisoning of their blood. . . .

Those who want to live, must also fight, and those who will not fight in this world of eternal struggle do not deserve to live. . . . All that we see before us today of human culture, all the achievements of art, science, and technology, is almost exclusively the creative product of the Aryan race. . . . [H]e alone was the founder of all higher forms of humanity, and thus represents the very prototype of all that we understand by the word "human." He is the Prometheus of mankind from whose bright forehead the divine spark of genius has always sprung. . . .

Everything in this world that is not of good race is chaff. All occurrences in world history, for better and for worse, are simply the expression of the racial instinct for self-preservation. . . .

The Jew represents the most formidable opponent of the Aryan. . . . Because the Jew . . . has never possessed a culture of his own, the foundations of his intellectual work have always been provided by others. . . . If the Jews were alone in this world, not only would they suffocate in filth and offal, but they would also seek, in their hate-filled struggles, to cheat and to destroy each another. . . . [T]he Jew is led by nothing more than the naked egoism of the individual. . . .

The black-haired Jewish youth, satanic joy in his face, lurks in wait for the unsuspecting girl whom he defiles with his blood, thus stealing her from her people. He uses every means to taint the racial foundations of the people he has set out to subjugate. . . . And thus he tries to systematically lower the racial level [of a people] by the continuous poisoning of individuals. . . . He has found, in the organized masses of Marxism, the weapon that allows him . . . to subjugate and to "govern" the peoples with a dictatorial and brutal fist. . . .

If we mentally review all the reasons for the German collapse [defeat in World War I], the ultimate and most decisive remains the failure to recognize the racial problem and especially the Jewish menace. . . . The lost purity of the blood is enough to destroy the inner happiness [of a people] forever . . . the consequences of which can never be eliminated from body and from spirit. . . . All really significant symptoms of decay from the prewar period can be traced back to racial causes. . . .

. . . [T]he state is a means to an end. Its purpose lies in the preservation and advancement of a society of physically and spiritually homogenous beings. . . . States that do not serve this purpose are misbegotten, indeed they are monstrosities. . . .

The highest purpose of the folkish state is therefore concern for the preservation of those original cultural-bestowing racial elements that create the beauty and dignity of higher humanity. We, as Aryans, conceive of the state simply as the living organism of a nation that not only ensures the preservation of the nation, but through the development of its spiritual and intellectual abilities leads it to the highest freedom. . . .

This world is surely moving toward a great revolution. And the only question is whether it will rebound to the salvation of Aryan mankind or to the profit of the eternal Jew. . . .

. . . [T]he folkish state must accordingly free the political leadership . . . entirely from the parliamentarian principle of majority or mass rule, and instead absolutely guarantee the right of the personality. . . . The best state constitution and state form is the one with the instinctual certainty to raise the best minds of the national community to leading prominence and influence. . . . There will be no majority decisions, only responsible individuals, and the word "counsel" will be restored to its original meaning. Every man will have advisers by his side to be sure, but the decision will be made by one man. . . .

With respect to the feasibility of these ideas, I beg you not to forget that the parliamentary principle of democratic majority rule has not always governed mankind, but rather is to be found only in the briefest periods of history, which are invariably eras of decay of peoples and states.

Source: Adolf Hitler, *Mein Kampf. Zwei Bände in einem Band,* translated by Sarah Panzer (München: Zentralverlag der NSDAP, 1943), 311, 312–13, 316, 317, 324, 329, 330, 331, 357, 359, 360, 433, 434, 475, 500, 501, 502.

■ ■ ■

SOURCE 11.3 Nazi Anti-Semitism

Hatred of Jews was central to Nazi ideology. This image, which served as the cover of a Nazi publication titled *Der Ewige Jude* (The Eternal Jew), summed up many of the themes in Nazi anti-Semitism.

1. How does this image illustrate Hitler's understanding of Jews as expressed in Source 11.2?

2. Notice particular aspects of the image: the coins in the man's right hand, the whip in his left hand, the map of Russia with a hammer and sickle. What does each of these suggest about the Nazi case against the Jews?

3. Notice also the general appearance and dress of the figure. What does this contribute to the image of Jews that Nazis are trying to convey?

H. SCHLUTER | *Der Ewige Jude (The Eternal Jew)* | **1937**

akg-images

■ ■ ■

SOURCE 11.4   The Japanese Way

In the Japanese language, the word *kokutai* is an evocative term that refers to the national essence or the fundamental character of the Japanese nation and people. Drawing both on long-established understandings and on recently developed nationalist ideas, the Ministry of Education in 1937 published a small volume, widely distributed in schools and homes throughout the country, titled *Kokutai No Hongi* (Cardinal Principles of the National Entity of Japan). That text, excerpted in Source 11.4, defined the uniqueness of Japan and articulated the philosophical foundation of its authoritarian regime. When the Americans occupied a defeated and devastated Japan in 1945, they forbade the further distribution of the book.

- According to *Cardinal Principles*, what is *kokutai*? How does the document define the national essence of Japan? How do its authors compare Japan to the West?

- What was the ideal role of the individual in Japanese society?

- Why do you think the American occupation authorities banned the document?

Cardinal Principles of the National Entity of Japan | *1937*

[T]he foreign ideologies imported into our country are in the main ideologies of the [European] Enlightenment. . . . The views of the world and of life that form the basis of these ideologies . . . lay the highest value on, and assert the liberty and equality of, individuals. . . .

We subjects [of the Japanese emperor] are intrinsically quite different from the so-called citizens of the Occidental [Western] countries. . . .

Our country is established with the Emperor. . . . For this reason, to serve the Emperor and to receive the Emperor's great august Will as one's own is the rationale of making our historical "life" live in the present. . . .

Loyalty means to reverence the Emperor as [our] pivot and to follow him implicitly. . . . Hence, offering our lives for the sake of the Emperor does not mean so-called self-sacrifice, but the casting aside of our little selves to live under his august grace and the enhancing of the genuine life of the people of a State. . . . An individual is an existence belonging to the State and her history, which forms the basis of his origin, and is fundamentally one body with it. . . .

We must sweep aside the corruption of the spirit and the clouding of knowledge that arises from setting up one's "self" and from being taken up with one's "self" and return to a pure and clear state of mind that belongs intrinsically to us as subjects, and thereby fathom the great principle loyalty. . . .

Indeed, loyalty is our fundamental Way as subject, and is the basis of our national morality. Through loyalty are we become Japanese subjects; in loyalty do we obtain life and herein do we find the source of all morality.

Source: J. O. Gauntlett, trans., and R. K. Hall, ed., *Kokutai No Hongi* (*Cardinal Principles of the National Entity of Japan*) (Cambridge, MA: Harvard University Press, 1949), 52, 80–83.

■ ■ ■

Japanese Imperialism

Empire was a major theme in Japanese ideology of the 1930s and 1940s. It began to be put into practice in the early 1930s, when Japanese forces seized parts of northeastern China, calling it Manchukuo. Source 11.5 presents a Japanese propaganda poster, created in 1933, showing anti-Japanese Manchurians in hell (on the left), while pro-Japanese supporters (on the right) enjoy a blissful paradise.

1. What contrasts can you identify between the two panels? How does the imagery in both panels enhance the message of the poster? What kinds of figures dominate each panel of the image, and what are they doing?

2. To whom might this image be directed?

3. How does this portrayal of Japanese empire building compare with that of Italian imperialism in Source 11.1?

Japanese Propaganda Poster of Manchuria under Japanese Occupation | **1933**

ullstein bild/Getty Images

DOING HISTORY

1. **Making comparisons:** What broad similarities and differences in outlook can you identify among these sources? What aspects of the Japanese *Cardinal Principles* text might Hitler have viewed with sympathy, and what parts of it might he have found distasteful or offensive?

2. **Criticizing the West:** In what ways did Mussolini, Hitler, and the authors of *Cardinal Principles* find fault with mainstream Western societies and their political and social values?

3. **Considering ideas and action:** To what extent did the ideas articulated in these sources find expression in particular actions or policies of political authorities?

4. **Placing sources in context:** To what extent were the ideas in these sources new and revolutionary? In what respects did they draw on long-standing traditions? In what ways did they embrace modern life, and what aspects of it did they reject? Have these ideas been completely discredited, or do they retain some resonance in contemporary political discourse?

Anti-Semitism

Because hatred and fear of Jews were central to Nazi ideology, the history of anti-Semitism and its relationship to the Holocaust have loomed large in historians' efforts to understand the Nazi phenomenon. Voice 11.1, by historian Beth A. Griech-Polelle, shows how Nazi anti-Semitism drew on ideas built up over centuries to create a sense of Jews as radically "other" and threatening. Voice 11.2, derived from a book by the prominent historian Christopher Browning, takes a shorter-term perspective by exploring why Nazi policies were at least tacitly supported by millions of Germans upon whom the fate of the Jews "weighed lightly or not at all."

1. In what ways did anti-Semitism define Jews as radically "other"?

2. Why does Browning believe that many millions of "ordinary" Germans at least tacitly accepted Nazi anti-Semitic policies?

3. What elements of the Nazi program were most widely criticized by "ordinary" Germans and why?

4. **Integrating primary and secondary sources:** How might these two historians use Sources 11.2 and 11.3 to support their arguments?

VOICE 11.1

Beth A. Griech-Polelle on Anti-Semitism Creating "Otherness" | 2017

In this "Us" vs "Them" world, insiders are told that their very existence is threatened by an enemy who seeks to define, pollute, and destroy the coherence of "us." The threatening imagery of "the Jew" . . . was built up over the course of centuries. Destructive legends, myths, and stereotypes all contributed to a type of acceptable language about Jews that enabled Hitler to play on well-established tropes. Images of the "diabolical, cunning" Jew could be used to instill fear and anxiety and could serve as an explanation as to why an average German person felt stymied in their personal and professional development. They were told repeatedly that the enemy, the Jew, was standing in their way of creating a peaceful harmonious society. . . . In order for the German people to live, Jews had to die. . . .

The "other" is portrayed in language that suggests Jews are dirty, foreign, corrupt, corrupting, and never to be trusted. They are depicted as being in league with the devil, perpetrating every evil known to mankind. . . . Germans had to attack Jews in a kind of preemptive strike. . . . The Germans were only acting in self-defense to protect themselves from an imagined future annihilation. . . .

The image of "the Jew" was now a figure standing outside of history, an eternal enemy of "us."

Source: Beth A. Griech-Polelle, *Anti-Semitism and the Holocaust* (London: Bloomsbury Academic, 2017), 1–2.

Christopher Browning on Why Many Ordinary Germans Tacitly Supported Nazi Anti-Semitic Policies | 2004

Hitler's coming to power would not only "unleash" the Nazis and their right-wing allies . . . to harm the Jews, but would do so with the tacit support of millions of Germans for whom the fate of the Jews weighed lightly or not at all . . . and increasingly with the support of millions of Germans eager to catch the political tide. . . . Germany ceased to be a pluralistic society, and there were no significant "countervailing" forces outside the alliance of Nazis and conservative nationalists on which the regime rested.

. . . It is most unlikely that the conservatives on their own would have proceeded beyond the initial discriminatory measures of 1933–34 that drove the Jews out of the civil and military services, the professions, and cultural life . . . [but] with strikingly few exceptions they had no remorse or regret for the fate of the Jews.

What can be said of the German people at large in the 1930s? . . . The majority of "ordinary" Germans . . . accepted the legal measures of the regime . . . yet this majority was critical of the hooliganistic violence of activists. . . . Many Germans who were indifferent or even hostile toward Jews were not indifferent to the public flouting of deeply ingrained values concerning the preservation of order, propriety, and property. But anti-Semitic measures carried out in an orderly and legal manner were widely accepted. . . . This was a major accomplishment for the regime, but it still did not offer the prospect that most ordinary Germans would approve of, much less participate in, the mass murder of European Jewry.

Source: Christopher R. Browning, *The Origins of the Final Solution: The Evolution of Nazi Jewish Policy, September 1939–March 1942* (Lincoln: University of Nebraska Press, 2004), 8–10.

NOTES

1. Benito Mussolini, *The Political and Social Doctrine of Fascism* (London: Hogarth Press, 1933), 25.

2. Quoted in Christopher Kelly, *The Roman Empire* (Oxford: Oxford University Press, 2006), 124.

CHAPTER 12

Articulating Independence

For millions of people in Africa, Asia, Oceania, and the Caribbean, the achievement of political independence from colonial rule and foreign domination marked a singular moment in their personal lives and in their collective histories. That achievement took shape in many different ways, with variation in the duration and intensity of the struggle, in the tactics of the independence movements, and in the ideologies that they espoused. Here, we focus less on the process by which independence was acquired, and more on the various meanings ascribed to it. In all of these regions, the moment of independence represented a surprising triumph against great odds and an awakening to the possibility of building new lives and new societies. The sources that follow reflect the hopes, aspirations, and warnings of that remarkable moment. Many of the most ambitious goals subsequently went unfulfilled or were betrayed, fueling immense disappointment. Nonetheless, it is worth reflecting on the varied meanings associated with the coming of independence, for in human affairs, almost always, our reach exceeds our grasp.

SOURCE 12.1 Declaring Vietnam's Independence

Just a few weeks after the end of World War II in Asia, Ho Chi Minh, the nationalist and communist leader of his country's independence movement, declared Vietnam free of both five years of Japanese control and more than sixty years of French colonial rule. The date was September 2, 1945, and the place was Hanoi, the colonial capital of French Indochina. More than thirty more years of struggle lay ahead, first against French efforts to reestablish colonial rule over Vietnam, and then against American military intervention in the country. But the Declaration of 1945 spoke to the meaning of that struggle, largely by referring to the colonial past, to the legacy of the Atlantic revolutions, and to the proclaimed values of the victors in World War II.

1. In what ways does the Declaration seek to legitimate Vietnam's independence?

2. Why do you think Ho Chi Minh began his Declaration with references to the American and French revolutions?

3. What critique of colonial rule is contained in the Declaration?

4. How does the Declaration seek to situate Vietnam's independence struggle both historically and in terms of the global politics of 1945?

HO CHI MINH | *Declaration of Independence of the Democratic Republic of Vietnam* | September 2, 1945

"All men are created equal. They are endowed by their Creator with certain inalienable rights, among them are Life, Liberty, and the pursuit of Happiness." This immortal statement was made in the Declaration of Independence of the United States of America in 1776. In a broader sense, this means: All the peoples on the earth are equal from birth, all the peoples have a right to live, to be happy and free.

The Declaration of the French Revolution made in 1791 on the Rights of Man and the Citizen also states: "All men are born free and with equal rights, and must always remain free and have equal rights." Those are undeniable truths.

Nevertheless, for more than eighty years, the French imperialists, abusing the standard of Liberty, Equality, and Fraternity, have violated our Fatherland and oppressed our fellow-citizens. They have acted contrary to the ideals of humanity and justice.

In the field of politics, they have deprived our people of every democratic liberty.

They have enforced inhuman laws; they have set up three distinct political regimes in the North, the Center and the South of Vietnam in order to wreck our national unity and prevent our people from being united.

They have built more prisons than schools. They have mercilessly slain our patriots; they have drowned our uprisings in rivers of blood.

To weaken our race they have forced us to use opium and alcohol.

In the field of economics, they have fleeced us to the backbone, impoverished our people, and devastated our land.

They have robbed us of our rice fields, our mines, our forests, and our raw materials. They have monopolized the issuing of bank-notes and the export trade.

They have invented numerous unjustifiable taxes and reduced our people, especially our peasantry, to a state of extreme poverty.

They have hampered the prospering of our national bourgeoisie; they have mercilessly exploited our workers.

In the autumn of 1940, when the Japanese Fascists violated Indochina's territory to establish new bases in their fight against the Allies, the French imperialists went down on their bended knees and handed over our country to them.

Thus, from that date, our people were subjected to the double yoke of the French and the Japanese. Their sufferings and miseries increased. . . . Notwithstanding all this, our fellow-citizens have always manifested toward the French a tolerant and humane attitude. . . . The Vietminh League helped many Frenchmen to cross the frontier, rescued some of them from Japanese jails, and protected French lives and property. From the autumn of 1940, our country had in fact ceased to be a French colony and had become a Japanese possession.

After the Japanese had surrendered to the Allies, our whole people rose to regain our national sovereignty and to found the Democratic Republic of Vietnam. The truth is that we have wrested our independence from the Japanese and not from the French.

Our people have broken the chains which for nearly a century have fettered them and have won independence for the Fatherland. Our people at the same time have overthrown the monarchic regime that has reigned supreme for dozens of centuries. In its place has been established the present Democratic Republic.

For these reasons, we, members of the Provisional Government, representing the whole Vietnamese people, declare that from now on we break off all relations of a colonial character with France; we repeal all the international obligations that France has so far subscribed to on behalf of Vietnam and we abolish all the special rights the French have unlawfully acquired in our Fatherland.

The whole Vietnamese people, animated by a common purpose, are determined to fight to the bitter end against any attempt by the French colonialists to reconquer their country.

We are convinced that the Allied nations which at Tehran [where Roosevelt, Churchill, and Stalin met] and San Francisco [where the United Nations was established] have acknowledged the principles of self-determination and equality of nations, will not refuse to acknowledge the independence of Vietnam.

A people who have courageously opposed French domination for more than eighty years, a people who have fought side by side with the Allies against the Fascists during these last years, such a people must be free and independent.

For these reasons, we, members of the Provisional Government of the Democratic Republic of Vietnam, solemnly declare to the world that Vietnam has the right to be a free and independent country—and in fact is so already. The entire Vietnamese people are determined to mobilize all their physical and mental strength, to sacrifice their lives and property in order to safeguard their independence and liberty.

Source: Ho Chi Minh, *Selected Works*, vol. 3 (Hanoi: Foreign Languages Publishing House, 1960–1962), 17–21.

■ ■ ■

SOURCE 12.2   An Image of Vietnam's Independence: Fifty Years Later

In 1995, Vietnam marked the fiftieth anniversary of its earlier Declaration of Independence, an event celebrated by this poster. Pictured on the right side of the poster is Ho Chi Minh, the principal author of the earlier Declaration, who had died in 1969. The caption refers to a "National Day" commemoration for what had become a "unified and socialist" country, almost twenty years after the victory over American forces in the Vietnam War.

1. What does the poster suggest have been the country's major achievements since independence?

2. What is the significance of the tanks and soldiers shown in red at the upper left of the poster?

3. Does the poster emphasize Vietnam's nationalist or its communist achievements?

Fiftieth Anniversary of Vietnamese Independence | 1995

(Poster for the 50th Anniversary of Vietnamese Independence, 1995 (color litho)/ Phuong Luong Van (fl. 1995)/Private Collection/Bridgeman Images)

■ ■ ■

SOURCE 12.3 India's "Tryst with Destiny"

Just two years after Ho Chi Minh announced Vietnam's independence, Jawaharlal Nehru did the same for India, shortly before midnight on August 14, 1947. Hovering over this joyful event was the tragedy of the bloody partition between India and Pakistan and the absence at the celebration of India's great nationalist leader, Gandhi, who was in Calcutta, praying, fasting, and seeking to stem the violence between Muslims and Hindus.

1. How does Nehru's speech compare with Ho Chi Minh's Declaration?

2. What kind of India does Nehru foresee emerging from the struggle for independence? How does his vision compare with that of Gandhi? (See Source 9.5 in the Thinking through Sources feature for Chapter 9.)

3. What aspects of Indian society posed a challenge for the India of Nehru's hopes?

JAWAHARLAL NEHRU | *Independent Day Speech* | August 14, 1947

Long years ago we made a tryst with destiny, and now the time comes when we shall redeem our pledge, not wholly or in full measure, but very substantially. At the stroke of the midnight hour, when the world sleeps, India will awake to life and freedom. A moment comes, which comes but rarely in history, when we step out from the old to the new, when an age ends, and when the soul of a nation, long suppressed, finds utterance. It is fitting that at this solemn moment we take the pledge of dedication to the service of India and her people and to the still larger cause of humanity. . . .

Before the birth of freedom we have endured all the pains of labour and our hearts are heavy with the memory of this sorrow. Some of those pains continue even now. Nevertheless, the past is over and it is the future that beckons to us now.

That future is not one of ease or resting but of incessant striving so that we may fulfil the pledges we have so often taken and the one we shall take today. The service of India means the service of the millions who suffer. It means the ending of poverty and ignorance and disease and inequality of opportunity. The ambition of the greatest man of our generation [Gandhi] has been to wipe every tear from every eye. That may be beyond us, but as long as there are tears and suffering, so long our work will not be over.

And so we have to labour and to work, and work hard, to give reality to our dreams. Those dreams are for India, but they are also for the world, for all the nations and peoples are too closely knit together today for any one of them to imagine that it can live apart. Peace has been said to be indivisible; so is freedom, so is prosperity now, and so also is disaster in this One World that can no longer be split into isolated fragments.

To the people of India, whose representatives we are, we make an appeal to join us with faith and confidence in this great adventure. This is no time for petty and destructive criticism, no time for ill-will or blaming others. We have to build the noble mansion of free India where all her children may dwell.

The appointed day has come—the day appointed by destiny—and India stands forth again, after long slumber and struggle, awake, vital, free and independent. The past clings on to us still in some measure and we have to do much before we redeem the pledges we have so often taken. Yet the turning-point is past, and history begins anew for us, the history which we shall live and act and others will write about.

It is a fateful moment for us in India, for all Asia and for the world. A new star rises, the star of freedom in the East, a new hope comes into being, a vision long cherished materializes. . . . On this day our first thoughts go to the architect of this freedom, the Father of our Nation [Gandhi], who, embodying the old spirit of India, held aloft the torch of freedom and lighted up the darkness that surrounded us. We have often been unworthy followers of his and have strayed from his message, but not only we but succeeding generations will remember this message and bear the imprint in their hearts of this great son of India, magnificent in his faith and strength and courage and humility. . . .

The future beckons to us. Whither do we go and what shall be our endeavour? To bring freedom and opportunity to the common man, to the peasants and workers of India; to fight and end poverty and ignorance and disease; to build up a prosperous, democratic and progressive nation, and to create social, economic and political institutions which will ensure justice and fullness of life to every man and woman.

We have hard work ahead. There is no resting for any one of us till we redeem our pledge in full, till we make all the people of India what destiny intended them to be. We are citizens of a great country on the verge of bold advance, and we have to live up to that high standard. All of us, to whatever religion we may belong, are equally the children of India with equal rights, privileges and obligations. We cannot encourage communalism or narrow-mindedness, for no nation can be great whose people are narrow in thought or in action.

To the nations and peoples of the world we send greetings and pledge ourselves to cooperate with them in furthering peace, freedom and democracy.

And to India, our much-loved motherland, the ancient, the eternal and the ever-new, we pay our reverent homage and we bind ourselves afresh to her service.

JAI HIND [Hail India]

Source: Jawaharlal Nehru, "A Tryst with Destiny," August 14, 1947, "Great Speeches of the 20th Century," *Guardian*, http://www.theguardian.com/theguardian/2007/may/01/greatspeeches.

■ ■ ■

SOURCE 12.4 Another View of India's Struggle for Independence

Nehru's vision of India as a secular and modernizing state that provided a secure home for all of its religious communities was not the only image of the country's struggle for independence. Gandhi was widely viewed as a religious figure, the *mahatma*, or great soul, and the fight against British colonialism, which he led, was often portrayed in distinctly religious and Hindu terms, as Source 12.4, a poster from 1930–1931, illustrates. Here Gandhi is cast as the great Hindu deity Shiva and is portrayed saving a female character representing Mother India from British imperialism, depicted as Yama, the lord of death. This image appropriates the widely known Hindu mythological story of Markandeya, a young and pious sage, who is attacked by Yama, riding a buffalo and seeking to take his soul by casting a rope around the young man. But the great god Shiva rescues Markandeya, grants him eternal life, and slays Yama.

1. What features of this legend can you identify in Source 12.4?

2. Why might this image be appealing to Indians in the several decades before independence? To what groups in India might this image raise suspicions or be offensive?

3. How does this image differ from Nehru's depiction of independent India in Source 12.3?

Gandhi and the Fight against British Colonialism | *ca. 1930–1931*

SOURCE 12.5 | One Africa

For Kwame Nkrumah, the leader of Ghana's anticolonial movement and the new West African country's first president, independence meant an opportunity to challenge the common assumption that Europe's African colonies should become nation-states within their existing borders. He was convinced that only by forming a much larger union could the African continent achieve substantial economic development and genuine independence. In doing so, Nkrumah was drawing on the notion of a broader African identity, Pan-Africanism, which had emerged among educated people during the colonial era.

1. What kind of union did Nkrumah seek?

2. Why did he think that union was so essential? What benefits would it bring to Africa in its efforts at modern development?

3. What challenges did Nkrumah identify to his soaring vision of a United States of Africa?

KWAME NKRUMAH | *Africa Must Unite* | 1963

There are those who maintain that Africa cannot unite because we lack the three necessary ingredients for unity, a common race, culture, and language. It is true that we have for centuries been divided. The territorial boundaries dividing us were fixed long ago, often quite arbitrarily, by the colonial powers. Some of us are Moslems, some Christians; many believe in traditional, tribal gods. Some of us speak French, some English, some Portuguese, not to mention the millions who speak only one of the hundreds of different African languages. We have acquired cultural differences which affect our outlook and condition our political development. . . .

In the early flush of independence, some of the new African states are jealous of their sovereignty and tend to exaggerate their separatism in a historical period that demands Africa's unity in order that their independence may be safeguarded. . . .

[A] united Africa—that is, the political and economic unification of the African Continent—should seek three objectives: Firstly, we should have an overall economic planning on a continental basis. This would increase the industrial and economic power of Africa. So long as we remain balkanized, regionally or territorially, we shall be at the mercy of colonialism and imperialism. The lesson of the South American Republics vis-à-vis the strength and solidarity of the United States of America is there for all to see.

The resources of Africa can be used to the best advantage and the maximum benefit to all only if they are set within an overall framework of a continentally planned development. An overall economic plan, covering an Africa united on a continental basis, would increase our total industrial and economic power. We should therefore be thinking seriously now of ways and means of building up a Common Market of a United

Africa and not allow ourselves to be lured by the dubious advantages of association with the so-called European Common Market. . . .

Secondly, we should aim at the establishment of a unified military and defense strategy. . . . For young African States, who are in great need of capital for internal development, it is ridiculous—indeed suicidal—for each State separately and individually to assume such a heavy burden of self-defense, when the weight of this burden could be easily lightened by sharing it among themselves. . . .

The third objective: [I]t will be necessary for us to adopt a unified foreign policy and diplomacy to give political direction to our joint efforts for the protection and economic development of our continent. . . . The burden of separate diplomatic representation by each State on the Continent of Africa alone would be crushing, not to mention representation outside Africa. The desirability of a common foreign policy which will enable us to speak with one voice in the councils of the world, is so obvious, vital and imperative that comment is hardly necessary. . . .

Under a major political union of Africa there could emerge a United Africa, great and powerful, in which the territorial boundaries which are the relics of colonialism will become obsolete and superfluous, working for the complete and total mobilization of the economic planning organization under a unified political direction. The forces that unite us are far greater than the difficulties that divide us at present, and our goal must be the establishment of Africa's dignity, progress, and prosperity.

Source: Kwame Nkrumah, *Africa Must Unite* (London, UK: Heinemann, 1963), 132, 148, 218–21.

■ ■ ■

SOURCE 12.6 South African "Independence"

Independence in South Africa had a somewhat different meaning than elsewhere in the colonial world, for that country had already ended its colonial relationship with Great Britain in 1910. The struggle in South Africa was against a local entrenched and dominant white minority that had imposed a regime of harsh racial oppression, known as apartheid, which had no parallel in other parts of the world. When that system of government ended in April 1994 with the country's first genuinely democratic elections, its demise marked the conclusion of an era in world history in which Europeans exercised formal political control in the African, Asian, Caribbean, and Pacific worlds. This photograph shows a man standing in line preparing to vote in that historic election by displaying his identification document. Such photographs, of which there were thousands, articulated what was for many the essential meaning of that moment.

1. Africans had long resented and resisted the requirement to produce on demand an identity card—a kind of internal passport—during the apartheid era. Why, then, do you think that the man in the foreground is proudly displaying his identification document in this photograph?

2. How does the image of several whites, also waiting to vote, enhance the message of the photograph?

3. Notice that the two African men in the foreground are shown in clear focus, while the whites in the background are displayed in a somewhat blurred fashion. Do you think this was deliberate on the part of the photographer? How does this feature of the photo contribute to the message it conveys?

First Post-Apartheid South African Election | *1994*

Peter Turnley/Getty Images

■ ■ ■

SOURCE 12.7 Independence as Threat

Independence had meaning not only for those who sought it, but also for those who opposed it. In 1961, a Portuguese archbishop in Mozambique, Alvim Pereira, distributed a document to local seminary students and priests that outlined his opposition to independence for Mozambique and other Portuguese colonies.

1. How would you summarize the reasons for Pereira's hostility to independence?

2. What role does the archbishop prescribe for the Catholic Church in confronting independence movements?

3. What kind of future for Mozambique does he imply?

ALVIM PEREIRA | *Ten Principles* | 1961

1. Independence is irrelevant to the welfare of man. It can be good if the right conditions are present (the cultural conditions do not yet exist in Mozambique).

2. While these conditions are not being produced, to take part in movements for independence is acting against nature.

3. Even if these conditions existed, the Metropole has the right to oppose independence if the freedoms and rights of man are respected, and if it [the Metropole] provided for the well-being, for civil and religious progress of all.

4. All the movements which use force (terrorists) are against the natural law....

5. When the movement is a terrorist one, the clergy have the obligation, in good conscience, not only to refrain from taking part but also to oppose it....

6. Even when the movement is peaceful, the clergy must abstain from it in order to have spiritual influence on all people....

7. The native people of Africa have the obligation to thank the colonists for all the benefits which they receive from them.

8. The educated have the duty to lead those with less education from all the illusions of independence.

9. The present independence movements have, almost all of them, the sign of revolt and of Communism; they have no reason....

10. The slogan "Africa for the Africans" is a philosophical monstrosity and a challenge to the Christian civilization, because today's events tell us that it is Communism and Islamism which wish to impose their civilization upon the Africans.

Source: Eduardo Mondlane, *The Struggle for Mozambique* (Hammondsworth, UK: Penguin Books, 1969), 74–75.

DOING HISTORY

1. **Making comparisons:** What do the independence movements described in these sources share? In what ways do they differ?

2. **Defining points of view:** Independence was a widely shared value in the colonial world, but the meanings attached to it varied considerably. How could you use these sources to support this statement?

3. **Imagining a conversation:** Choose three or four of the sources and construct a dialogue between their authors or creators.

HISTORIANS' VOICES

Assessing African Independence

The coming of independence in Africa (1955–1975) was greeted initially with something approaching euphoria. This enthusiastic excitement was captured by the African historian and activist Basil Davidson in Voice 12.1. By the early 1990s, however, that euphoria had turned for many people to disappointment, despair, and anger as widespread corruption, ethnic conflict, political instability, elite enrichment, and mass poverty seemed to betray the great promise of independence. This sensibility found expression in the work of George Ayittey, a Ghanaian economist and historian, and is reflected in Voice 12.2.

1. How does Davidson describe the euphoria attending the coming of independence in Africa of the 1960s?

2. How does Ayittey account for the rather different mood of the early 1990s?

3. **Integrating primary and secondary sources:** To what extent do the primary sources in this feature illustrate the kind of optimism that Davidson describes in Voice 12.1? In what ways are they more cautious?

VOICE 12.1

Basil Davidson on the Promise of Independence | 1978

The coming of independence could in those days seem a climactic moment dividing the past from an altogether different future when all things would be possible . . . [T]he most blatant [European] control was gone or could now be removed. This was the rule that all things must be ordered as though whites were naturally and inherently superior to blacks: the cultural bludgeon of colonial government. Now the bludgeon had no local hand to wield it, and with this there came a profound sense of cultural rebirth. . . .

[T]he overall impression one retains of those sunsets when the imperial flags came down, and the banners of nationhood climbed to mastheads lit with flares and fireworks, stays firm and clear. Independence spelt renewal, the flinging down of racist barriers, the fraught emotion of swaying crowds, dancing, drumming, for whom their own ideas, beliefs, and abilities could now be clothed in a new respect and value.

This may be seen as the chief achievement of the 'political classes'. They had asserted the right of Africans to stand level with other peoples in all ways cultural or psychological. They had struck down the old spectre of a 'natural' inferiority, and banished the haunting fear that racist teachings, so grimly argued over so many decades, might after all contain a truth . . . [T]he doorway to equality was open. There came a vivid consciousness of having grasped destiny by the hand so that Africa's history could begin again.

Source: Basil Davidson, *Let Freedom Come* (New York, NY: Little Brown, 1978), 283–84.

VOICE 12.2

George Ayittey on the Betrayal of Independence | 1992

Three decades of independence from colonial rule have produced nothing but economic misery and disintegration, political chaos, and institutional and social disintegration. The decline in per-capita income has been calamitous for many African countries. Agricultural growth has been dismal, producing chronic food shortages and an ever-present threat of famine. . . . The proportion of state spending devoted to health and education fell. . . .

For most Africans, independence did not bring a better life or even greater political or civil liberties. . . . Since independence in the 1960s, there has been a systematic curtailment and virtual banishment across Africa of freedom and civil liberties. . . . One word of criticism of an African government may earn a death sentence.

Africa has been betrayed. Freedom from colonial rule has evolved into ghastly tyranny, arbitrary rule, denial of civil liberties, brutal suppression of dissent, and the wanton slaughter of peasants. . . . But the most painful was the cultural insult. . . . African elites who replaced them [colonial rulers] deprecated the indigenous as "backward" and "primitive." In many places the elites sought the destruction of the indigenous by imposing alien systems on Africa. . . . To replace western institutions, many African leaders marched off to the East and adopted socialist and communist systems for transplantation into Africa. . . .

Most analysts now agree that although colonialism was evil, it offered comparatively more freedom than did many independent African countries in the 1980s.

Source: George Ayittey, *Africa Betrayed* (New York, NY: St. Martin's Press, 1992), 8–10, 12.

13 Global Feminism

With its focus on equal rights and opportunities for women, modern feminism has challenged the most ancient and perhaps deeply rooted of human inequalities—that of patriarchy or the dominance of men over women. Beginning in Western Europe and the United States during the nineteenth century, it was born in the context of democratic gains for men from which women were excluded. Like science, industrialism, socialism, and electoral democracy, feminism was a Western cultural innovation that acquired a global reach during the most recent century.

In doing so, feminism has found expression in many voices, giving rise to much controversy and many questions within feminist circles. How relevant has mainstream Western feminism been to women of color in the West and in the developing countries? To what extent do all women share common interests? In what ways do differences of class, race, nation, religion, sexual orientation, and economic condition generate quite distinct feminist agendas? How important is sexual freedom to the feminist cause? What tactics are most effective in realizing the varying goals of feminists? The documents that follow provide a sample of the divergent voices in which global feminism has been articulated during the past century.

SOURCE 13.1 Western Feminism in the Twenty-First Century

In the West, where modern feminism had begun, a new phase of that movement took shape during the 1960s and after. Moving well beyond the earlier focus on suffrage and property rights, second-wave feminists gave voice to a wide range of new issues: the value of housework, discrimination in the workplace, media portrayal of women, sexuality and the family, reproductive rights, lesbianism, violence against women, pornography, and prostitution.

At the opening of the twenty-first century, Western feminists continued to advance a broad agenda, as reflected in the two images that constitute Source 13.1. Source 13.1A depicts a 2012 "slutwalk" in London protesting against rape culture. This march was one of many around the world, the first of which occurred in Canada in 2011 when a policeman told a group of students that in order to avoid being raped "women should avoid dressing like sluts." Source 13.1B documents a 2017 protest in Toulouse, France, that advocated for women's rights in the workplace, another major goal of modern Western feminism. The banner in the foreground reads, "Precarious, underpaid, harassed. It's enough!"

1. What strategies are these protesters employing to secure the changes that they advocate for?

2. What do the issues raised by participants and the types of protest depicted in these images reveal about Western feminism in the first decades of the twenty-first century?

SOURCE 13.1A

A "Slutwalk" in London, a Global Protest against Rape Culture | **2012**

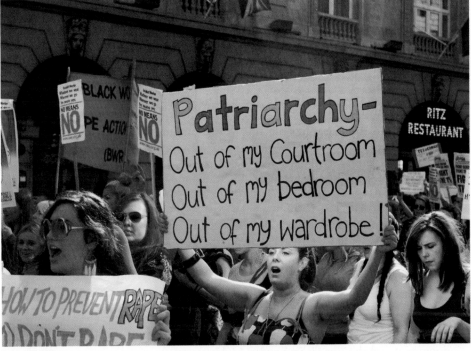

Patricia Phillips/Alamy

SOURCE 13.1B

A Demonstration for Women Workers' Rights in Toulouse, France | 2017

PRÉCARISÉES, SOUS PAYÉES, HARCELÉES,
Y'EN A ASSEZ !

NurPhoto/Getty Images

■ ■ ■

SOURCE 13.2   Black American Feminism

Within North American feminism, a distinctive voice arose among women of color—especially Blacks and Hispanics. Many among them resented the claims of white, middle-class feminists to speak for all women and objected to the exclusive promi-nence given to gender issues. Capitalism, race, class, and compulsory heterosexuality, they insisted, combined with patriarchy to generate an interlocking system of oppression that was unique to women of color. Such a perspective is reflected in the 1977 statement of the Combahee River Collective, a Black feminist organization.

1. What similarities and differences in perspective can you identify between this document and the images in Source 13.1?

2. What issues divide Black and white feminists in the United States?

3. What difficulties have Black American feminists experienced in gaining support for their movement?

4. On what basis might this Black feminist statement generate opposition and controversy?

COMBAHEE RIVER COLLECTIVE │ *A Black Feminist Statement* │ 1977

We are a collective of Black feminists who have been meeting together since 1974. . . . [W]e are actively committed to struggling against racial, sexual, heterosexual, and class oppression . . . based upon the fact that the major systems of oppression are interlocking. . . .

[W]e find our origins in the historical reality of Afro-American women's continuous life-and-death struggle for survival and liberation. . . . Black women have always embodied an adversary stance to white male rule. . . . Black feminist politics also have an obvious connection to movements for Black liberation, particularly those of the 1960s and 1970s. . . . It was our experience and disillusionment within these liberation movements, as well as experience on the periphery of the white male left, that led to the need to develop a politics that was anti-racist, unlike those of white women, and anti-sexist, unlike those of Black and white men. . . . [A]s we developed politically we [also] addressed ourselves to heterosexism and economic oppression under capitalism. . . .

Although we are feminists and Lesbians, we feel solidarity with progressive Black men and do not advocate the fractionalization that white women who are separatists demand. . . . We struggle together with Black men against racism, while we also struggle with Black men about sexism. . . . We are socialists because we believe that work must be organized for the collective benefit of those who do the work and create the products, and not for the profit of the bosses. . . . We need to articulate the real class situation of persons . . . for whom racial and sexual oppression are significant determinants in their working/economic lives. . . . No one before has ever examined the multilayered texture of Black women's lives. . . . "Smart-ugly" crystallized the way in which most of us had been forced to develop our intellects at great cost to our "social" lives. . . . We have a great deal of criticism and loathing for what men have been socialized to be in this society . . . [b]ut we do not have the misguided notion that it is their maleness, per se—i.e., their biological maleness—that makes them what they are.

The major source of difficulty in our political work is that we are . . . trying . . . to address a whole range of oppressions. . . . We do not have racial, sexual, heterosexual, or class privilege to rely upon. . . . The psychological toll of being a Black woman and the difficulties this presents in reaching political consciousness and doing political work can never be underestimated. . . . As an early group member once said, "We are all damaged people merely by virtue of being Black women." . . . The material conditions of most Black women would hardly lead them to upset both economic and sexual arrangements that seem to represent some stability in their lives. . . . Accusations that Black feminism divides the Black struggle are powerful deterrents to the growth of an autonomous Black women's movement.

The inclusiveness of our politics makes us concerned with any situation that impinges upon the lives of women, Third World and working people. . . . One issue that is of major concern to us and that we have begun to publicly address is racism in the white women's movement. . . . Eliminating racism in the white women's movement is by definition work for white women to do, but we will continue to speak to and demand accountability on this issue. . . .

Source: Zillah R. Eisenstein, ed., *Capitalist Patriarchy and the Case for Socialist Feminism* (New York: Monthly Review Press, 1979), 362–72.

■ ■ ■

SOURCE 13.3 Communist Feminism

Following the Russian Revolution of 1917, the communist Soviet Union was the site of a remarkable experiment in state-directed feminism. Early on women were granted full legal and political equality with men, divorce was legalized, and pregnancy leave was mandated for employed women. As part of a determined drive to industrialize the country, authorities also sought to liberate women from household responsibilities so that they could work outside the home. This poster from 1949 advertises the support available to Soviet women who chose to pursue careers in industry. The poster caption reads, "The broad development of a network of nursery schools, kindergartens, dining rooms and laundries will provide for the participation of women in socialist construction."

1. How would you describe the woman in the center of the poster? What do you think that the artist wanted to convey about her?

2. How are the specific services promised to women in the poster text depicted in the image? How might state provision of these services alter the daily life and family dynamics of working women?

3. How might the protesters in Source 13.1B react to this poster?

Soviet Poster Advertising Support for Women Workers | 1949

Photo 12/Getty Images

■ ■ ■

SOURCE 13.4 Islamic Feminism

Beyond the Western world and the communist world, modern feminism has also found expression in the developing countries. Nowhere has this provoked greater controversy than in the Islamic world. For a few women, exposure to Western gender norms and liberal thought has occasioned the abandonment of Islam altogether. Far more common have been efforts to root gender equality in both personal and public life within the traditions of Islam. Such was the argument of Benazir Bhutto, several times the prime minister of Pakistan, in a speech delivered to a United Nations conference on women in 1995.

1. What message does Bhutto feel her election and the election of other female Muslim heads of state provide to Muslim women everywhere?

2. How does Bhutto account for the manifest inequality of women in so many Muslim societies?

3. How might you compare Bhutto's case for feminism with those of Westerners and communists in the preceding documents?

BENAZIR BHUTTO | *Politics and the Muslim Woman* | 1995

I stand before you not only as a Prime Minister but as a woman and a mother proud of her cultural and religious heritage. . . . Muslim women have a special responsibility to help distinguish between Islamic teachings and social taboos spun by the traditions of a patriarchal society. . . .

[W]e must remember that Islam forbids injustice; injustice against people, against nations, against women. It shuns race, colour, and gender as a basis of distinction amongst fellow men. It enshrines piety as the sole criteria for judging humankind. It treats women as human beings in their own right, not as chattels. A woman can inherit, divorce, receive alimony and child custody. Women were intellectuals, poets, jurists and even took part in war. The Holy Book of the Muslims refers to the rule of a woman, the Queen of Sabah. The Holy Book alludes to her wisdom and to her country being a land of plenty. The Holy Prophet (peace be upon him) himself married a working woman. And the first convert to Islam was a woman, Bibi Khadija. Prophet Muhammad (peace be upon him) emphatically condemned and put an end to the practice of female infanticide in pre-Islamic Arabia. The Holy Quran reads:

When news is brought to one of them, of the birth of a female (child),
his face darkens and he is filled with inward grief what shame does he
hide himself from his people because of the bad news he has had.
Shall he retain it on sufferance and contempt, or bury it in the dust.
Ah! what an evil choice they decide on (Surah Al-Nahl, Ayat 57, 58, 59)

Ladies and gentlemen! How true these words ring even today.

How many women are still "retained" in their families "on sufferance and contempt" growing up with emotional scars and burdens. How tragic it is that the pre-Islamic practice of female infanticide still haunts a world we regard as modern and civilized. Girl children are often abandoned or aborted. Statistics show that men now increasingly out-number women in more than 15 Asian nations. . . . Boys are wanted because their worth is considered more than that of the girl. Boys are wanted to satisfy the ego: they carry on the father's name in this world. Yet too often we forget that for Muslims on the Day of Judgement, each person will be called not by their father's name but by the mother's name. . . . And it [the aborting or killing of female babies] continues, not because of religion in the case of Pakistan, but because of social prejudice. The rights Islam gave Muslim women have too often been denied.

Source: United Nations, Fourth World Conference on Women, September 4, 1995, http://www.un.org/esa/gopher-data/conf/fwcw/conf/gov/950904202603.txt, made available by the United Nations.

■ ■ ■

SOURCE 13.5 | Mexican Zapatista Feminists

Mexican feminists, like those in much of Latin America, have operated in societies shaped by widespread poverty, sharp class inequalities, racial and ethnic conflict, and frequently authoritarian or corrupt governments. Thus feminists have often sought to address the ways in which multiple sources of oppression, not only gender relations, affect both women and men. Such was the case in the Zapatista rebellion that erupted in 1994 among the Maya people in the Chiapas region of southern Mexico. It was a protest against a long history of injustice and impoverishment for Indigenous peoples. Women activists within this largely peasant movement had to confront the sexist attitudes of their male comrades as well as an oppressive Mexican government that marginalized its Maya citizens. Although they usually rejected the "feminist" label, these women articulated their demands in an Indigenous Women's Petition (Source 13.5A) and succeeded in embedding their concerns in a Women's Revolutionary Law (Source 13.5B).

1. How would you describe the issues that these documents articulate? How do they reflect class, ethnic, and gender realities of Mexican life?

2. Should these documents be regarded as feminist? Why or why not? Why might Zapatista women be reluctant to call themselves feminists?

3. Which of these demands might provoke the strongest male resistance? Why?

4. With which of the previous feminist sources might Zapatista women be most sympathetic?

Indigenous Women's Petition | **March 1, 1994**

We, Indigenous campesino women, demand the immediate solution to our urgent needs, which the government has never resolved:

A: Childbirth clinics with gynecologists. . . .

B: That child care facilities be built in the communities.

C: We ask the government to send sufficient food for the children in all rural communities including: milk, cornflour, rice, corn, soy, oil, beans, cheese, eggs, sugar, soup, oats, etc.

D: That kitchens and dining halls be built for the children in the communities. . . .

E: We demand the construction of community corn dough mills and tortillerías based on the number of families in each community.

F: That they give us poultry, rabbit, sheep and pig farm projects, and also that we be provided with technical assistance and veterinarians.

G: We ask for bakery projects, which include the provision of ovens and ingredients.

H: We want artisan workshops to be built, equipped with machinery and raw materials.

I: Markets in which to sell our crafts at fair prices.

J: That schools be built where women can get technical training.

K: That there be preschools and maternal schools in rural communities, where children can play and grow in a morally and physically healthy way.

L: That as women we have sufficient transportation for the products we produce in our various projects.

Source: *Zapatistas! Documents of the New Mexican Revolution (December 31, 1993–June 12, 1994)* (New York: Autonomedia, 1994), 243, accessed January 9, 2018, http://lanic.utexas.edu/project/Zapatistas/Zapatistas_book.pdf.

The Women's Revolutionary Law | **January 1, 1994**

[T]aking into account the situation of the woman worker in Mexico, the revolution supports their just demands for equality and justice in the following Women's Revolutionary Law.

First: Women, regardless of their race, creed, color or political affiliation, have the right to participate in the revolutionary struggle in a way determined by their desire and capacity.

Second: Women have the right to work and receive a just salary.

Third: Women have the right to decide the number of children they will have and care for.

Fourth: Women have the right to participate in the affairs of the community and hold positions of authority if they are freely and democratically elected.

Fifth: Women and their children have the right to primary attention in matters of health and nutrition.

Sixth: Women have the right to an education.

Seventh: Women have the right to choose their partner, and are not to be forced into marriage.

Eighth: Women shall not be beaten or physically mistreated by their family members or by strangers. Rape and attempted rape will be severely punished.

Ninth: Women will be able to occupy positions of leadership in the organization and hold military ranks in the revolutionary armed forces.

Source: *Zapatistas! Documents of the New Mexican Revolution (December 31, 1993–June 12, 1994)* (New York: Autonomedia, 1994), 38–39, accessed January 9, 2018, http://lanic.utexas.edu/project/Zapatistas/Zapatistas_book.pdf.

DOING HISTORY

1. **Identifying similarities:** What common concerns animate these sources?

2. **Defining differences:** What variations or conflicting feminist perspectives can you identify in these sources? What accounts for those differences?

3. **Considering change over time:** How do you think nineteenth-century Western feminists would have responded to each of these twentieth-century statements?

4. **Evaluating global feminism:** What aspects of global feminism were most revolutionary, liberating, or threatening to established authorities and ways of living? To what extent do you think the goals of these varying feminist efforts have been realized?

Feminism: Tensions and Resistance

The globalization of the feminist movement after 1960 has transformed its scope and impact while also creating new tensions both within the movement and in the wider society. The two historians' voices that follow offer broad assessments of feminism. In Voice 13.1 Merry Wiesner-Hanks examines the movement's globalization after 1960 and the tensions that emerged among feminists. In Voice 13.2 Peter Stearns explores the different countercurrents that have resisted feminism since the 1960s.

1. According to Voice 13.1, what roles did the United Nations play in the modern feminist movement?

2. What motivations for opposing some goals of international feminism does Voice 13.2 identify?

3. **Integrating primary and secondary sources:** How might Wiesner-Hanks and Stearns use the sources in this feature to support their overviews of the modern global feminist movement?

VOICE 13.1

Merry Wiesner-Hanks on International Feminism | 2011

By the 1960s, women in many parts of the world were dissatisfied with the pace at which they were achieving political and legal equality, and a second-wave women's movement began, often termed the "women's liberation movement." Women's groups pressured for an end to sex discrimination in hiring practices, pay rates, inheritance rights, and the granting of credit, they opened shelters for battered women, day care centers, and rape crisis centers, and pushed for university courses on women, and laws against sexual harassment. In Western countries they pushed for abortion rights, and in India they mobilized against dowries and dowry-related deaths. By the early 1970s, advocates of rights for homosexuals had also mobilized in many countries, sponsoring demonstrations, political action campaigns, and various types of self-help organizations. The United Nations declared 1975–1985 to be the International Decade for Women, and meetings discussing the status of women around the world were held under UN auspices in Mexico City (1975), Copenhagen (1980), Nairobi (1985), and Beijing (1995). These meetings were sometimes divisive, pointing out the great differences in women's concerns around the world, with sexual orientation and female genital cutting often the most explosive issues. The official Platform for Action of the Beijing Conference sought to avoid some of these divisions by calling for a general "empowerment of women," noting that this would mean different things in different areas of the world.

Source: Merry E. Wiesner-Hanks, *Gender in History: Global Perspectives*, 2nd ed. (Oxford: Wiley Blackwell, 2011), 157–58.

VOICE 13.2

Peter Stearns on Resistance to Global Feminism | 2015

Two related trends emerged. The first . . . was the resurgence of religious and other conservatism, often directed explicitly against changes in gender relations. . . . Islamic, Hindu and many Christian fundamentalists all urged more traditional gender hierarchy and the importance of female modesty. . . .

Equally interesting, if less important numerically, was the growing group of women's leaders who objected to international standards because they were too Western and too individualistic. These were people who wanted women to have an active voice in their lives and societies but who did not find the international formulas persuasive. An Indian women's magazine thus objected to global consumerism on the grounds that it tended to force women to waste time and effort on personal beauty in the hope of finding and keeping men. Far better, in terms of real women's interests, was the Indian custom of arranged marriages, which made the Western appearances game irrelevant. . . .

Finally . . . at the grass-roots level, many ordinary women sought to effect compromise, using new standards to a degree but combining them with older goals. Thus a grandmother in Kenya talks of the importance of education for women, so they can fend for themselves, and also accepts new levels of birth control. But beneath this interestingly cosmopolitan surface she hopes not for individual fulfillment for her granddaughters, but for a revived family cohesion in which different generations of women will take care of each other, regardless of what the men do. International influences have had some effect here, but more on the means by which goals were to be met than on the purposes themselves.

Source: Peter N. Stearns, *Gender in World History*, 3rd ed. (New York: Routledge, 2015), 194–95.

chapter 14

Experiencing International Migration

WORKING WITH EVIDENCE

The long-distance movement of people has been a prominent feature of the human story, and never more so than in the seven decades since the end of World War II. This immense stream of people in motion has been and remains the product of many elements in recent world history: an awareness of global inequality and the perceived promise of a better life abroad; the pressures of population growth and the harsh realities of poverty; environmental degradation; war, repression, and political crises. These and other factors have given rise to many kinds of migrants: economic migrants seeking work in new lands; political migrants or refugees seeking safety or freedom; legal and undocumented migrants; migrant victims of sex trafficking. These migrant streams have moved in many directions. Russia has been the destination for many millions, many of them Russian speakers from the countries of the former Soviet Union. Small but wealthy states such as Hong Kong, Singapore, Kuwait, and the United Arab Emirates have attracted large numbers of immigrants, who represent now a substantial proportion of their populations—some 88 percent in the United Arab Emirates and 73 percent in Kuwait. Global sex trafficking has become a big and profitable business, moving millions of women and girls across international boundaries. Western retirement migrants, seeking warmer and inexpensive locations for their later years, have generated expatriate communities in various countries of Latin America and Asia.

But the largest stream of international migrants has involved people from the Global South of Africa, Asia, the Middle East, and Latin America seeking new homes and new lives in the more developed countries of the Global North, including Europe and North America. The United States has been the target destination for the largest number of the world's migrants; by 2015, it was home to some 46.6 million migrants, or approximately 14.5 percent of the total U.S. population. For many of the world's migrants, the journey to their new homes has been harrowing and often deadly—trekking across burning deserts of northern Mexico, the southwestern United States, or the Sahara, or navigating the treacherous Mediterranean Sea in flimsy boats.

The sources that follow focus less on these journeys and more on the experience of the migrants in their new homes, the response of the host societies, and the impact of migration on those left behind in their countries of origin.

SOURCE 14.1   Hana in Holland

Once migrants arrive in their new location, many questions arise about how to live, fit in, accommodate, or resist the new and alien culture. Source 14.1 provides one example. Hana was a "multiple migrant." Born in Eritrea (then part of Ethiopia) around 1970, as a young girl she fled with her family to Sudan because of her father's political involvements. She spent some time in a Somali prison after being accused of spying for Ethiopia, and in 1990 made her way to Holland. There, her story, told to a British researcher, picks up.

1. What particular difficulties did Hana experience in Holland?

2. How did the events of September 11, 2001, affect Hana?

3. What does Hana imply about her expectations when she arrived in Holland?

HANA | *Adapting to Holland* | 2016

In Holland of course when I came it was a bit of a shock. After all that, you expect to come to a country which people will understand your situation or will support you, but when I came to Holland it was so shocking. I was put in a camp very far away from all other people. We were just us, all different kind of people, and most of them were from white European country or other. There was only one black woman from Somalia where I stayed. . . .

So it was the most depressive time of my life. Being locked in one place and then what you see is only from the window and you don't have enough clothes or enough warm jackets to go outside because when I came it was October 1990. . . . It took me I think nine months until I came to live in Amsterdam in a room with other Ethiopians and other nationalities.

[*Hana lived in the Netherlands for fourteen years, during which time she lived with a partner who was also Muslim, with whom she started a family. She worked in an accountancy firm until 2005.*]

I started to put a scarf on [a sign of Islamic modesty] and I was more deepened in my religion so at that time I was kicked off my job. And things got really really tough. First of all they found somebody who is Dutch [to replace her], and also kind of they didn't accept that I put on a scarf and I'm different, so that was my experience in Holland. . . .

In Holland you get stuck. There is a roof on your head, if you just move your head up more than you should, you just get pushed and you get pushed into a black hole that you never come out of. And after the incident of 11 September it was much worse. All even my neighbors they tried to, they started to treat my children differently and some of my friends in the road they were pulled and pushed and they took off their scarves and pulled their hair on the street and that is while the police is watching. And there are, where my child used to go was the Islamic school, that school had been bombed.

Imagine, you think you came to safe country to live safely and to have happiness at last in your life and it is being discriminated and you know I had to leave Holland. . . . And now I've started my life again here in England since 2005 March.

Source: Linda McDowell, *Migrant Women's Voices* (London, UK: Bloomsbury Publishing, 2016), 49–50.

■ ■ ■

SOURCE 14.2 Ayaan Hirsi Ali in Holland

A very different immigrant response to life in Holland can be seen in the experience of Ayaan Hirsi Ali, a Somali immigrant to the Netherlands and later to the United States who repudiated much of her Somali culture and its Islamic faith. Born in 1969, Hirsi Ali was the daughter of a prominent political opponent of the Somali government. Fleeing the country with her family, she spent much of her childhood in Saudi Arabia, Ethiopia, and Kenya, where she was attracted for a time to a strict form of Islam. As a teenager, she willingly wore a *hijab*, the traditional covering for modest Muslim women.

But in 1992, fleeing an arranged marriage to a man she regarded as a "bigot" and an "idiot," Hirsi Ali found political asylum in the Netherlands and was disowned by her father. As an immigrant, she flourished, moving from work as a cleaner to that of a translator in a refugee center and obtaining a master's degree in the process. Her encounter with Western individualism and Enlightenment thought produced a growing disenchantment with Islam, and Hirsi Ali came to see herself as an atheist. She got involved in politics, was elected to the Dutch parliament, and participated in the making of a film highly critical of Muslim treatment of women, for which she received numerous death threats. In 2006, she relocated to the United States, "in search of an opportunity to build a life and livelihood in freedom" and became an American citizen in 2013. By then a prominent public figure both in Europe and in North America, Hirsi Ali described her remarkable personal transformation as an immigrant in a number of books, articles, and interviews. In one of them, she penned "A Letter to My Grandmother," from which Source 14.2 is taken.

1. How would you describe the difference between Hirsi Ali's response to life in Europe and that of Hana in Source 14.1?

2. What elements of Western life does she appreciate?

3. What criticisms of Islam are disclosed in this passage?

AYAAN HIRSI ALI │ *A Letter to My Grandmother* │ 2010

I am sorry Grandmother that I was not there in your old age. . . . I would have summoned the spirits of my new world. Here they have salves to cleanse and sooth the itch in folded skin; they have hearing aids; they have walking sticks on wheels. . . ;

I have lived with the infidels for almost two decades. I have come to learn, appreciate, and adopt their way of life. . . .

Gone with you are the rigid rules of custom. . . . Gone with you is that bloodline [clan or tribal loyalties], for better or worse, and gone is the idiot tradition that meant you cherished mares and she-camels more than your daughters and granddaughters. . . .

The secret of the Dutchman's success is his ability to adapt, to invent. . . . We bow to a God who says we must not change a thing; it is he who has chosen it.

The infidel does not see life as a test, a passage to the hereafter, but as an end and a joy in itself. All his resources of money, mind, and organization go into making life here, on Earth, comfortable and healthy. . . . He is loyal to his wife and children; he may take care of his parents, but has no use for a memory filled with an endless chain of ancestors. All the seeds of his toil are spent on his own offspring, not those of his brothers or uncles.

Because the infidel trusts and studies new ideas, there is abundance in the infidel lands. . . . the birth of a girl is just fine. . . . The little girl sits right next to the little boy in school. . . . she gets to eat as much as he does . . . and when she matures, she gets the same opportunity to seek and find a mate as he does. . . .

Grandmother, I no longer believe in the old ways. . . .

Source: Ayaan Hirsi Ali, *Nomad: From Islam to America* (New York, NY: Atria Paperback, 2010), 86, 88–90, 92.

■ ■ ■

SOURCE 14.3 **Left Behind**

Migration had repercussions well beyond the circle of the migrants themselves, for those who remained in their homelands also felt the impact of those who had departed. One young Moroccan woman, whose new husband left for work in Europe in the early 1970s, expressed her anguish at his leaving. "I am afraid, afraid that my love forgets me in your paradise," she wrote. "With you he stays one year, with me just one month. . . . I am like a flower that withers more each day."[1]

More broadly, the repercussions of extensive migrations also echoed in fears within developing countries about the social and economic impact of losing many young, well-educated professional people to higher-paying and more prestigious positions in Europe and North America. Many who went abroad to study did not return home. Others were recruited—or seduced—by professional opportunities not available in their own countries. Frustration with such people boiled over in a novel by the Zimbabwean neurosurgeon and writer J. Nozipo Maraire. In her novel, *Zenzele: A Letter for My*

Daughter, the leading character sharply criticizes a friend who left Zimbabwe for a better life in the West.

1. What is her fundamental criticism of those who do not return home?

2. What does she fear for Africa if such practices continue?

3. Who does she feel is responsible for this situation?

J. NOZIPO MARAIRE | *Zenzele: A Letter for My Daughter* | **1996**

Africa needs the hearts and minds of its sons and daughters to nurture it. You were our pride. . . . When you did not return, a whole village lost its investment. Africa is all that we have. If we do not build it, no one else will. . . . Yes, you are just one, but it is thousands like you, whom our churches and governments pour money into, who ultimately drain our resources. If our brightest minds go and never return, then it is no wonder that we have poor leadership to guide our nations, that we have no engineers to run our machinery, no doctors to staff our hospitals, no professors to fill our universities, and no teachers to educate the generations to come. How can we move forward if our future Mandelas are content to spend their days sipping cappuccinos on Covent Gardens? If our potential Sembene's [a Senegalese film director] are happier shooting French films in Paris or our Achebes-to-be [a leading Nigerian novelist] prefer to tell stories of Americans, is it surprising that we appear to be culturally void? Who is left? You are the epitome of the brain drain.

Source: J. Nozipo Maraire, *Zenzele: A Letter for My Daughter* (New York, NY: Delta Books, 1996), 64–65.

■ ■ ■

SOURCE 14.4 The Politics of Immigration: A Cautious Welcome in Europe

Immigration has long found expression as a political issue in the receiving countries, and never more so than in early twenty-first century Europe. Fleeing civil war, poverty, drought, and oppression, a massive wave of desperate migrants from the Middle East and Africa, some 1.3 million people in 2015 alone, sought refuge in Europe. In many places, they received a warm and hospitable welcome. Angela Merkel, the chancellor of Germany and a citizen of the former communist state of East Germany, emerged as a spokesperson for a compassionate approach to this enormous humanitarian tragedy. That sensibility found expression in a speech she gave to the European Parliament in October of 2015.

1. How might you describe Merkel's posture toward the immigration crisis in Europe?

2. In what ways does her speech respond to those opposed to large-scale immigration in Europe?

3. What does she expect from those who seek a new home in Europe?

ANGELA MERKEL | *Speech to the European Parliament* | October 7, 2015

Not since the Second World War have so many people fled their homes as today — the number has now reached around 60 million. . . . We can rightly expect the people who come to us in Europe to become integrated into our societies. This requires them to uphold the rules that apply here, and to learn the language of their new homeland.

But, conversely, we also have a duty to treat the people who come to us in need with respect, to see them as human beings and not as an anonymous mass — regardless of whether they will be allowed to stay or not. . . . [T]his means that we must be guided by the values we have enshrined in the European treaties: human dignity, the rule of law, tolerance, respect for minorities and solidarity. . . .

. . . Today Europe is a region on which many people from all over the world pin their hopes and aspirations. . . . We have to deal responsibly with Europe's gravitational pull. In other words, we have to take greater care of those who are in need today in our neighbourhood.

Source: Statement by Federal Chancellor Angela Merkel to the European Parliament, October 7, 2015. Accessed at https://www.bundesregierung.de/Content/EN/Reden/2015/2015-10-07-merkel-ep_en.html?nn=393812.

■ ■ ■

SOURCE 14.5 The Politics of Immigration: Resentment and Resistance in Europe

A welcoming posture was not the only European response to the recent influx of immigrants, as a backlash against large-scale immigration, fueled by fears of a threat to national cultures, of the loss of jobs, and of terrorism, took shape across much of Europe. That backlash was reflected in Great Britain's decision to exit the European Union in 2015, and it was encouraged by the 2016 election of Donald Trump in the United States and his subsequent effort to restrict immigration from Muslim countries. That sensibility was articulated in a speech by Geert Wilders, a prominent Dutch politician and a leading figure in European anti-immigrant circles, delivered in early 2017 at a "Europe of Nations and Freedom" Conference in Germany.

1. What fears does Wilders articulate?

2. Who does he hold responsible for the influx of Muslims into Europe?

3. What is his posture toward the European Union? What kind of Europe does he favor?

4. How might Chancellor Merkel respond to Wilders' speech?

GEERT WILDERS | *Speech at the "Europe of Nations and Freedom" Conference* |
2017

[A]ll our European countries are faced with the question of their existence. My friends, the United Nations expects that the population of Africa will quadruple by the end of the century. . . . Many of them want to come to Europe in the future.

The question that none of our ruling politicians now ask is: How do we protect our country and our identity against mass immigration? How do we protect our values? How do we protect our civilization? Our culture? The future of our children? These are the fundamental questions we have to answer.

In recent years, our governments have allowed millions of people to flow uncontrollably into our countries. Our governments have conducted a dangerous open-borders policy. . . .

Our leaders . . . no longer value freedom.

Politicians from almost all of the established parties are promoting our Islamization. Almost the entire Establishment, the elite universities, the churches, the media, politicians, put our hard-earned liberties at risk. . . .

Day after day, for years, we are experiencing the decay of our cherished values. The equality of men and women, freedom of opinion and speech, tolerance of homosexuality — all this is in retreat. . . .

And then there is also the great danger of Islamic terrorism. A German undercover journalist recently revealed that some refugee housing centers have become breeding-grounds for terrorists. The consequences are visible to everyone. . . .

We are fed up with the elites, who offer you a beautiful ideal world, in which all cultures are morally equivalent. . . .

History calls on you to save Germany. History calls on us all to save Europe. To save our own humanistic Judeo-Christian culture and civilization, our liberties, our nations, the future of our children.

We are fed up with the Europhiles in Brussels, who want to abolish our countries and impose an undemocratic super-state, in which we become a single multicultural society.

To this Europe we say no! We stand for a Europe of national states and freedom! We will take our countries back. We will make sure that our countries will stay ours. . . .

My friends, we live in historic times. The people of the West are awakening. They are casting off the yoke of political correctness. They want their freedom back. They want their sovereign nations back. And we, the patriots of Europe, will be their instrument of liberation!

Source: Geert Wilders, "Speech at the 'Europe of Nations and Freedom' Conference," January 22, 2017. Accessed at https://www.gatestoneinstitute.org/9812/geert-wilders-koblenz-enf.

■ ■ ■

SOURCE 14.6 From the Holocaust to Israel

During the post–World War II era, and especially since the 1960s, the industrialized countries of Europe and North America have been the chief destinations for many millions of the world's migrants. Pakistanis, Indians, and West Indians moved to Great Britain; North Africans and West Africans to France; Turks and Kurds to Germany; Filipinos, Vietnamese, Koreans, Cubans, Mexicans, and Haitians to the United States. But there was one highly significant migrant stream moving outward from Europe—that of European Jews heading to Palestine/Israel. That migrant stream, known as Zionism, had begun in the late nineteenth and early twentieth centuries, but it expanded greatly in the wake of the Holocaust and the creation of the newly established State of Israel in 1948. There, these European migrants were joined by millions of other Jews hailing from the Islamic world and later from the former Soviet Union. Altogether, more than 3 million Jews have migrated to Israel since 1948, with the active support and encouragement of the Israeli government. Source 14.6 illustrates the connection between the Holocaust and this mass migration of European and other Jews. It was a fund-raising poster from circa 1950 for a Jewish settlement or *kibbutz* in northern Israel.

1. What is happening in the action of the poster? Note: The yellow armband worn by the older man was one of the signs of Jewish identity that the Nazis required Jews to wear. It served to isolate and dehumanize Jewish people.

2. How might this poster serve to encourage migration to Israel?

3. What image of the new Israeli state did the poster seek to convey?

Fund-Raising Poster from Israel | 1950

SOURCE 14.7 The Palestinian Diaspora

This large-scale Jewish migration to Israel prompted yet another migratory stream, as some 750,000 Palestinian Arabs fled or were expelled from their homes during the 1948 war that established the State of Israel. Many of them moved to often squalid refugee camps in Gaza, the West Bank, Syria, Lebanon, and Jordan, where millions of their descendants remain to this day. This forced migration of 1948, known to Palestinians as *Al-nakba* or "the catastrophe," is commemorated every year, with marchers carrying Palestinian flags and a key, symbolizing their "right to return" to the lands and homes from which they had been expelled. These two migrations have together generated one of the most intractable conflicts of the contemporary world—that between Israel and the Palestinians. Source 14.7 shows a Palestinian man from a refugee camp in the West Bank town of Hebron tenderly touching a poster announcing the sixty-seventh anniversary of Nakba in 2015.

1. What message is the poster intended to convey?

2. How might you imagine the thinking of the man touching the poster?

3. How might you compare the migratory journeys reflected in Sources 14.6 and 14.7? Construct a conversation between the creators of these two posters. What common ground might they share? On what issues might they never agree?

"The Catastrophe" Memorialized | 2015

HAZEM BADER/Getty Images

DOING HISTORY

1. **Comparing experiences:** In what different ways has migration been experienced by individuals during the past century?

2. **Considering consequences:** In what ways has migration had consequences well beyond the stories of individual migrants?

3. **Practicing empathy:** History, we often say, serves to awaken our empathy with people in a wide variety of circumstances. To what extent can you enter sympathetically into the experience of the people whose lives are depicted in these sources?

HISTORIANS' VOICES

Immigration to the United States and Europe

The principal destinations of twentieth-century migrants were the United States and, from the 1960s, Western Europe. The two Voices that follow assess attitudes toward migrants in these two regions. In Voice 14.1, Konrad H. Jarausch, a specialist in twentieth-century Europe, examines the societal tensions associated with Europe's shift from a continent of emigrants to an immigration continent. In Voice 14.2, Tobias Brinkmann and Annemarie Sammartino, specialists in migration and German history, compare American and German attitudes toward migration during the twentieth century and question common interpretations of both.

1. According to Jarausch, what fears inspired a nativist backlash toward immigration? In what ways have European governments and supporters of immigration reacted to this nativist backlash?

2. What differences between American and German attitudes toward migration and immigrants do Brinkmann and Sammartino identify?

3. **Integrating primary and secondary sources:** How might the primary sources presented earlier illustrate or explain the European and American reactions described in these Voices?

VOICE 14.1

Konrad Jarausch on Europe's Shift from Emigration to Immigration | 2015

The increasing pressure for immigration in the wake of globalization caught Europeans unprepared, because they continued to think of themselves as emigrants. Since the Old Continent had produced more hungry people than it could feed, migrants . . . had left for centuries populating distant shores from the United States to Australia. . . . But with fertility declining below replacement and longevity increasing substantially, an aging Europe turned from emigration to an immigration continent, needing foreign migrants to survive.

In response to growing immigration and economic downturn [after ca. 1970 and especially in the early twenty-first century], an ugly nativist backlash formed in many European countries. . . . Much of the motivation stemmed from irrational fear of losing one's job to the newcomers, envy of their purported welfare benefits or ignorance of their different customs. . . . Various rightist groups . . . capitalized on this widespread resentment to score surprising electoral victories. . . . While civil society groups of the Left rallied for tolerance, schools encouraged acceptance of strangers, and sports clubs tried to celebrate difference, established conservative parties profited from popular anger by proposing restrictive legislation.

The conflicting pressures of fear of foreigners and need for skilled immigration engendered a contradictory set of immigration policies. On the one hand, nativist backlash forced a tightening of ethnic remigration, family immigration, and recognition of asylum, decreasing the yearly influx. To stop the flow of illegal immigrants the EU agreed on a joint border regime, which sent asylum seekers back to "safe countries.". . . On the other hand, business lobbying forced the initiation of various "blue card" programs permitting university graduates to remain or professionals to enter. . . .

Source: Konrad H. Jarausch, *Out of Ashes: A New History of Europe in the Twentieth Century* (Princeton, NJ: Princeton University Press, 2015), 732–36.

VOICE 14.2

Tobias Brinkmann and Annemarie Sammartino on American and German Attitudes toward Immigration | 2010

There is no German counterpart to the image of the Statue of Liberty welcoming the "huddled masses" to America's shores. Yet behind the myths of American inclusion and German exclusion lurks a much more complicated portrait of two nations struggling with the challenges and opportunities of immigration.

The image of the United States as a beacon of freedom and tolerance for immigrants is a myth. From the earliest days until the present, forces of exclusion, deep-rooted racism and discrimination, and even brutal violence, especially against "non-white" immigrants, have been part of American history. For most of the twentieth century, U.S. immigration policy was restrictive, and the most deserving refugees and immigrants were excluded. Still, American immigration history proves the enormous potential of immigration from around the world. . . . Ethnic groups are not perceived as minorities but as distinctive parts of the dynamic and pluralist American mosaic. Since the late nineteenth century, immigrants have made America "their" home. Hyphenated identities are really an expression of a deeper link between a specific ethnicity and America. . . .

In contrast, Germans have never accepted immigration as part of their national identity, even as the long twentieth century bears witness to the reality of a large population of immigrants living and working on German soil. In Germany, as in many other countries, immigrants were and often still are expected to accommodate to their respective host societies, although prejudice has made such assimilation difficult if not impossible. Germans have rarely been entirely hospitable to migrants, but except for the Nazi years, they cannot be characterized as being completely unwelcoming either. As in the United States, economic, political, social, legal, and cultural imperatives all complicate any simple narrative of the German encounter with immigrants.

Source: Tobias Brinkmann and Annemarie Sammartino, "Immigration: Myth versus Struggles," in Cristof Mauch and Kiran Klaus Patel, *The United States and Germany during the Twentieth Century: Competition and Convergence* (Cambridge, UK: Cambridge University Press [German Historical Institute Copyright], 2010), 100.

NOTE

1. Quoted in Hazel Johnson and Henry Bernstein, *Third World Lives of Struggle* (London, UK: Heinemann Educational Books, 1982), 173–74.

Acknowledgments

Chapter 1

Source 1.5: "Sunita the Outcaste" (Thag 12.2), translated from the Pali by Thanissaro Bhikkhu. *Access to Insight (BCBS Edition)*, 30 November 2013, http://www.accesstoinsight.org/tipitaka/kn/thag/thag.12.02.than.html.

Chapter 2

Source 2.2: "The Chronicle of the Direct Descent of Gods and Sovereigns," from *Sources of Japanese Tradition, Volume 1,* compiled by William De Bary et al. Copyright © 2001 Columbia University Press. Reprinted with permission of Columbia University Press.

Source 2.3: From *The Pillow Book of Sei Shonagon* by Sei Shonagon, translated by Ivan I. Morris. Copyright © 1991 Columbia University Press. Reprinted with permission of Columbia University Press and reproduced with permission of Oxford University Press through PLSclear.

Source 2.5B: Carl Steenstrup, trans., "The Imagawa Letter," *Monumenta Nipponica* 28, no. 3 (1973): 295–316. Copyright © 1973 by Sophia University. Reproduced with permission of Sophia University.

Chapter 3

Source 3.1: Michael Dols, "Ibn al-Wardi's Risalah al-Nabah' 'an al-Waba; a Translation of a Major Source for the History of the Black Death in the Middle East," in *Near Eastern Numismatics, Iconography, Epigraphy and History: Studies in Honor of George C. Miles,* ed. Dickran K. Kouymjian (Beirut: American University of Beirut, 1974), 448–455. Reprinted by permission of Dickran K. Kouymjian.

Source 3.3: Christos S. Bartsocas, "Two Fourteenth-Century Descriptions of the 'Black Death.'" Republished with permission of Oxford University Press from *Journal of the History of Medicine and Allied Sciences*, 1966, permission conveyed through Copyright Clearance Center, Inc.

Source 3.7: Pistoia: "Ordinances for Sanitation in a Time of Mortality," translated by Duane Osheim, http://www2.iath.virginia.edu/osheim/pistoia.html. Used with permission of Duane Osheim.

Chapter 4

Source 4.4: Excerpt(s) from *Conquistadors*, edited by Patricia de Fuentes, translated by Patricia de Fuentes, translation copyright © 1963 by Penguin Random House LLC. Used by permission of Viking Books, an imprint of Penguin Publishing Group, a division of Penguin Random House LLC. All rights reserved.

Source 4.7: From *The Broken Spears* by Miguel León-Portilla. Copyright © 1962, 1990 by Miguel León-Portilla. Expanded and Updated Edition © 1992 by Miguel León-Portilla. Reprinted by permission of Beacon Press, Boston.

Chapter 10

Source 10.4: "Reflections on My Errors," from *Sources of Japanese Tradition, Volume 2,* compiled by William De Bary et al. Copyright © 2001 Columbia University Press. Reprinted with permission of Columbia University Press.

Chapter 13

Source 13.2: From *Combahee River Collective, a Black Feminist Statement,* 1977, in Zillah R. Eisenstein, ed., *Capitalist Patriarchy and the Case for Socialist Feminism* (New York: Monthly Review Press, 1979). Used by permission of Zillah R. Eisenstein.

Chapter 14

Source 14.1: Linda McDowell, *Migrant Women's Voices.* Copyright 2016 by Berg Publishers, Bloomsbury Academic, an imprint of Bloomsbury Publishing Plc. Reprinted by permission.

Source 14.5: Geert Wilders, "Speech at the 'Europe of Nations and Freedom' Conference," January 22, 2017. Accessed at https://www.gatestoneinstitute.org/9812/geert-wilders-koblenz-enf. Used by permission of The Tweede Kamer der Staten-Generaal.

Voice 14.2: Tobias Brinkmann and Annemarie Sammartino, "Immigration: Myth versus Struggles," in Cristof Mauch and Kiran Klaus Patel, *The United States and Germany during the Twentieth Century: Competition and Convergence.* Copyright © The German Historical Institute, 2010, published by Cambridge University Press. Reproduced with permission of Cambridge University Press through PLSclear.